"The Talented Tenth rises and pulls all that
are worth saving up to their vantage point."
                        —W.E.B. Du Bois

Library of Congress Cataloging-in-Publication Data

Gill, Joel Christian.
Bass Reeves / Joel Christian Gill.
pages cm. -- (Tales of the talented tenth ; volume 1)
Summary: "This is the first volume of a new series of graphic novels featuring notable and iconic African Americans. Each volume will focus on the individual, and will also include a discussion of the larger community to which the individual belonged and the historical relevance of the individual"-- Provided by publisher.

ISBN 978-1-938486-63-0 (paperback)

1. Reeves, Bass--Comic books, strips, etc. 2. African Americans--Indian Territory--Biography--Comic books, strips, etc. 3. African Americans--Oklahoma--Biography--Comic books, strips, etc. 4. Fugitive slaves--Indian Territory--Biography--Comic books, strips, etc. 5. United States marshals--Indian Territory--Biography--Comic books, strips, etc. 6. African American police--Indian Territory--Biography--Comic books, strips, etc. 7. Outlaws--Indian Territory--History--Juvenile literature. 8. Frontier and pioneer life--Indian Territory--Comic books, strips, etc. 9. Indian Territory--Biography--Comic books, strips, etc. 10. Graphic novels. I. Title.
F697.R44G55 2014
976.6'503092--dc23
[B]

2014029437

Printed in the United States
0 9 8 7 6 5 4 3 2 1

Fulcrum Publishing
4690 Table Mountain Dr., Ste. 100
Golden, CO 80403
800-992-2908 • 303-277-1623
www.fulcrumbooks.com

MIX
Paper from responsible sources
FSC
www.fsc.org
FSC® C002589

Bass Reeves:
TALES
of the
TALENTED
TENTH

words and pictures
Joel Christian Gill

Steady...

...you might want to aim
a little lower, Boss.

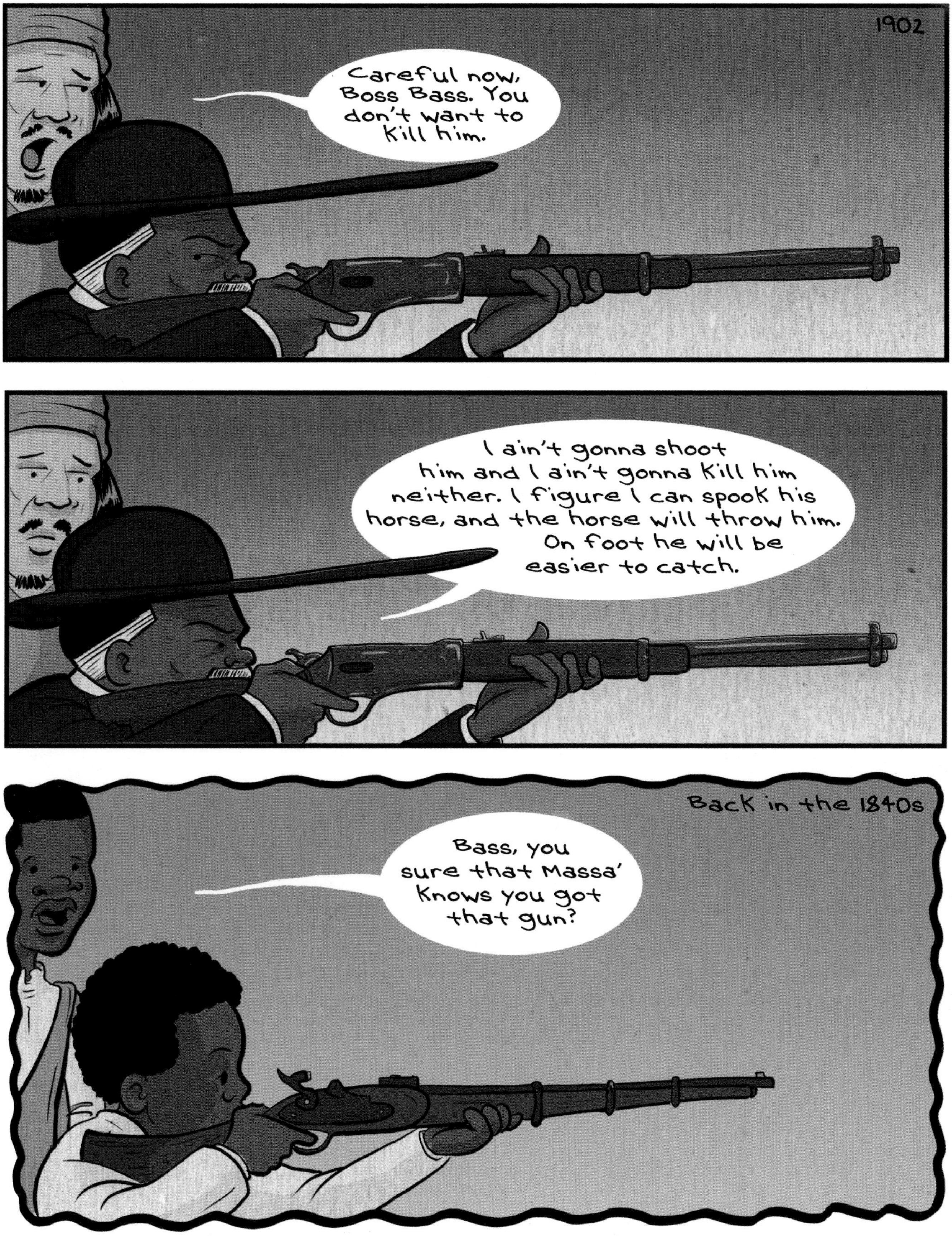
1902
Careful now, Boss Bass. You don't want to kill him.
I ain't gonna shoot him and I ain't gonna kill him neither. I figure I can spook his horse, and the horse will throw him. On foot he will be easier to catch.
Back in the 1840s
Bass, you sure that Massa' knows you got that gun?

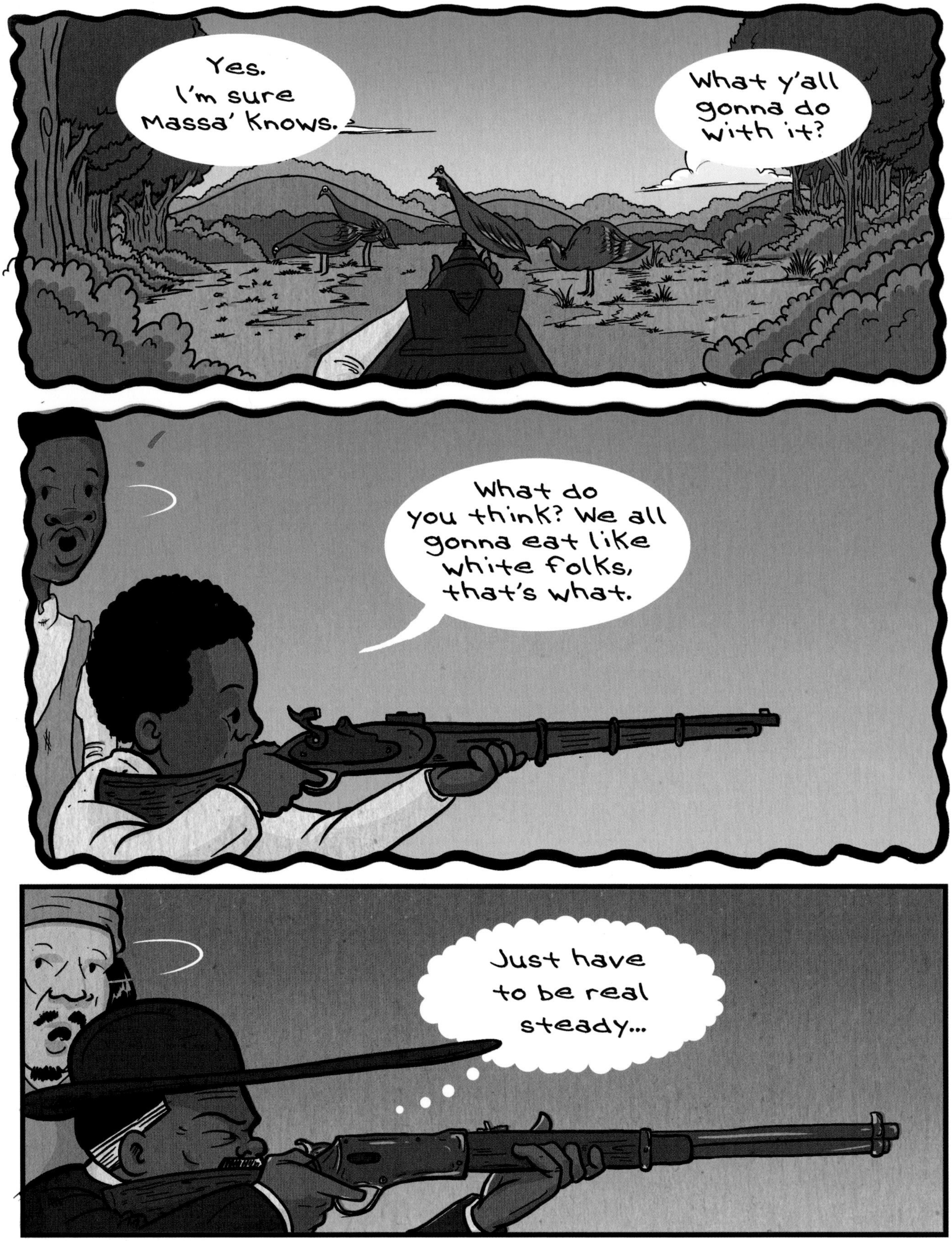
Yes. I'm sure Massa' Knows.
What y'all gonna do with it?
What do you think? We all gonna eat like white folks, that's what.
Just have to be real steady...

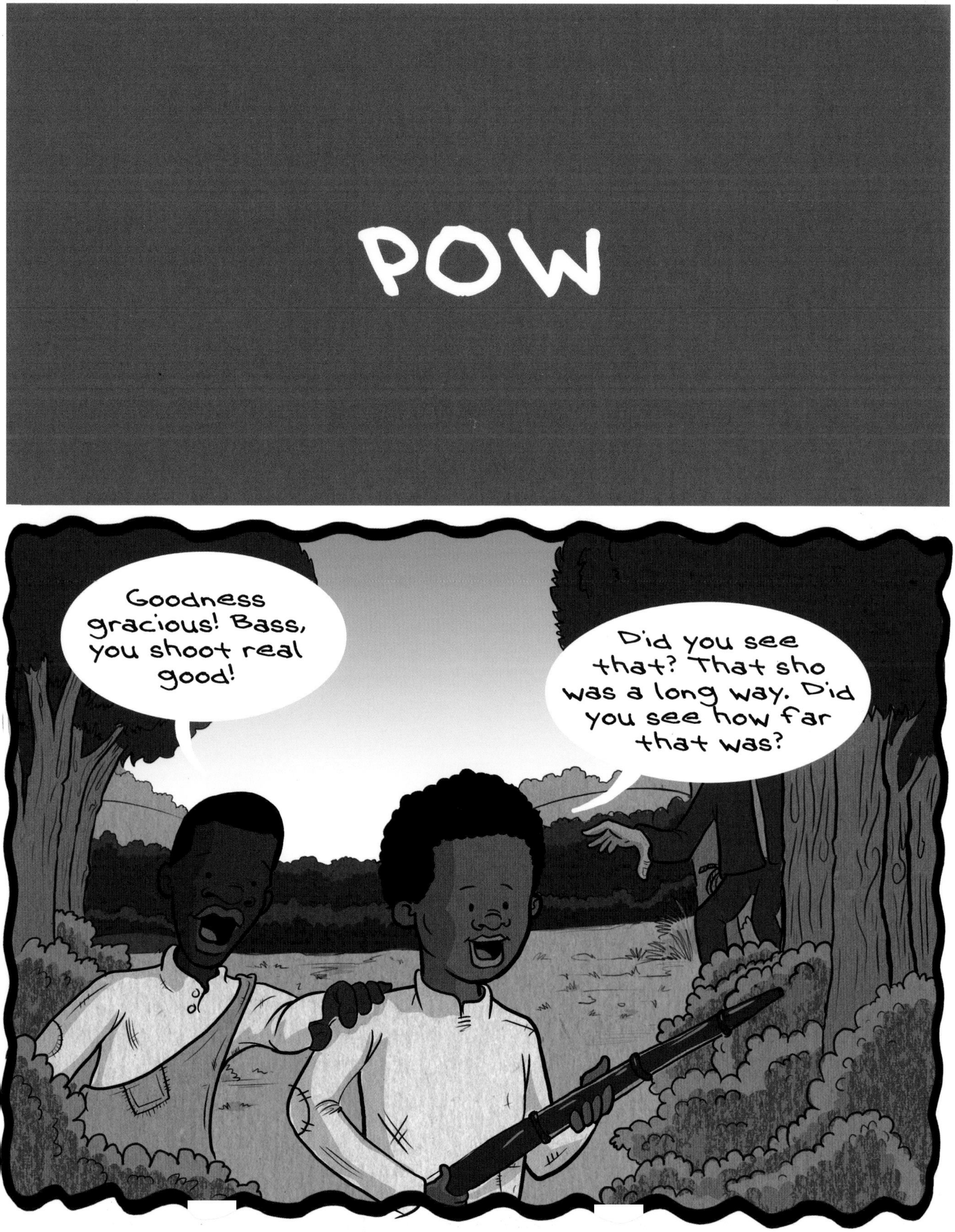
POW
Goodness gracious! Bass, you shoot real good!
Did you see that? That sho was a long way. Did you see how far that was?

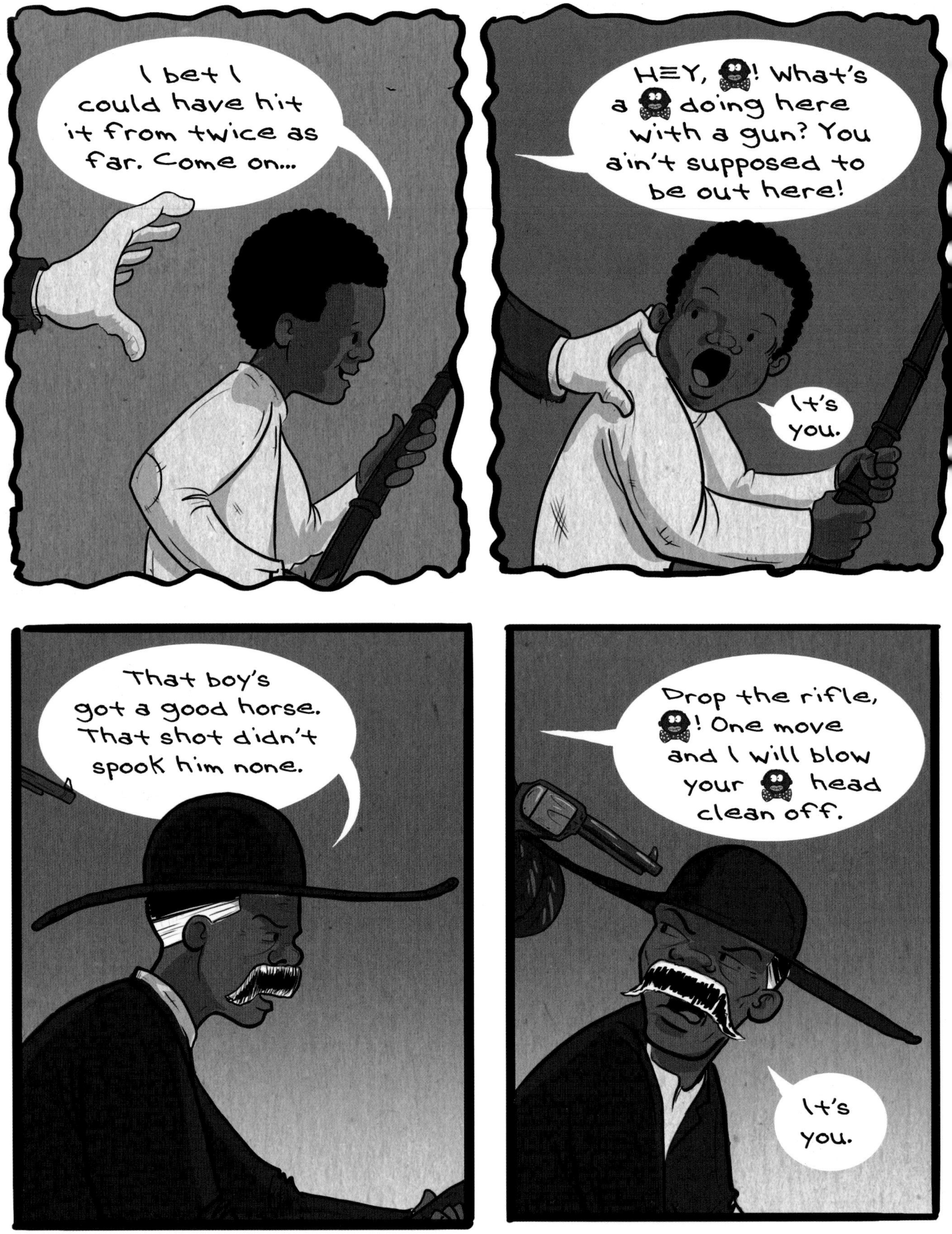
I bet I could have hit it from twice as far. Come on...
HEY, ! What's a doing here with a gun? You ain't supposed to be out here!
It's you.
That boy's got a good horse. That shot didn't spook him none.
Drop the rifle, ! One move and I will blow your head clean off.
It's you.

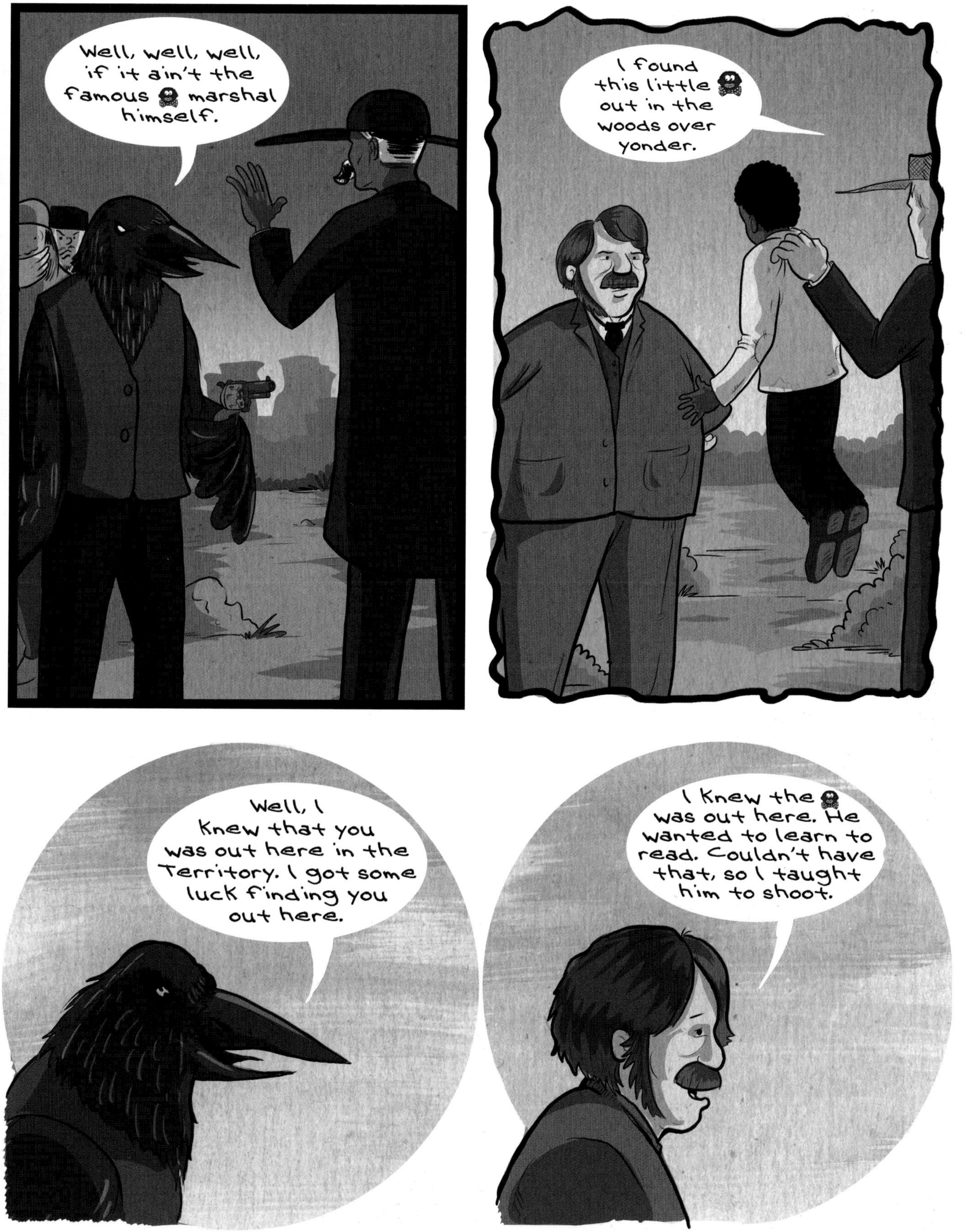
Well, well, well, if it ain't the famous marshal himself.
I found this little out in the woods over yonder.
Well, I Knew that you was out here in the Territory. I got some luck finding you out here.
I Knew the was out here. He wanted to learn to read. Couldn't have that, so I taught him to shoot.

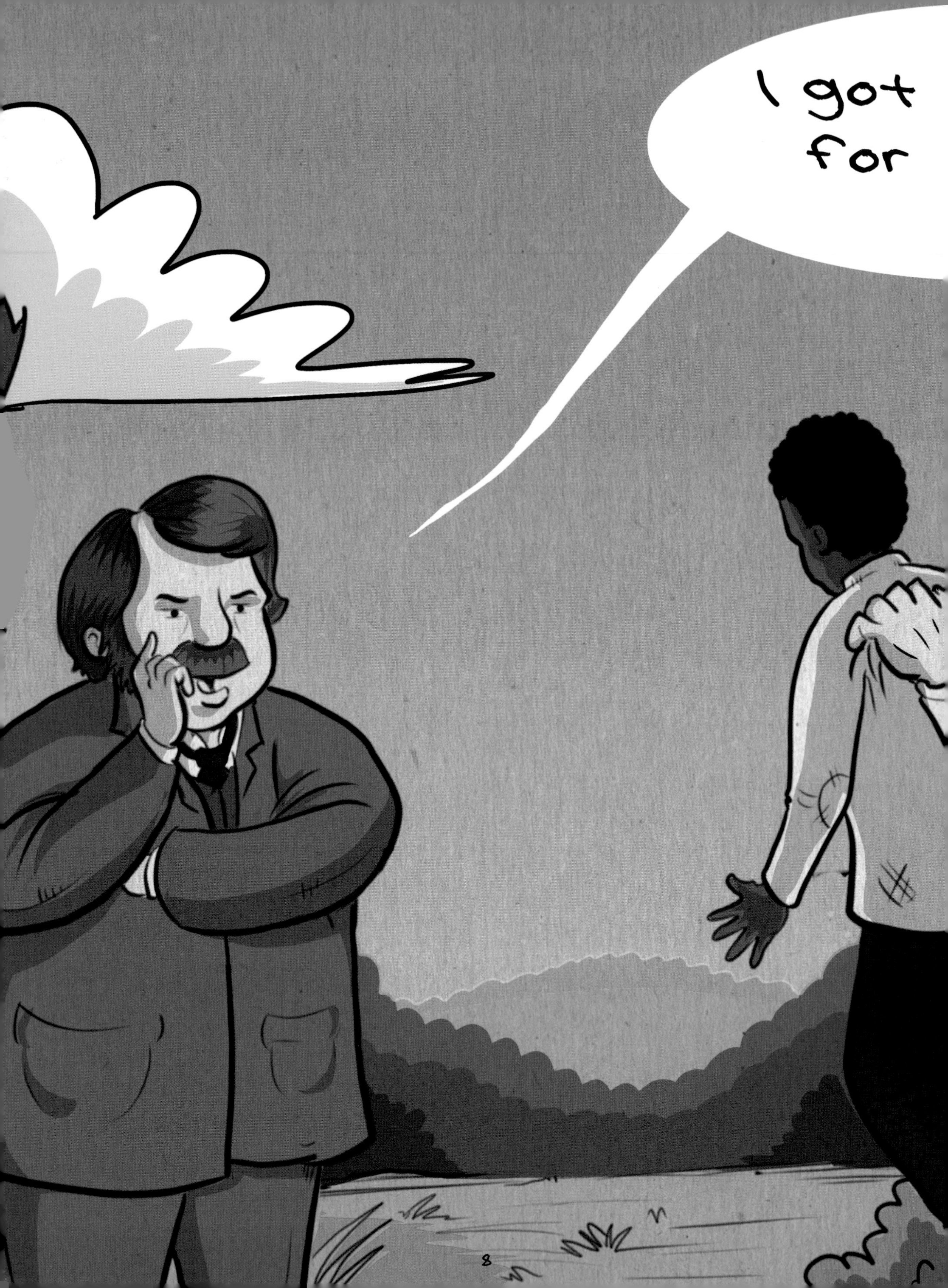
I got
for

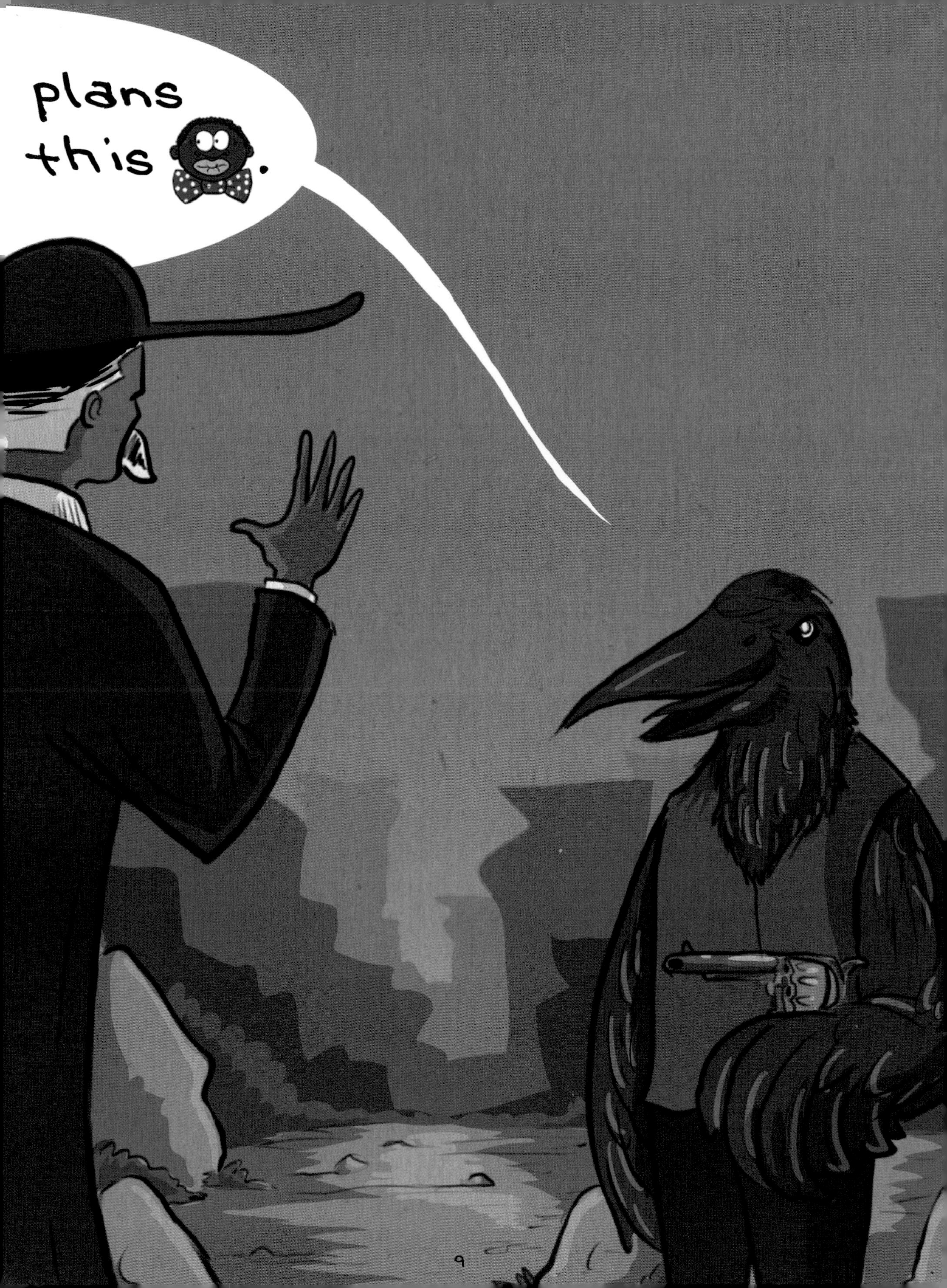
plans this .

Steady.

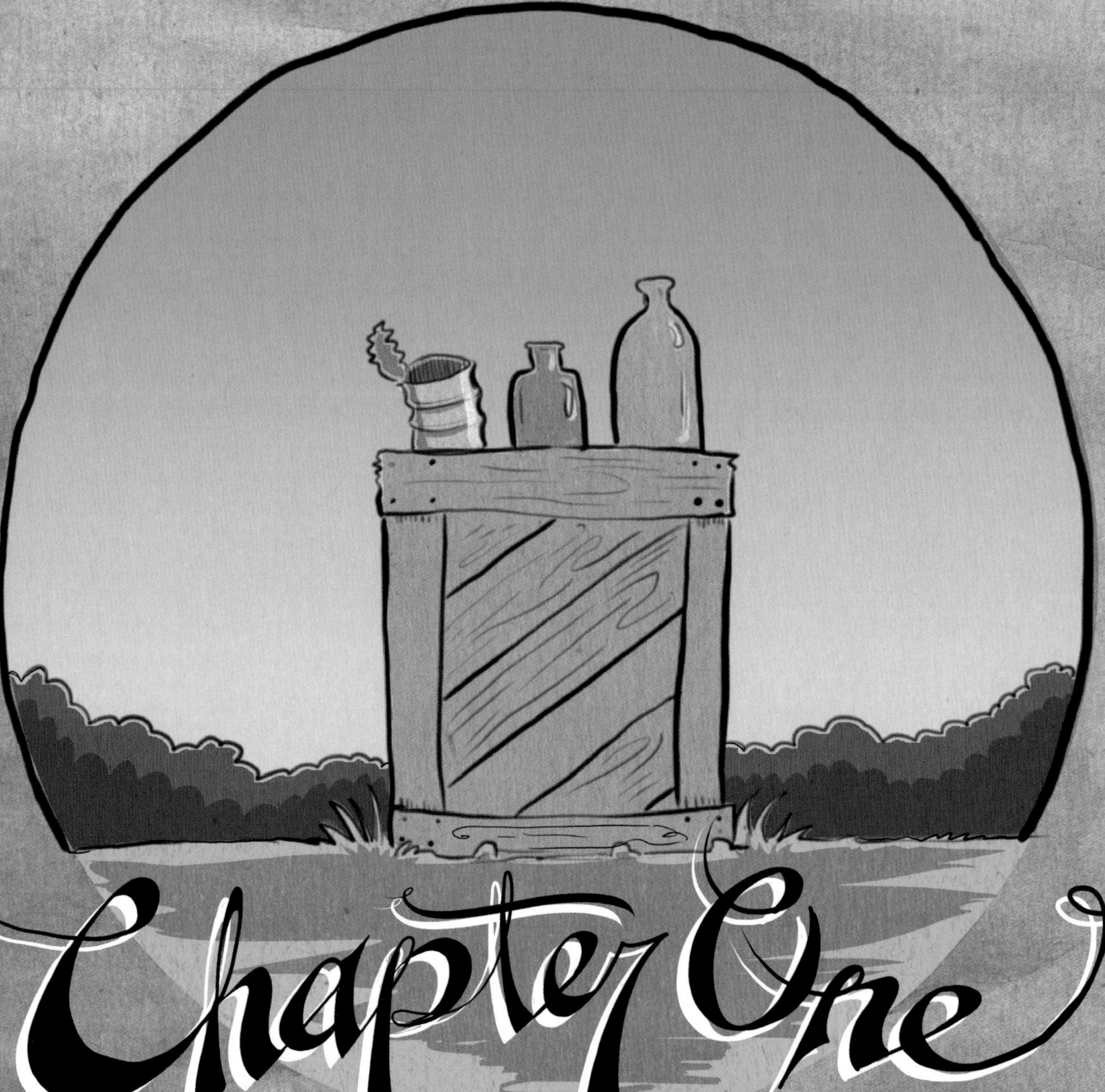

Chapter One

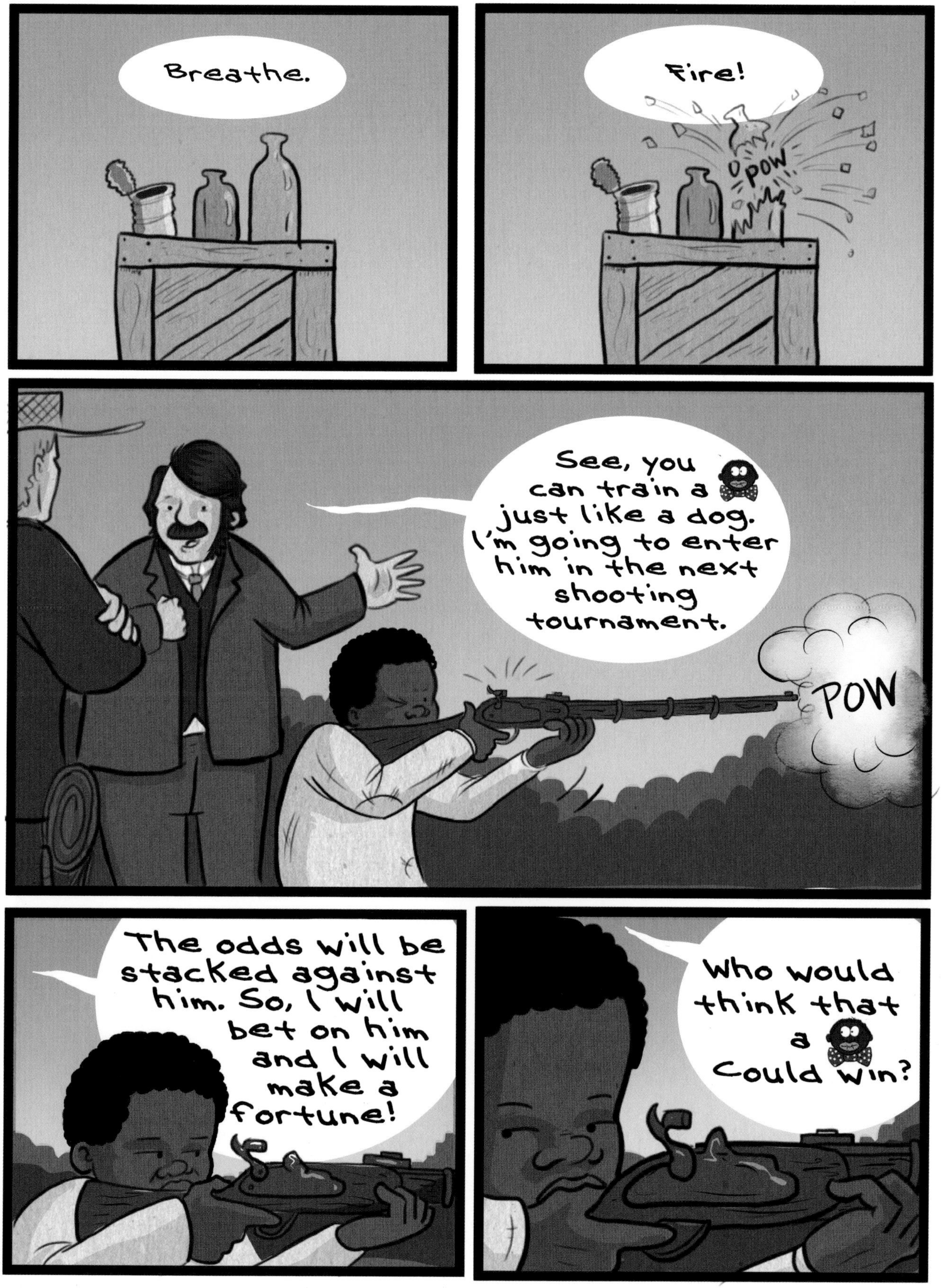

Breathe.
Fire!
POW
See, you can train a just like a dog. I'm going to enter him in the next shooting tournament.
POW
The odds will be stacked against him. So, I will bet on him and I will make a fortune!
Who would think that a Could win?

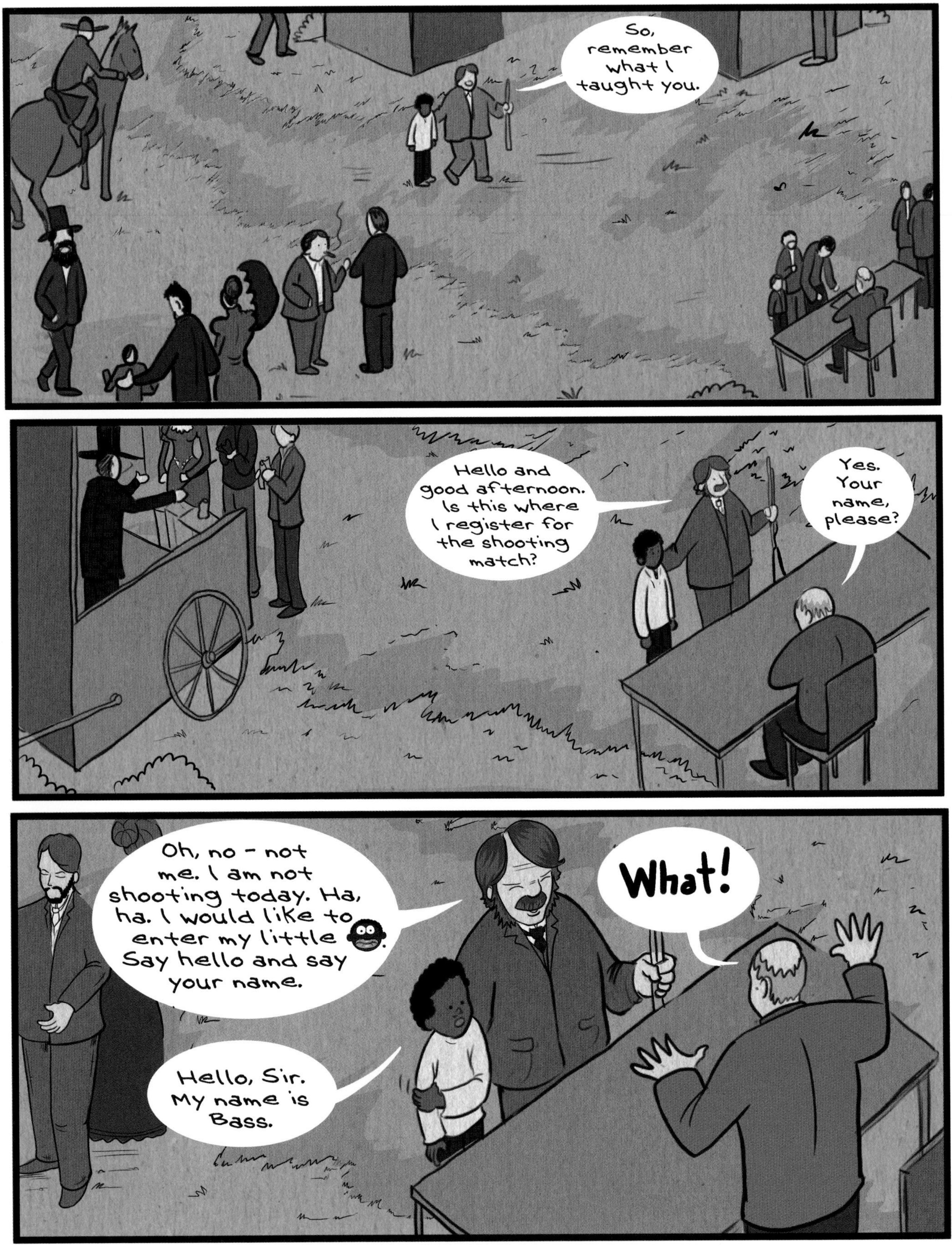

So, remember what I taught you.
Hello and good afternoon. Is this where I register for the shooting match?
Yes. Your name, please?
Oh, no - not me. I am not shooting today. Ha, ha. I would like to enter my little . Say hello and say your name.
Hello, Sir. My name is Bass.
What!

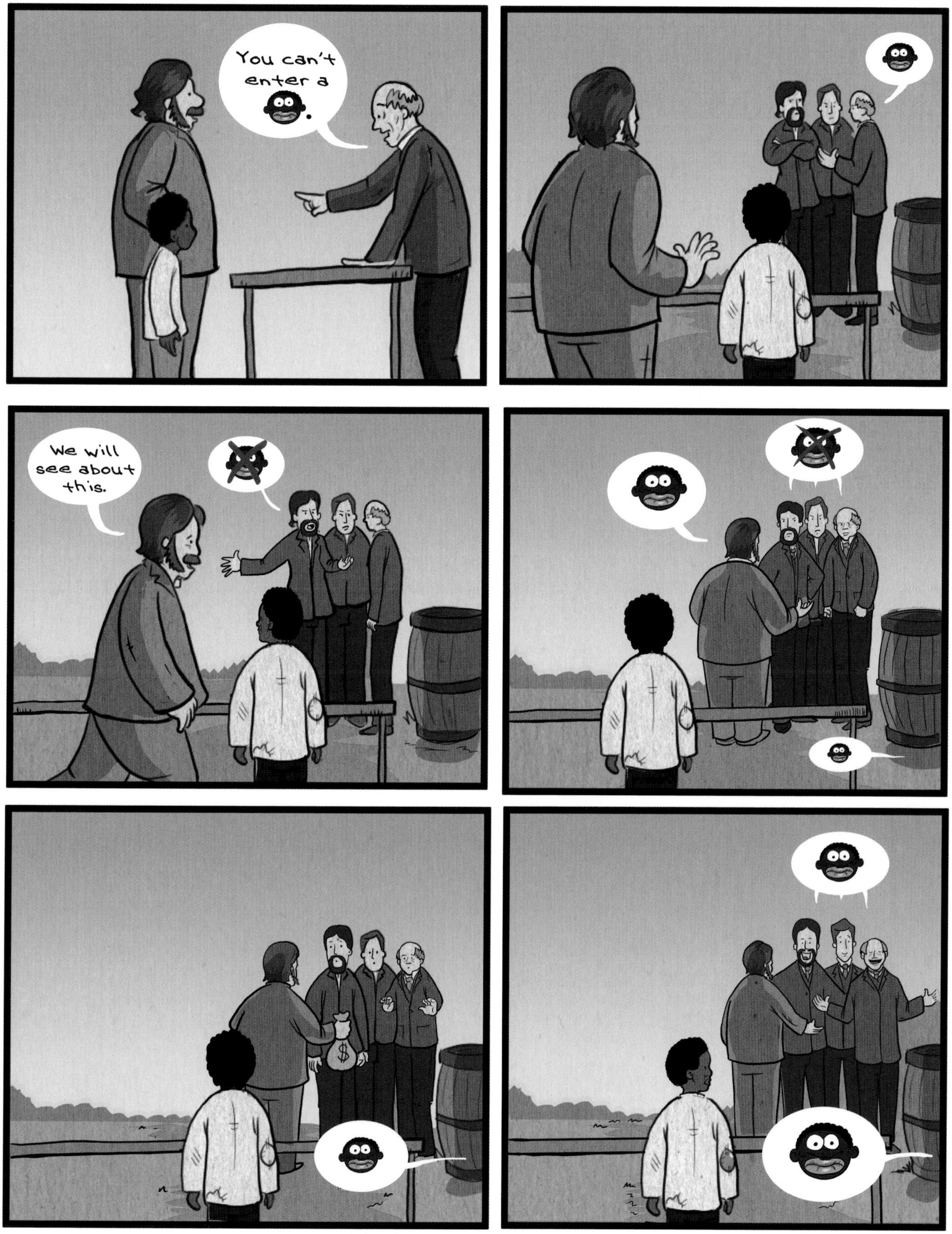
You can't enter a
We will see about this.

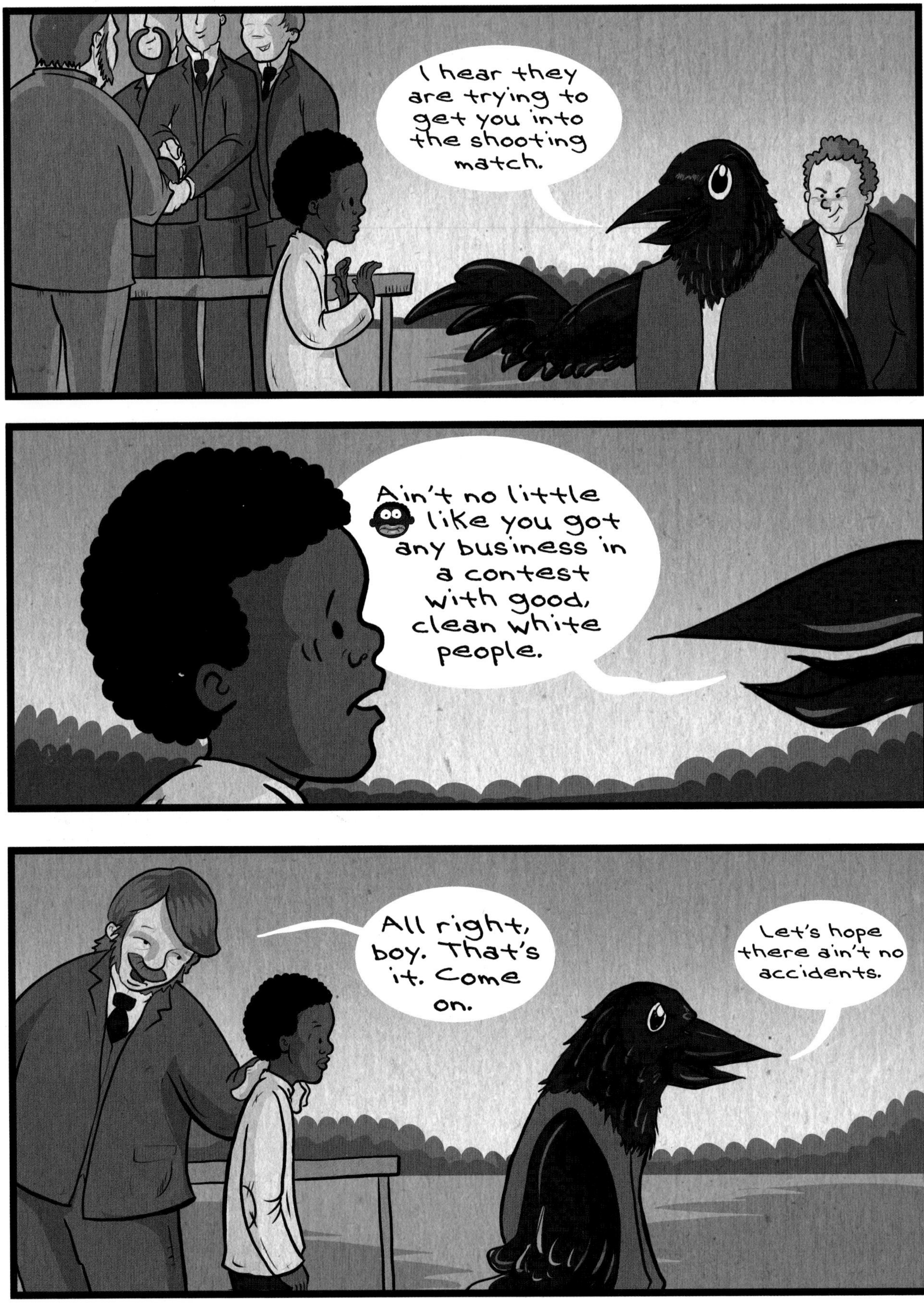
I hear they are trying to get you into the shooting match.
Ain't no little like you got any business in a contest with good, clean white people.
All right, boy. That's it. Come on.
Let's hope there ain't no accidents.

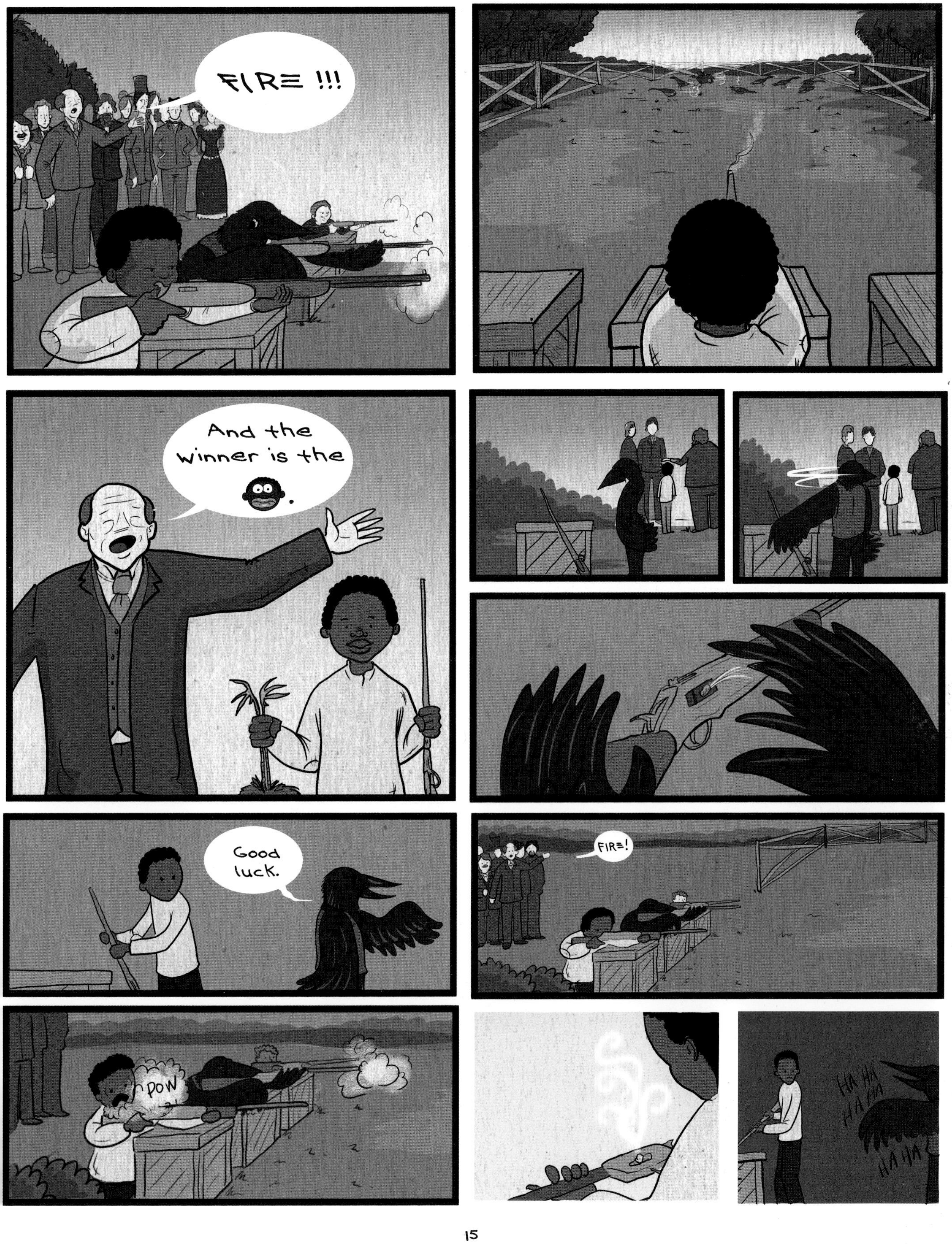

FIRE !!!
And the winner is the .
Good luck.
FIRE!
POW
HA HA
HA HA
HA HA

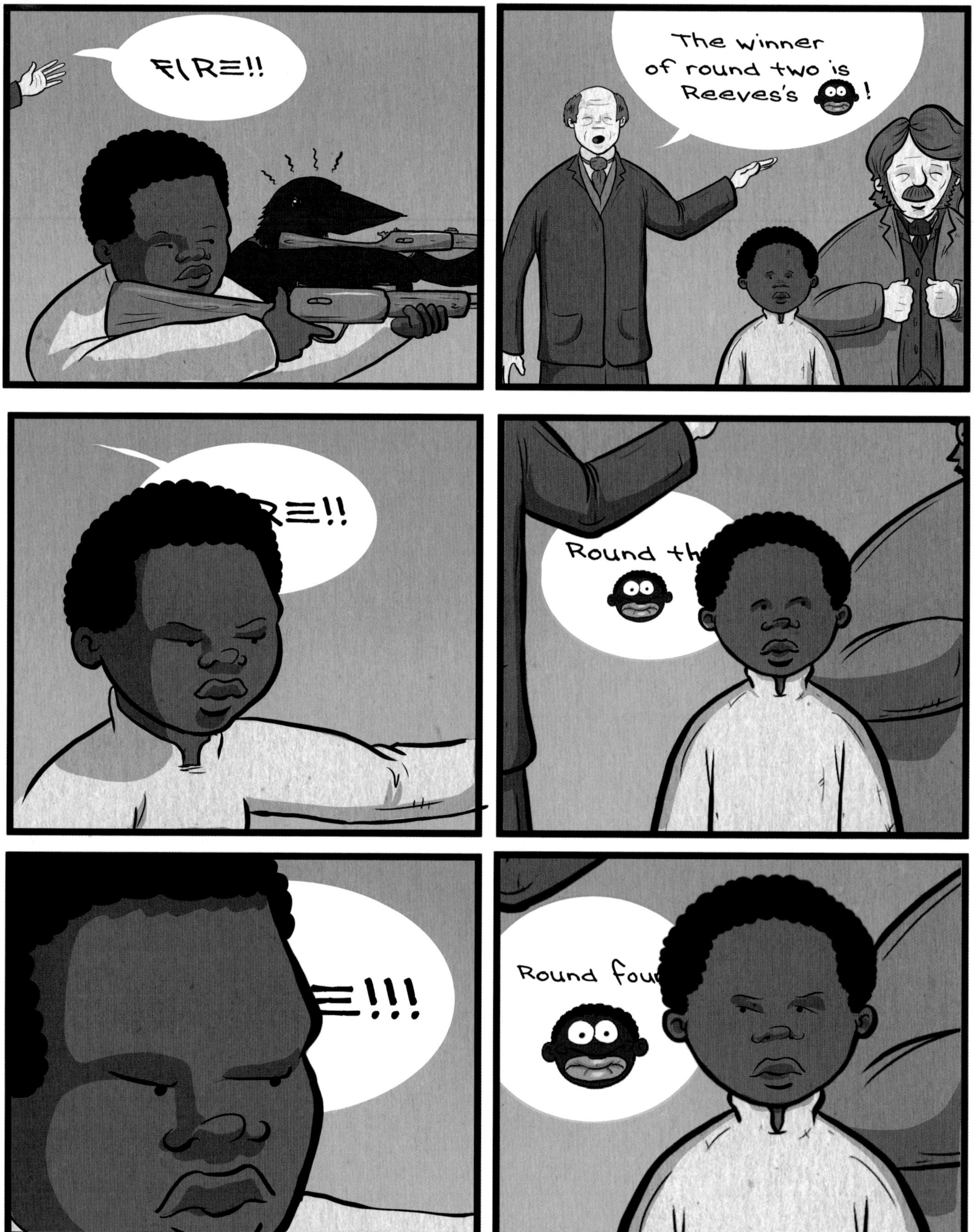

FIRE!!
The winner of round two is Reeves's !
RE!!
Round th
E!!!
Round fou

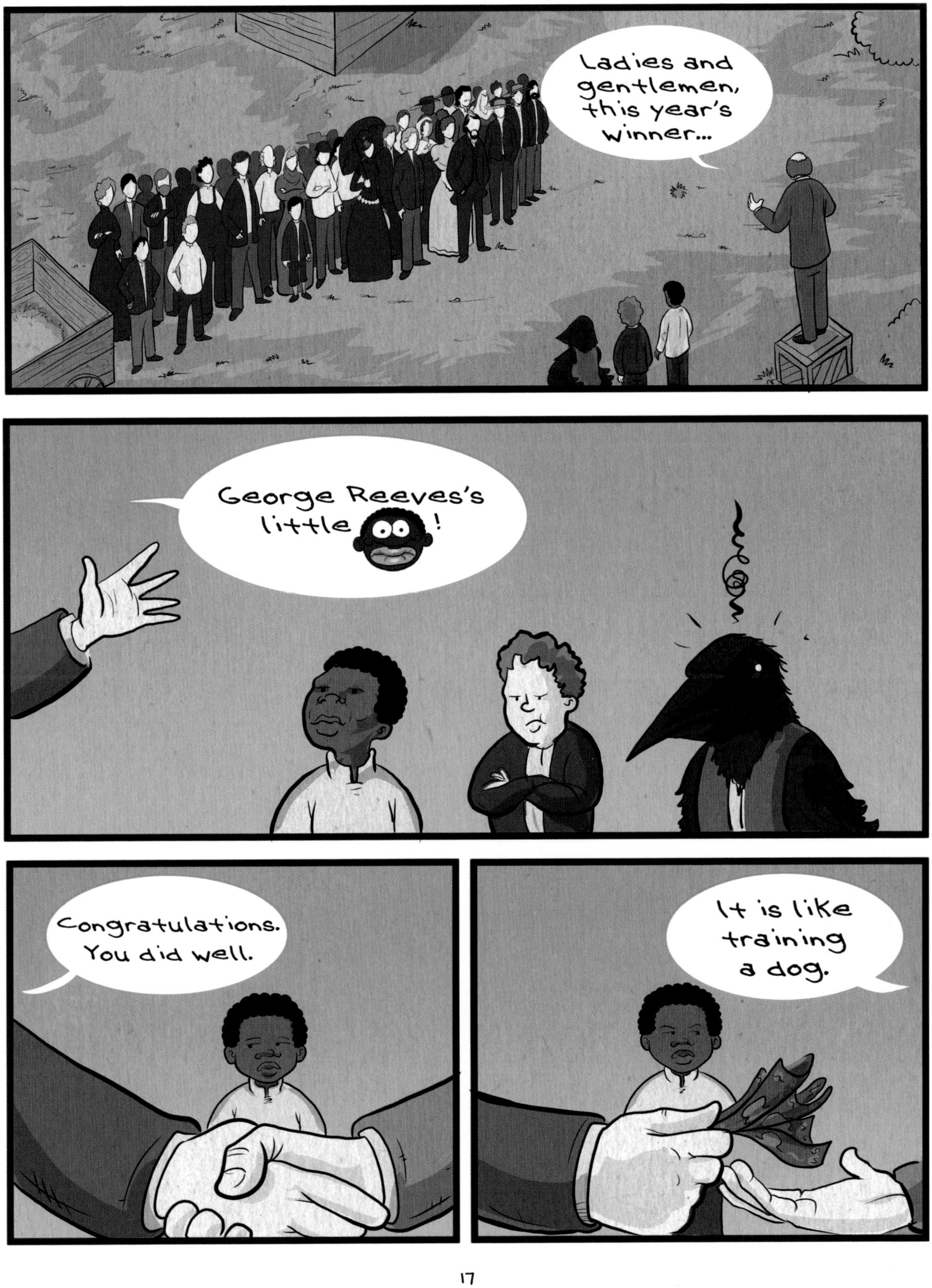
Ladies and gentlemen, this year's winner...
George Reeves's little !
Congratulations. You did well.
It is like training a dog.

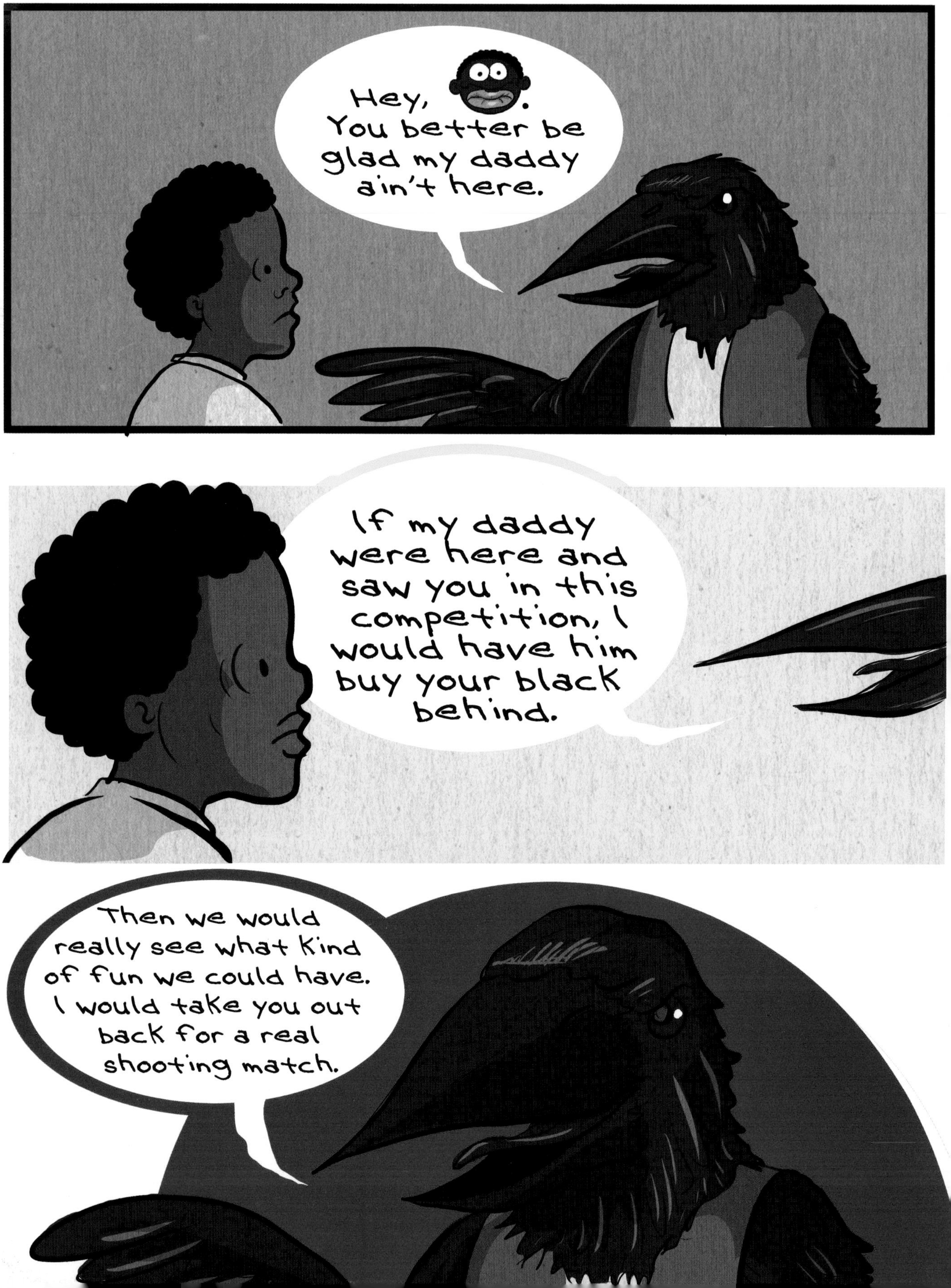
Hey, . You better be glad my daddy ain't here.
If my daddy were here and saw you in this competition, I would have him buy your black behind.
Then we would really see what kind of fun we could have. I would take you out back for a real shooting match.

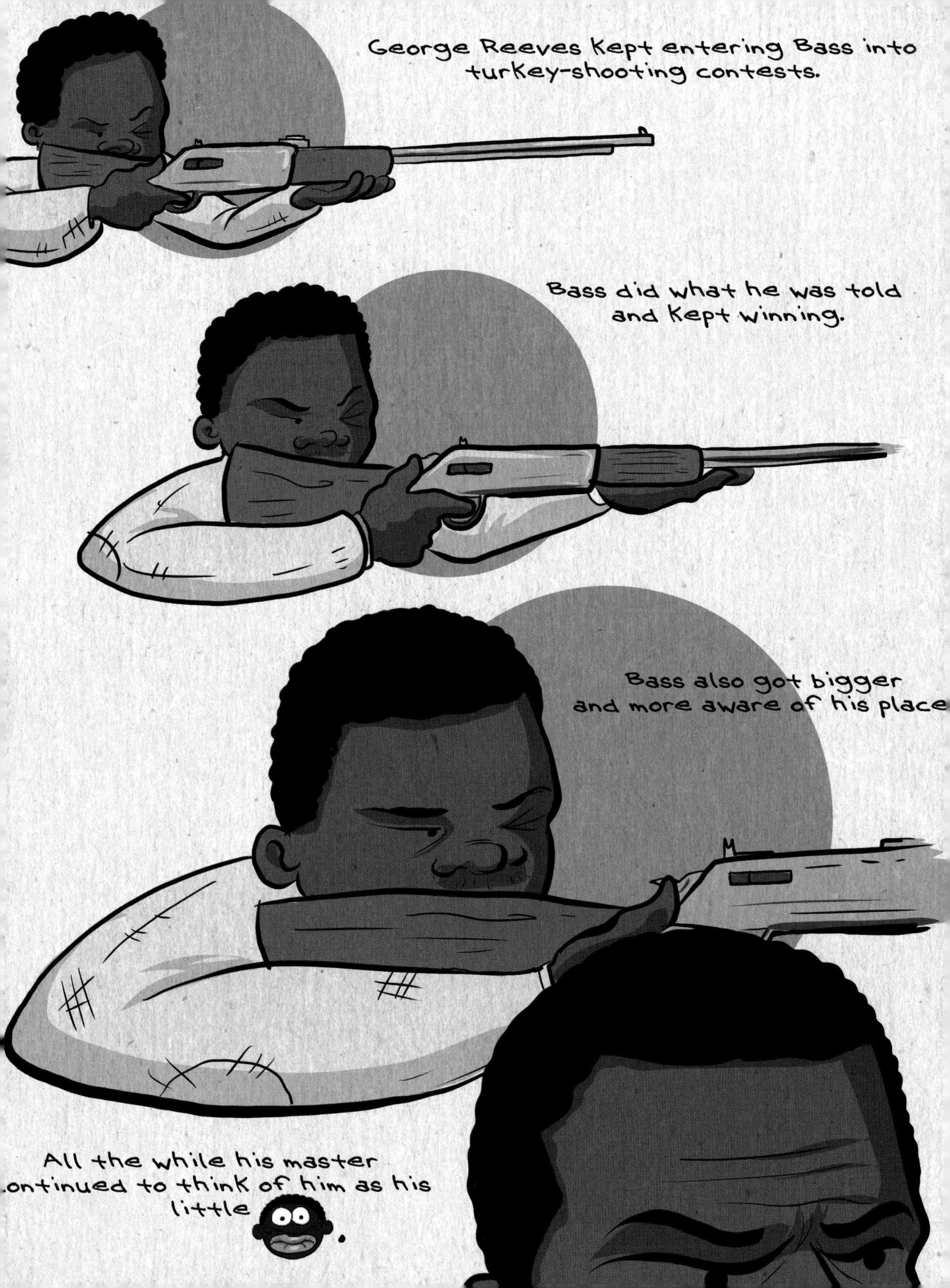
George Reeves Kept entering Bass into turkey-shooting contests.
Bass did what he was told and Kept winning.
Bass also got bigger and more aware of his place
All the while his master ontinued to think of him as his little

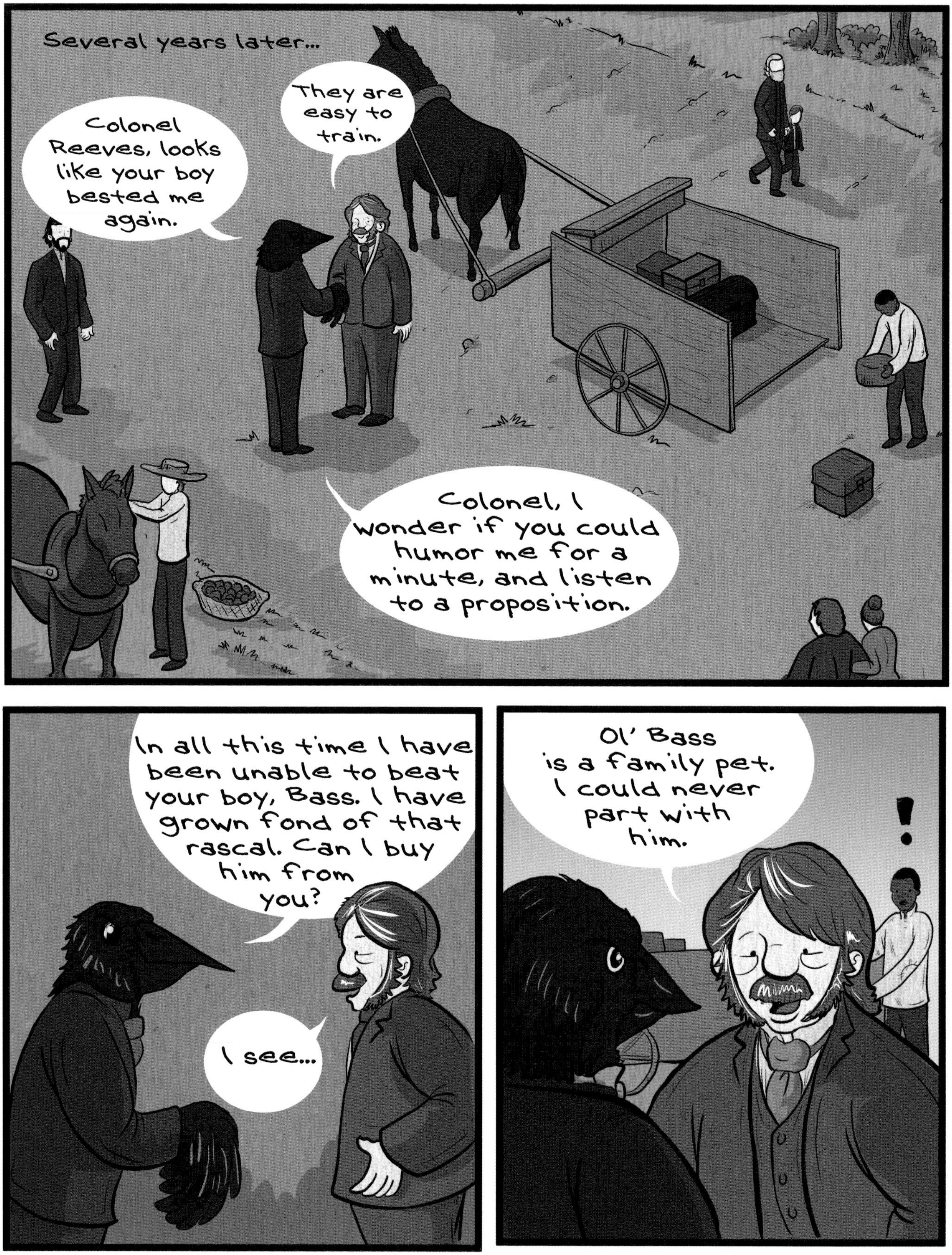
Several years later...
Colonel Reeves, looks like your boy bested me again.
They are easy to train.
Colonel, I wonder if you could humor me for a minute, and listen to a proposition.
In all this time I have been unable to beat your boy, Bass. I have grown fond of that rascal. Can I buy him from you?
I see...
Ol' Bass is a family pet. I could never part with him.
!

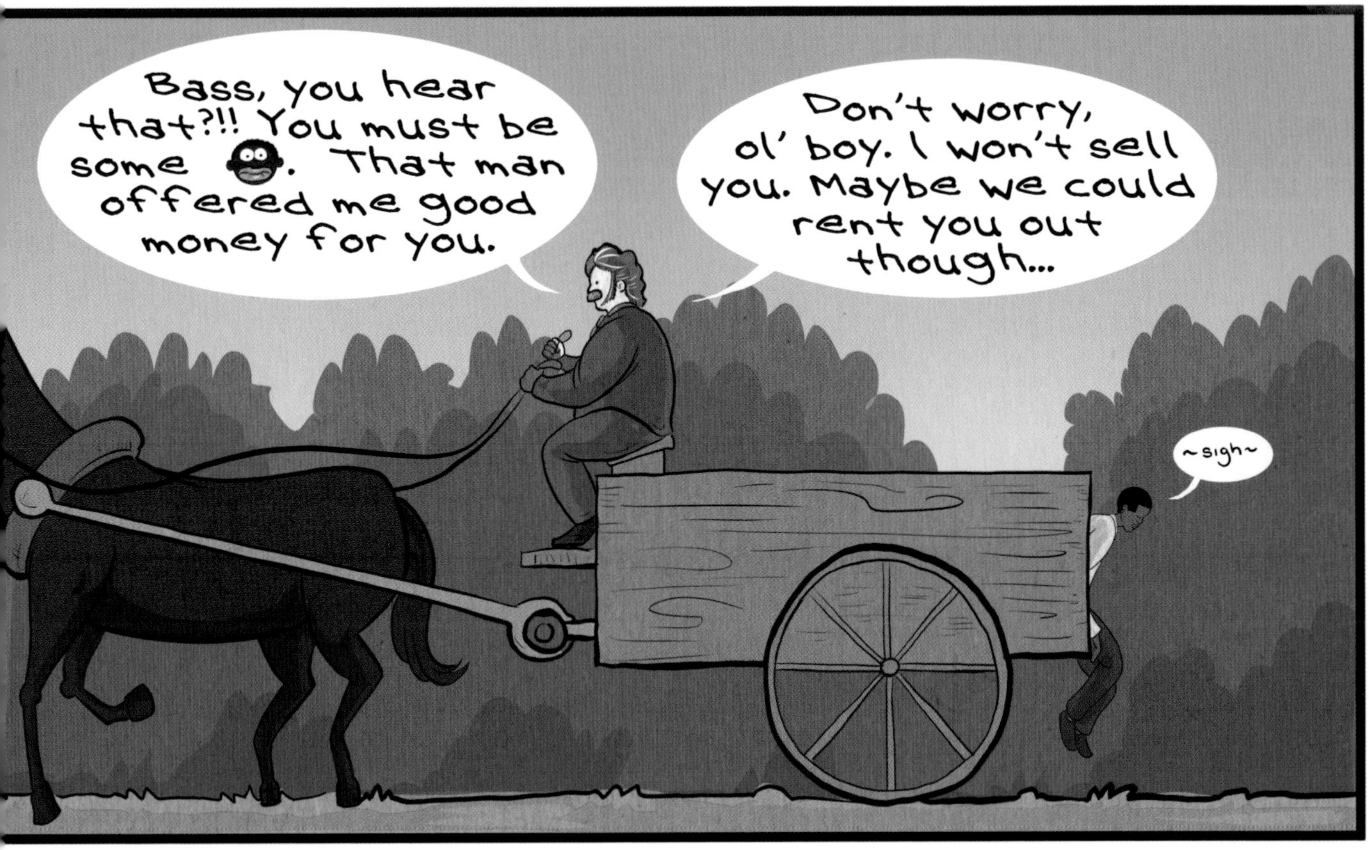
Bass, you hear that?!! You must be some . That man offered me good money for you.
Don't worry, ol' boy. I won't sell you. Maybe we could rent you out though...
~sigh~

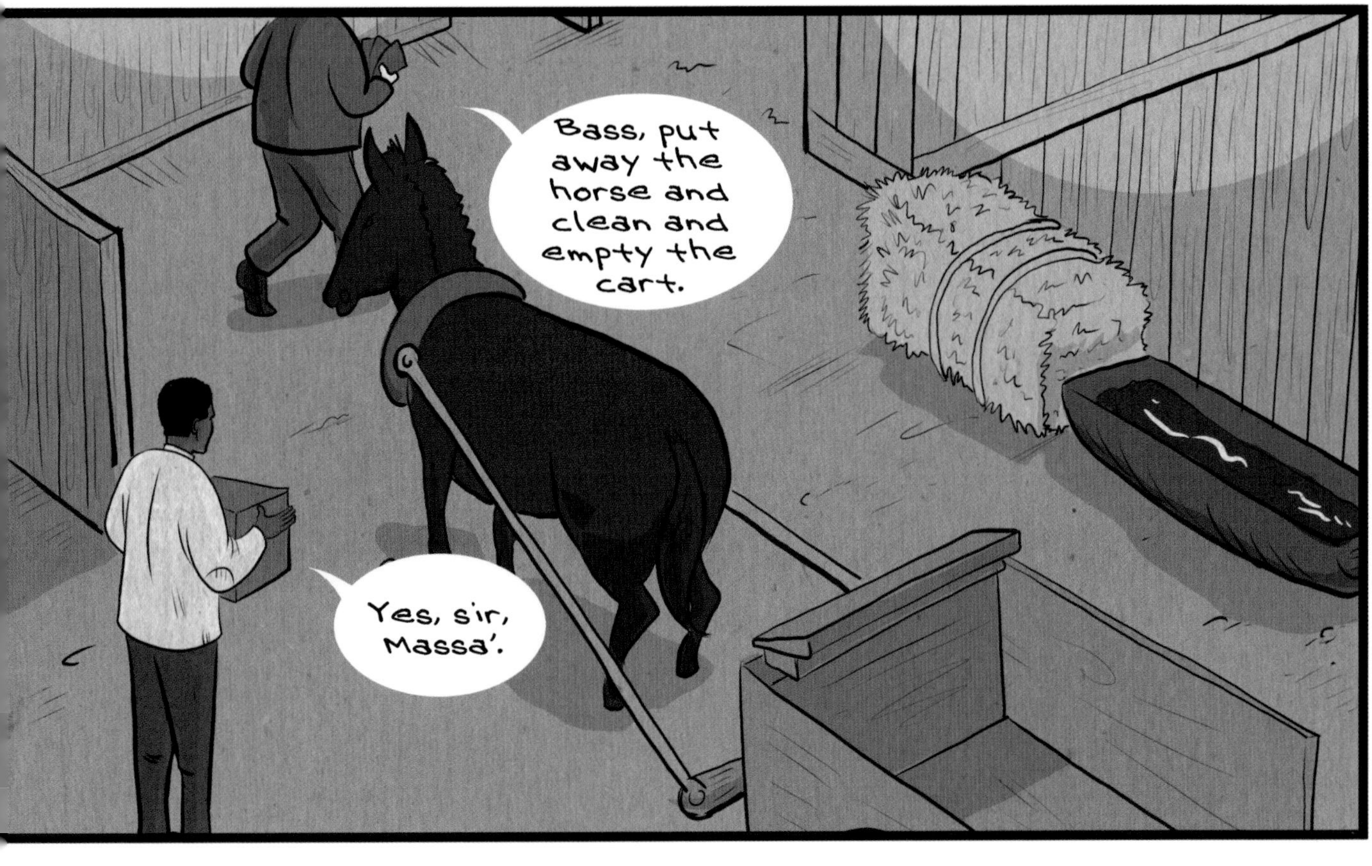
Bass, put away the horse and clean and empty the cart.
Yes, sir, Massa'.

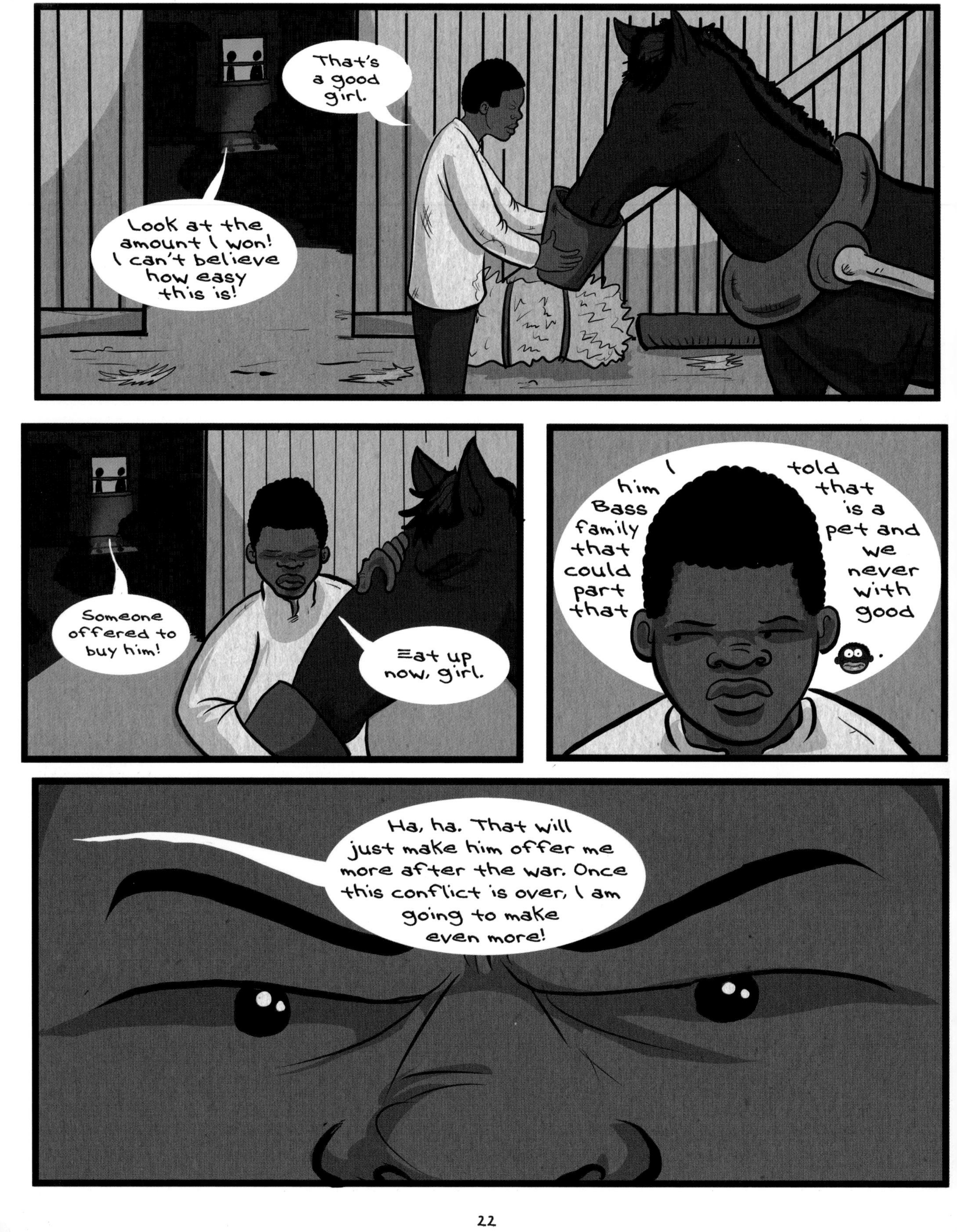
That's a good girl.
Look at the amount I won! I can't believe how easy this is!
Someone offered to buy him!
Eat up now, girl.
I told him that Bass is a family pet and that we could never part with that good
Ha, ha. That will just make him offer me more after the war. Once this conflict is over, I am going to make even more!

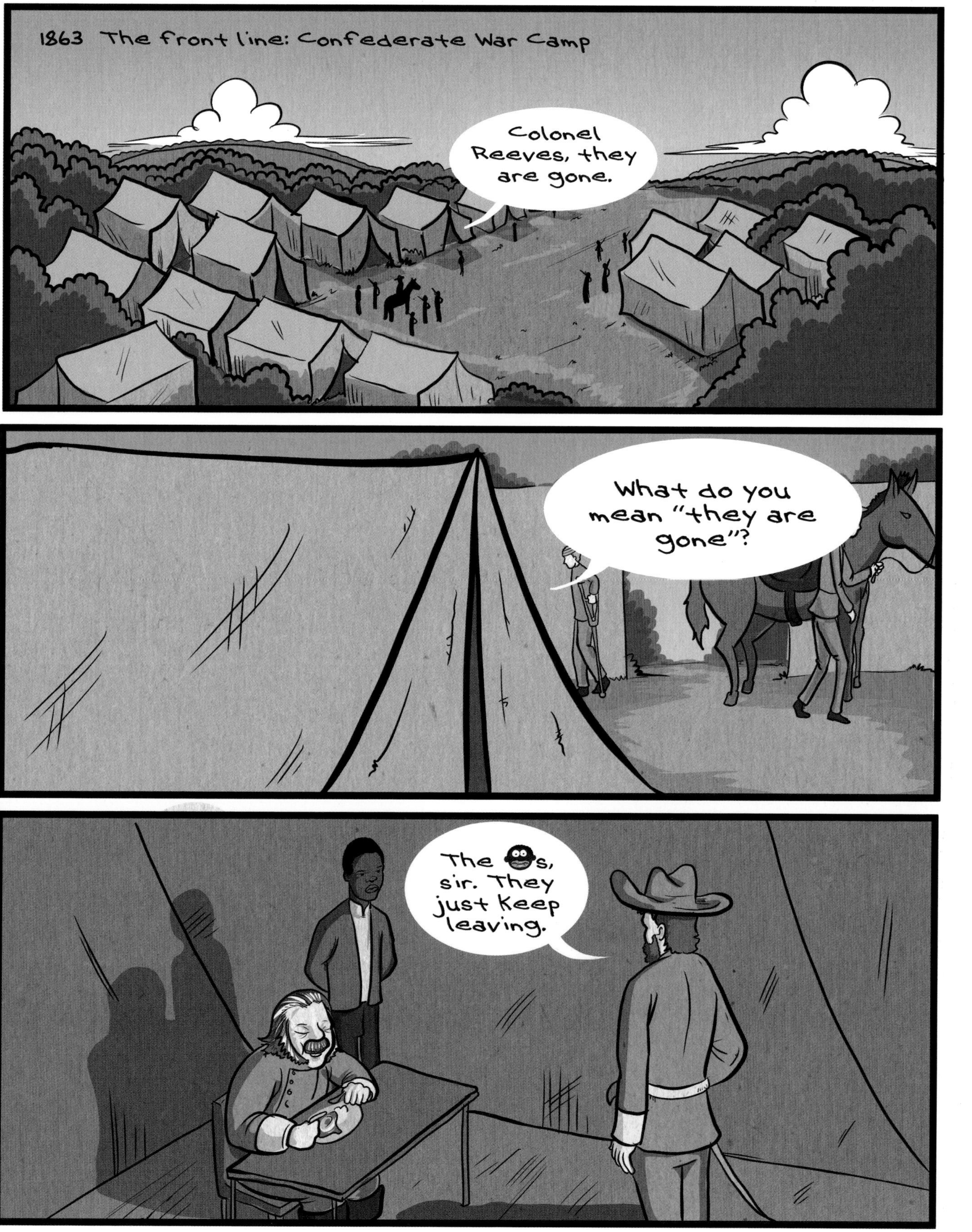
1863 The front line: Confederate War Camp
Colonel Reeves, they are gone.
What do you mean "they are gone"?
The s, sir. They just keep leaving.

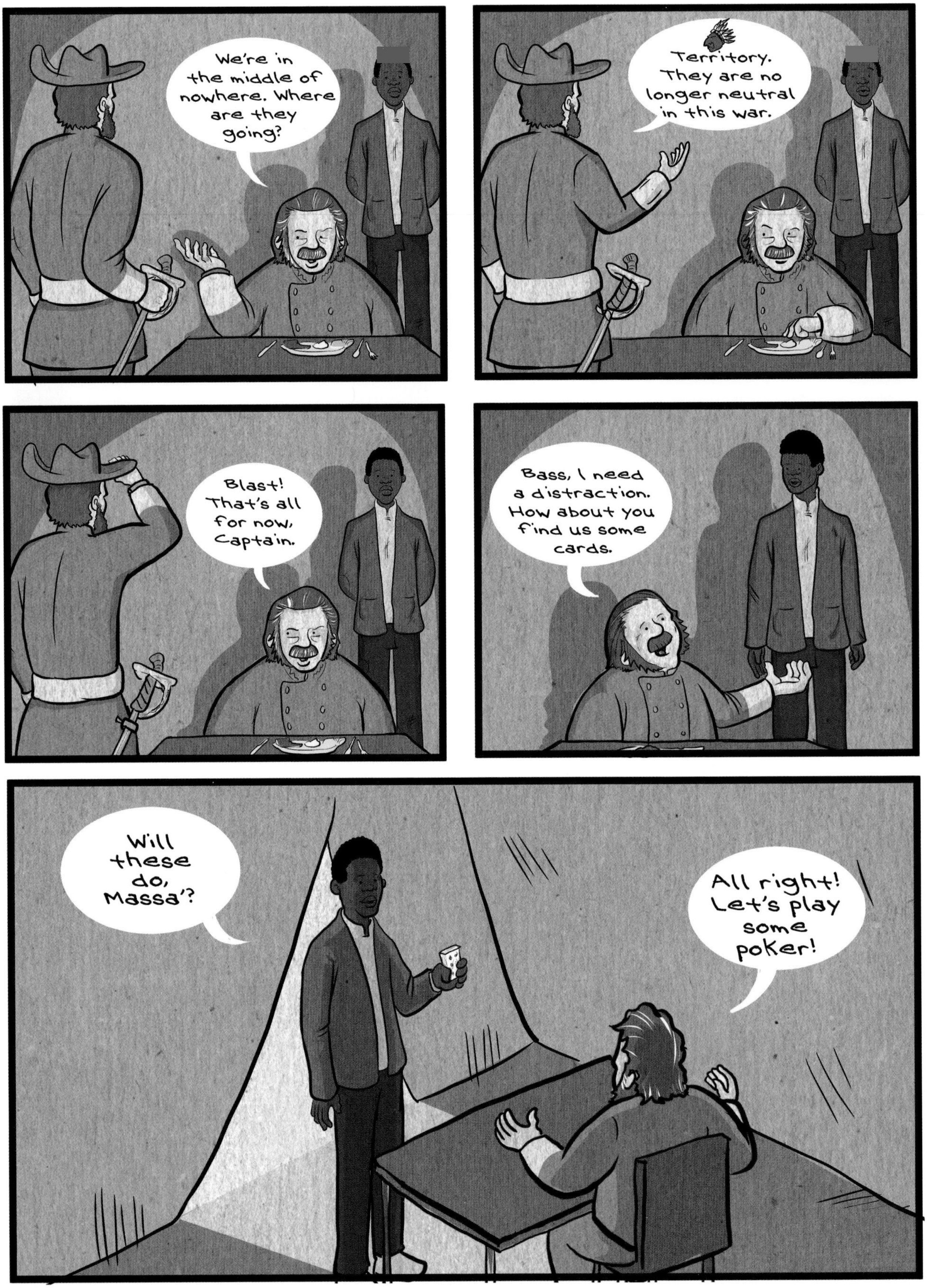
We're in the middle of nowhere. Where are they going?
Territory. They are no longer neutral in this war.
Blast! That's all for now, Captain.
Bass, I need a distraction. How about you find us some cards.
Will these do, Massa'?
All right! Let's play some poker!

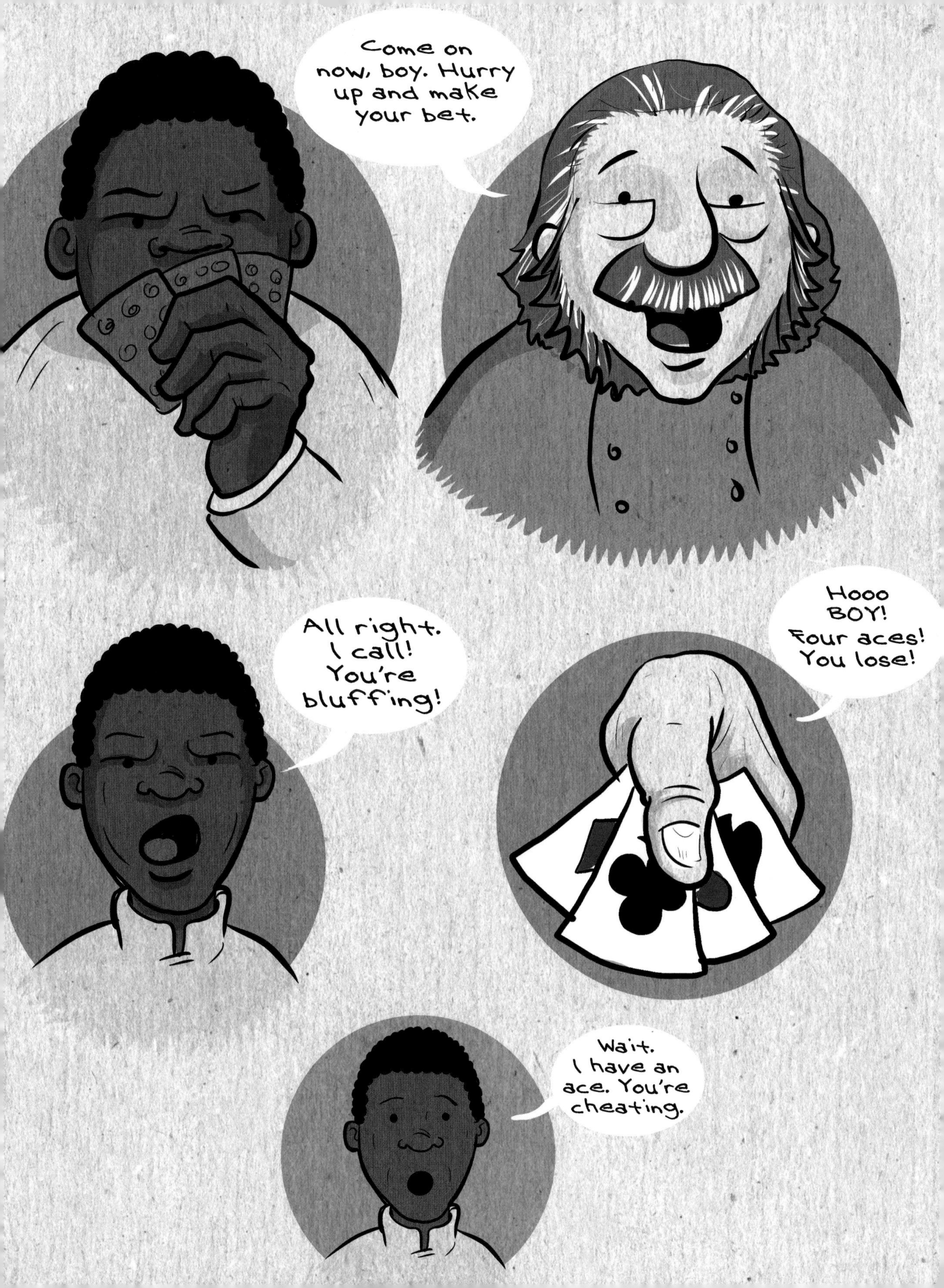
Come on now, boy. Hurry up and make your bet.
All right. I call! You're bluffing!
Hooo BOY! Four aces! You lose!
Wait. I have an ace. You're cheating.

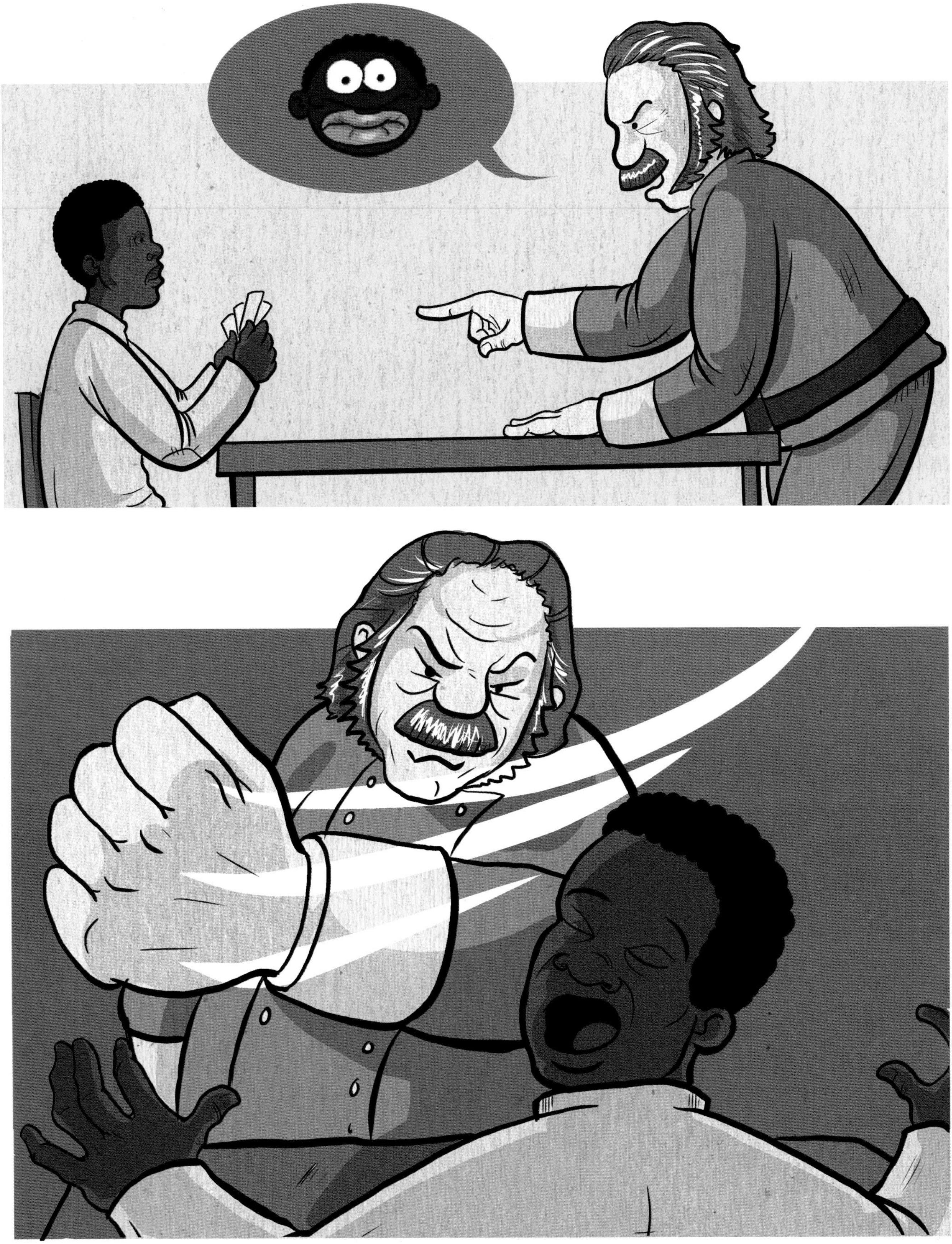

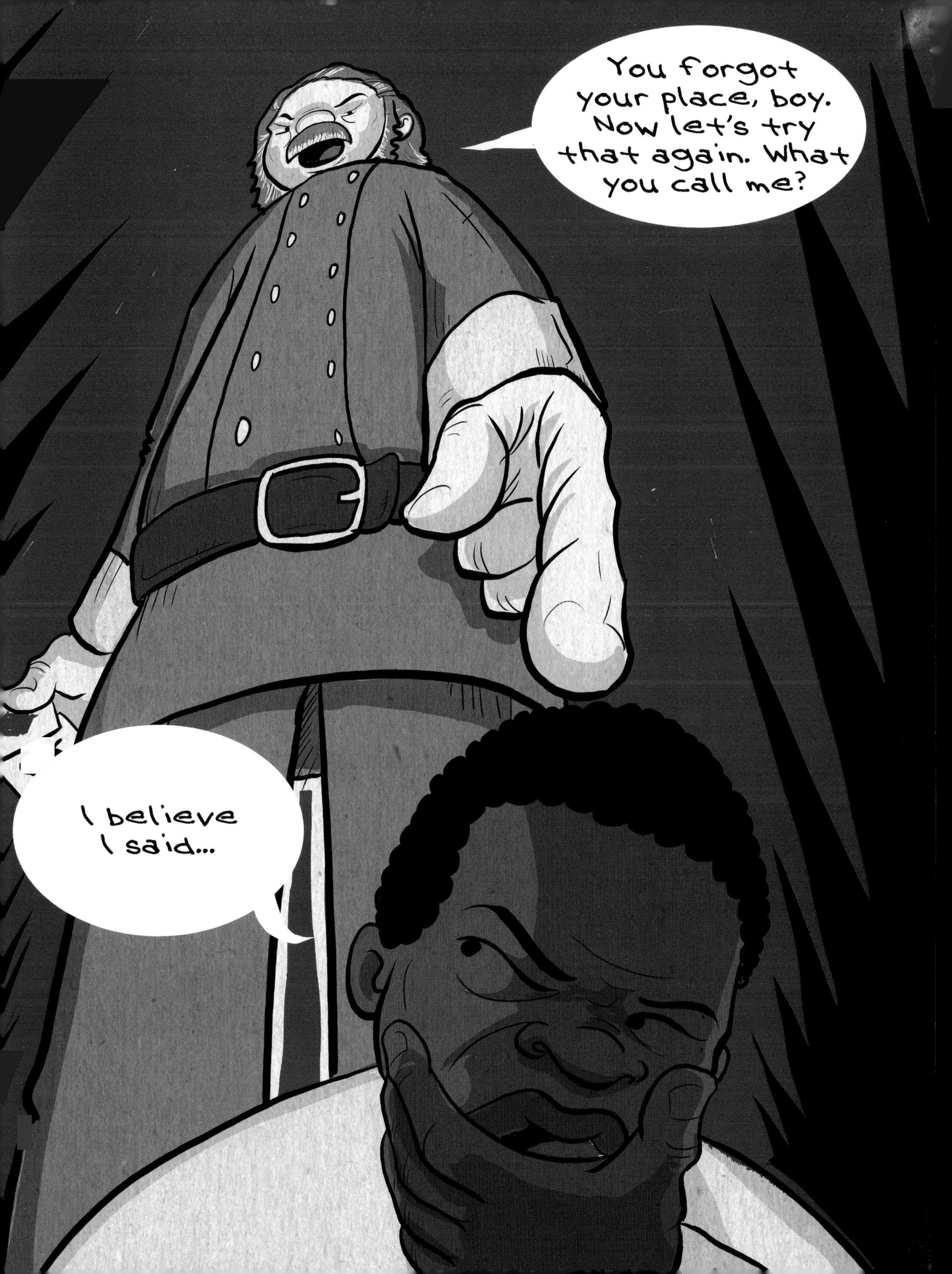
You forgot your place, boy. Now let's try that again. What you call me?
I believe I said...

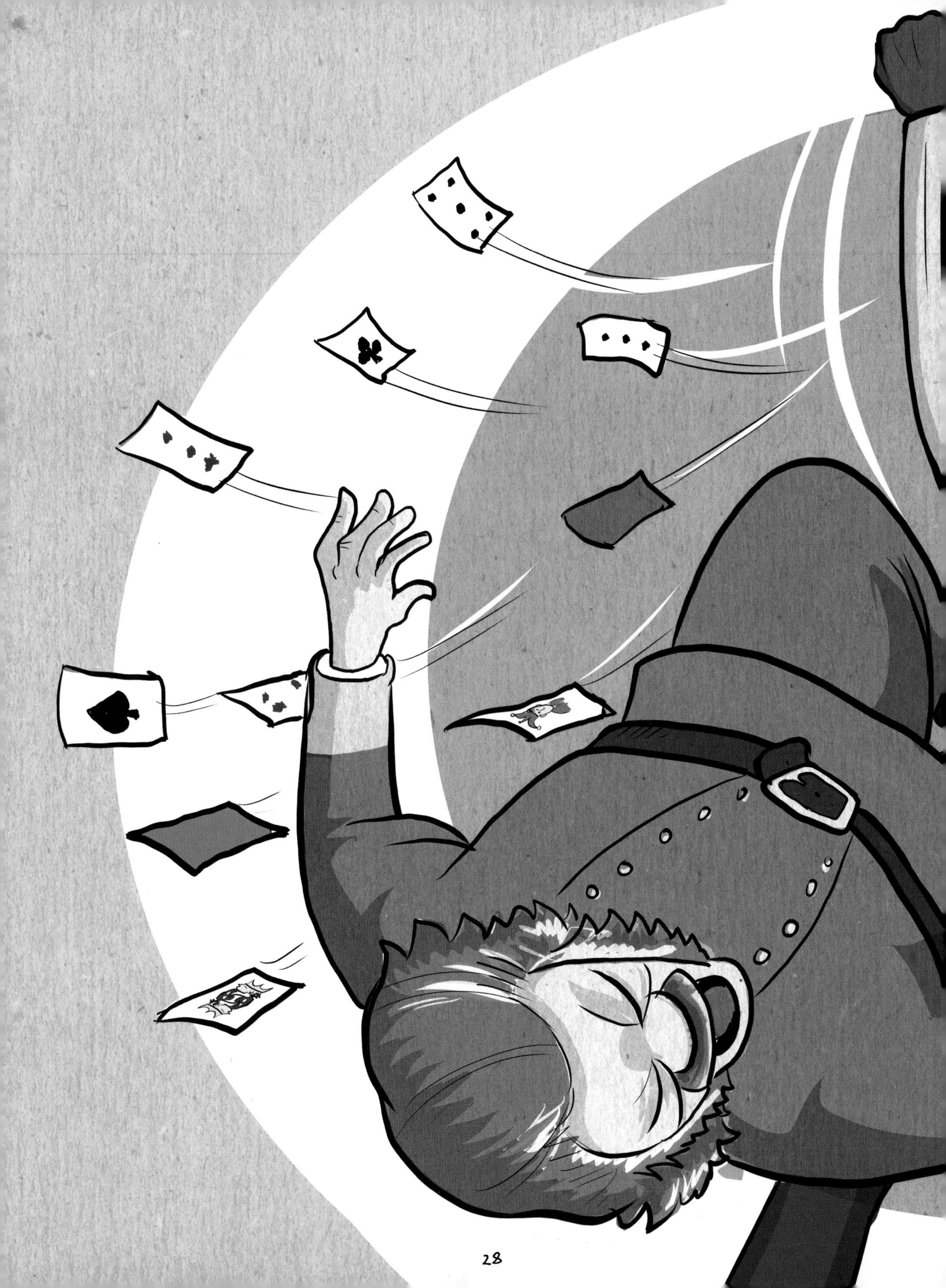

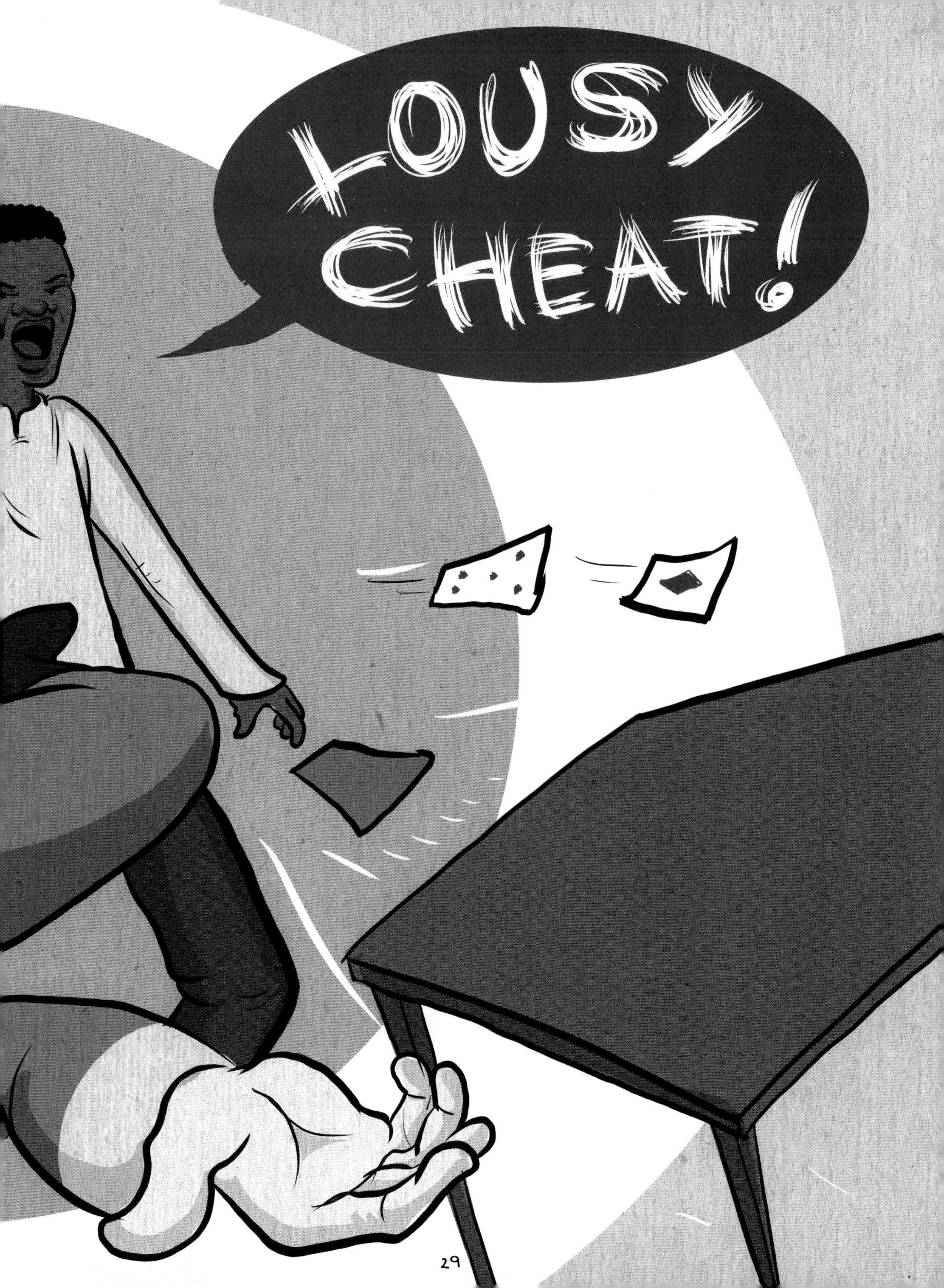
LOUSY CHEAT!

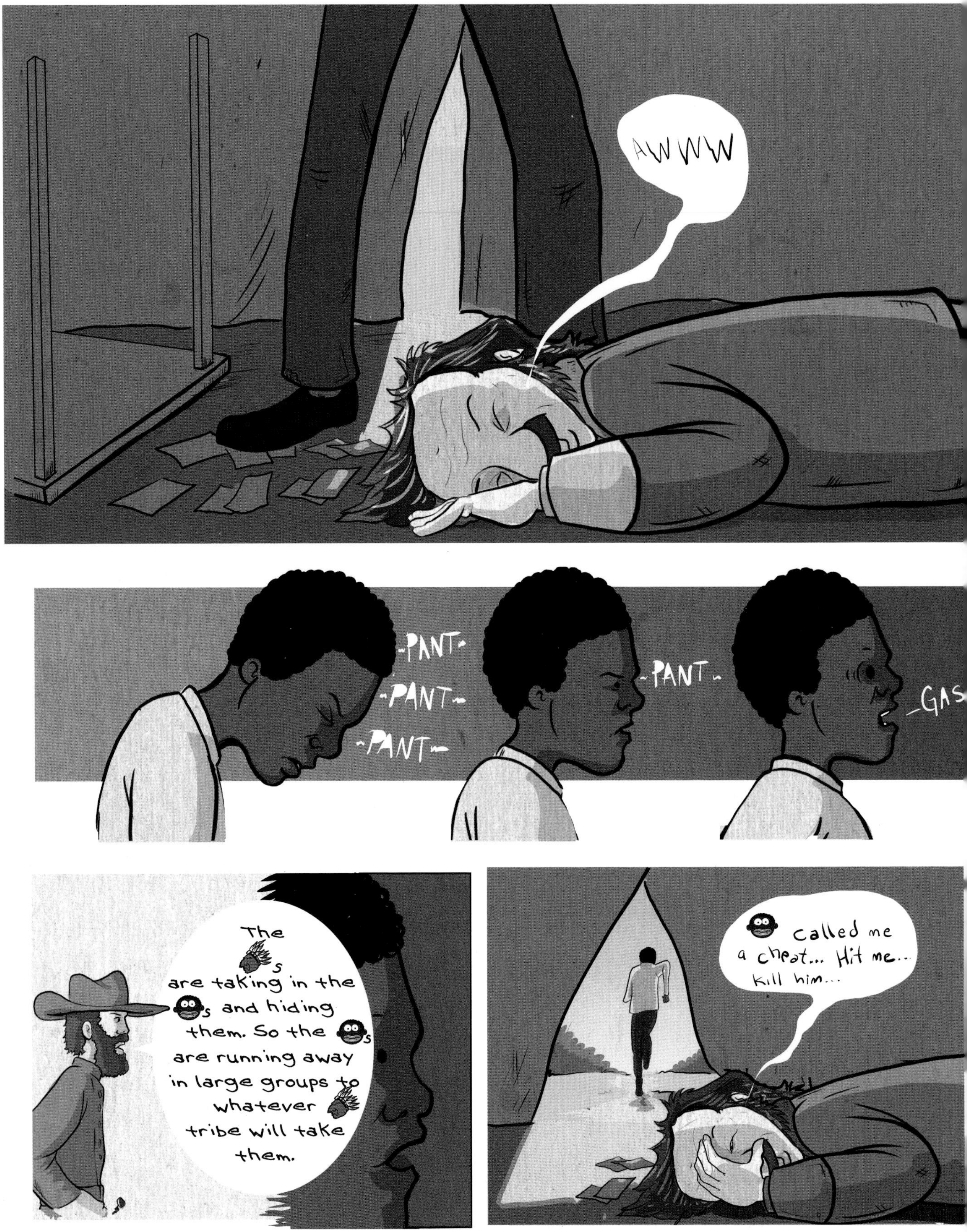
AWWW
-PANT-
-PANT-
-PANT-
-PANT-
-GAS
The s are taking in the s and hiding them. So the s are running away in large groups to whatever tribe will take them.
called me a cheat... Hit me... Kill him...

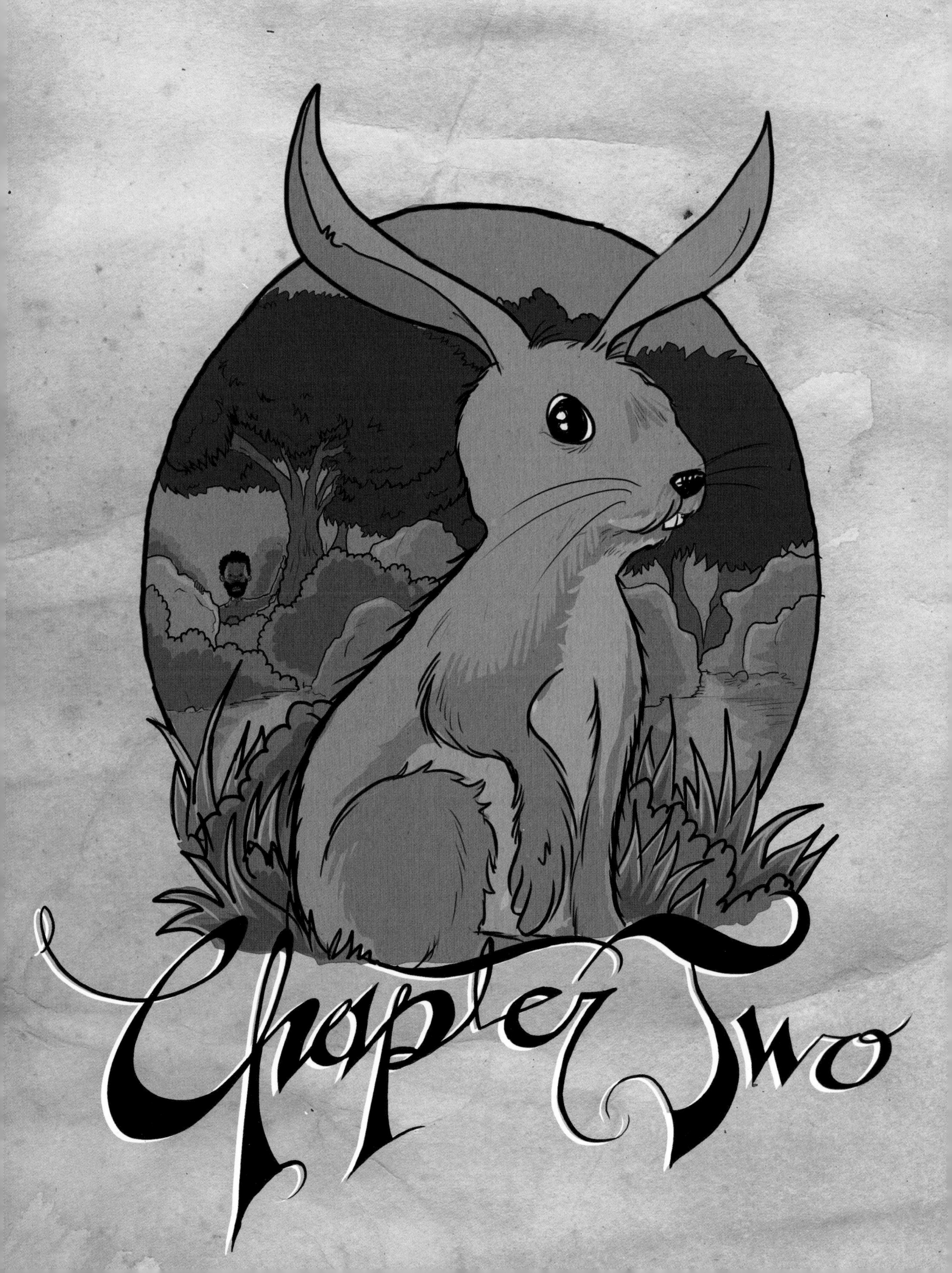

Chapter Two

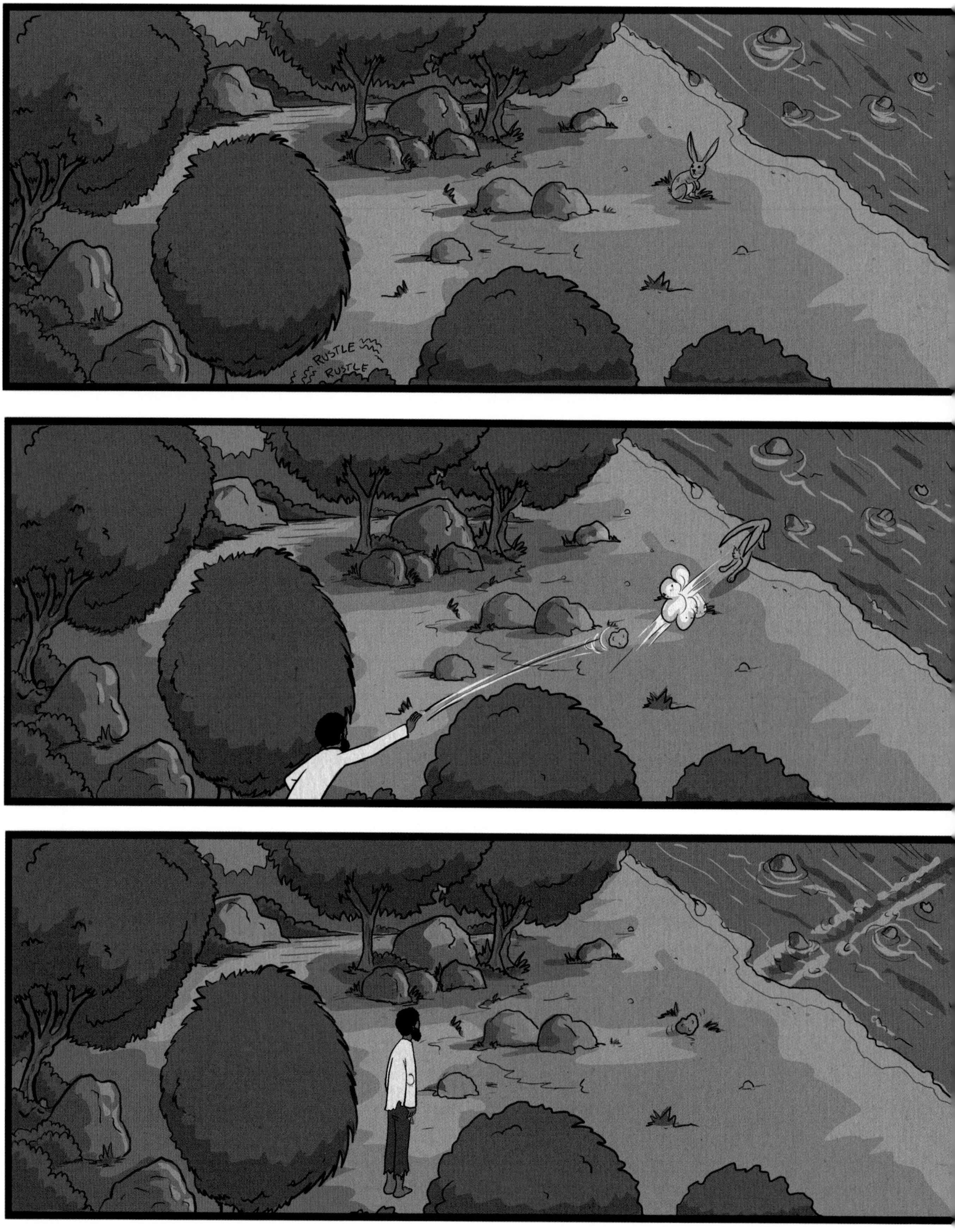
RUSTLE
RUSTLE

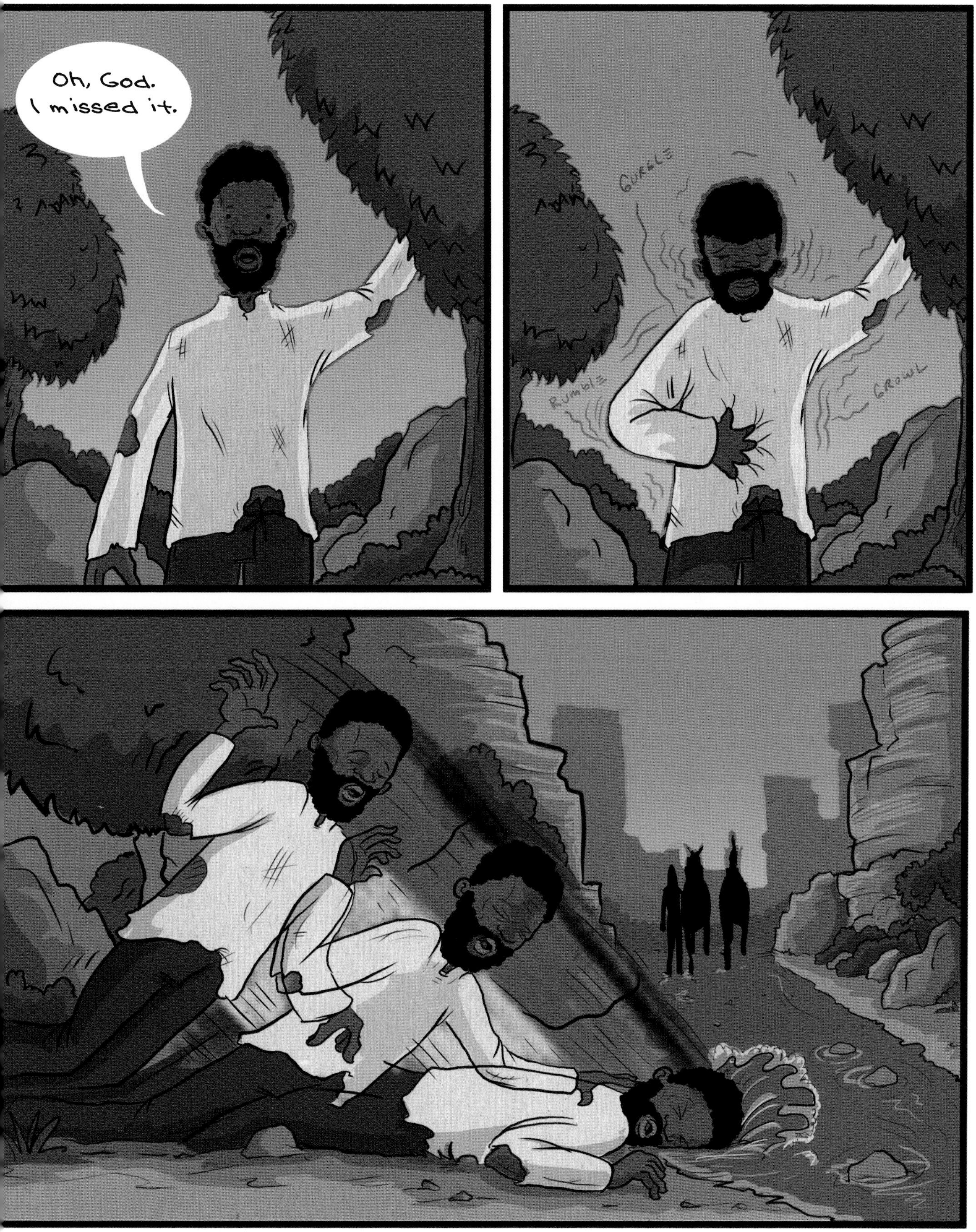

Oh, God.
I missed it.
GURGLE
RUMBLE
GROWL

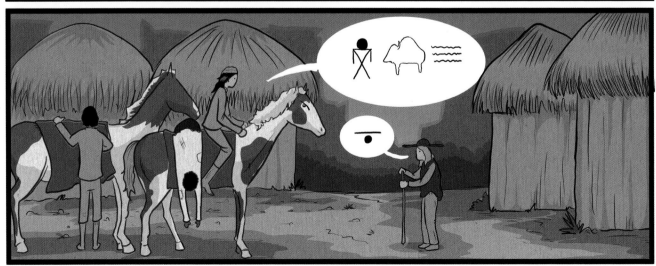

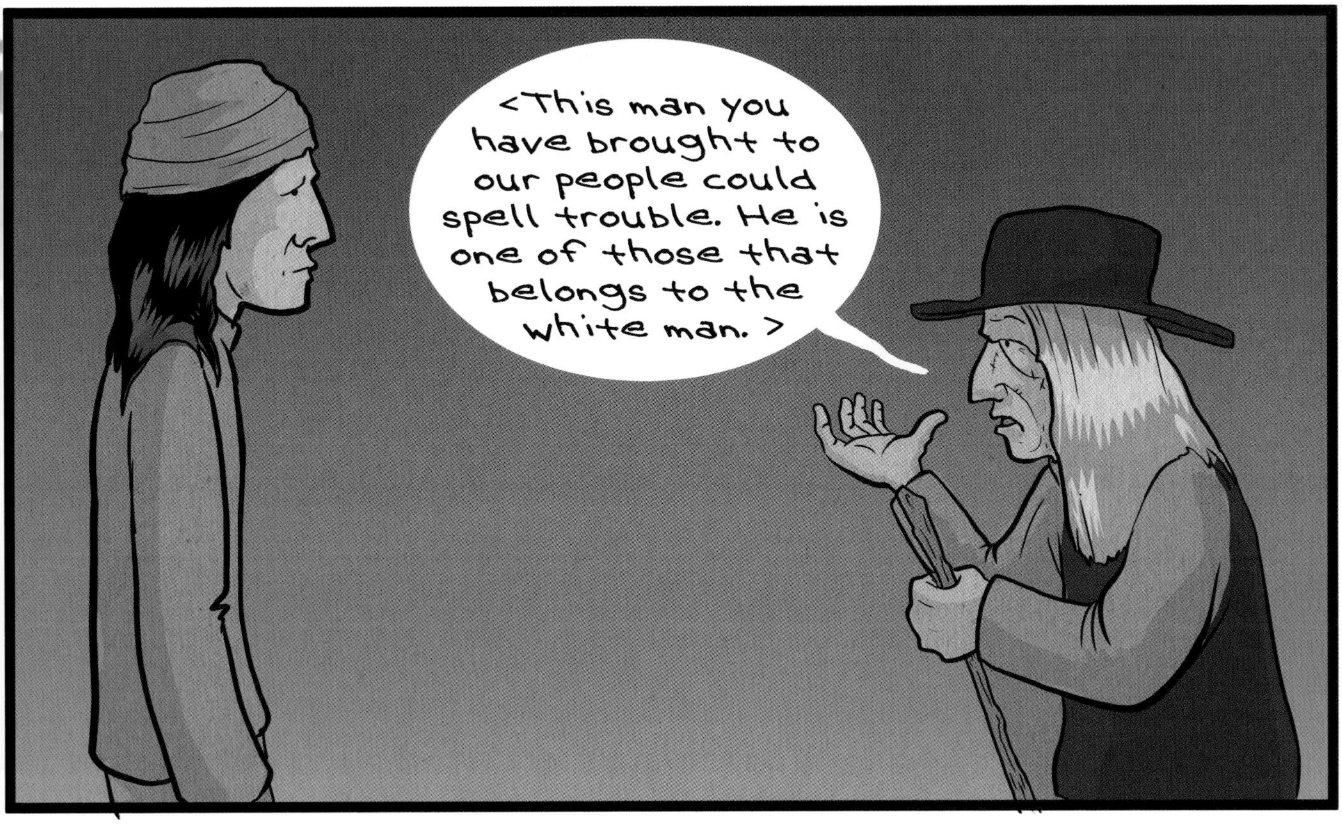
<This man you have brought to our people could spell trouble. He is one of those that belongs to the white man. >

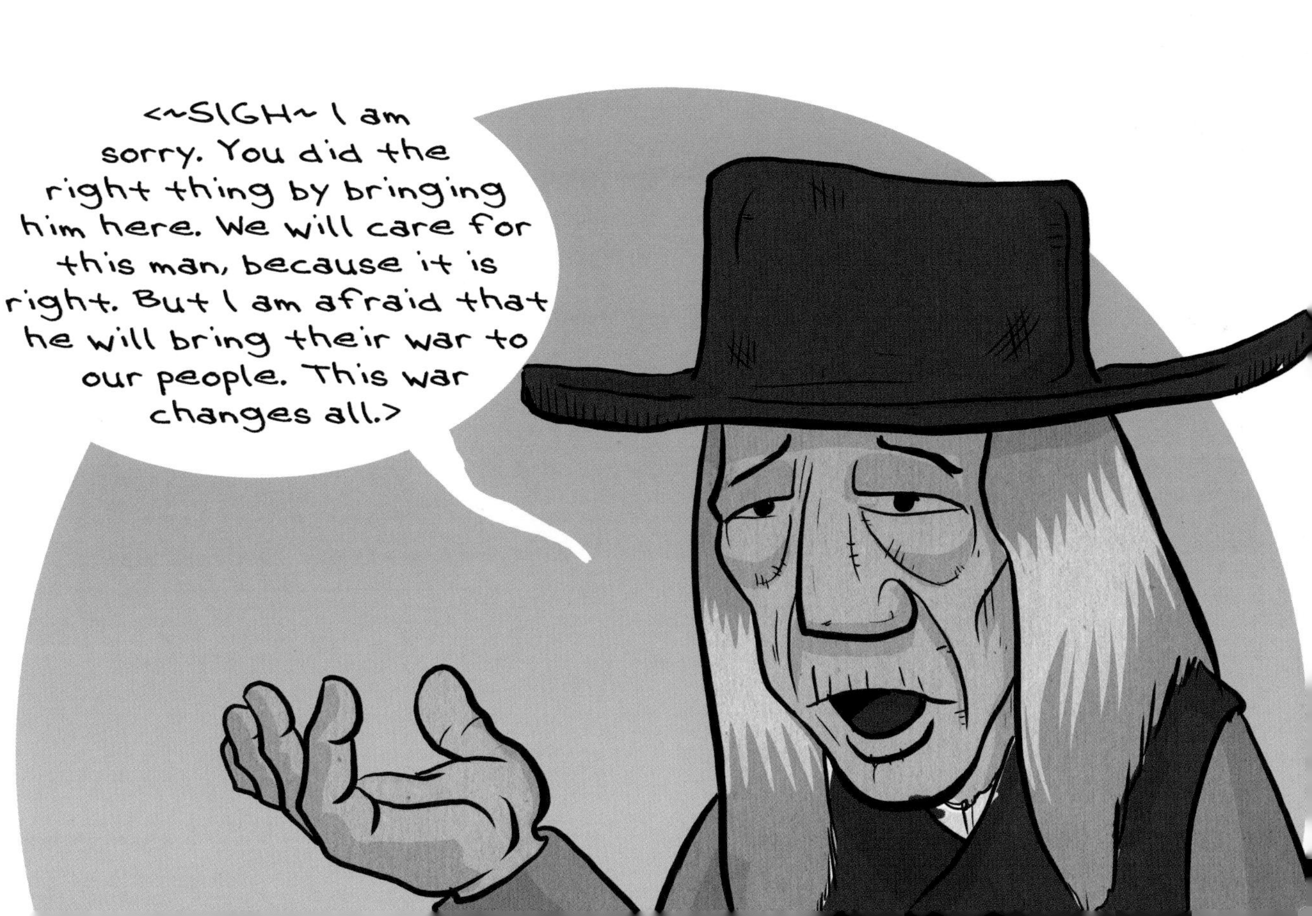
<~SIGH~ I am sorry. You did the right thing by bringing him here. We will care for this man, because it is right. But I am afraid that he will bring their war to our people. This war changes all.>

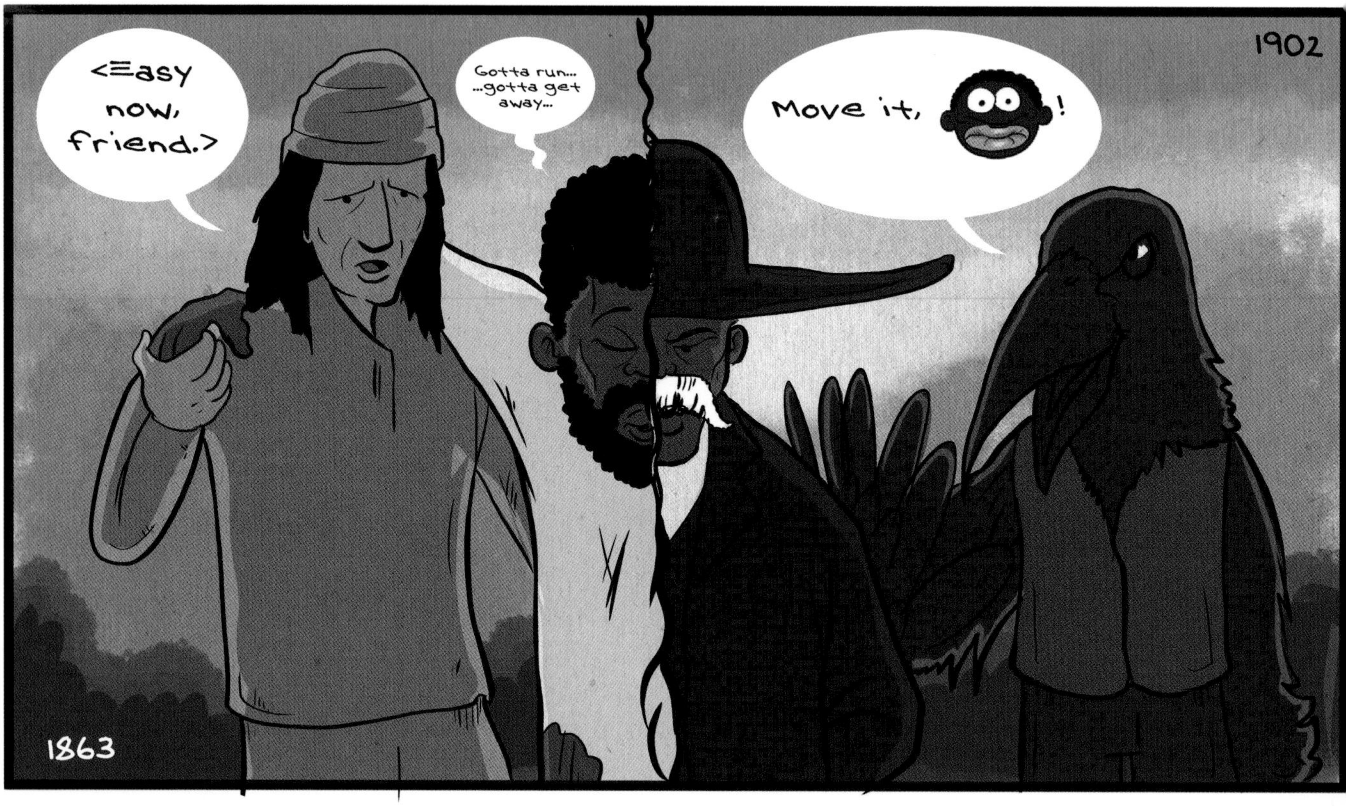
1902
<Easy now, friend.>
Gotta run... ...gotta get away...
Move it, !
1863

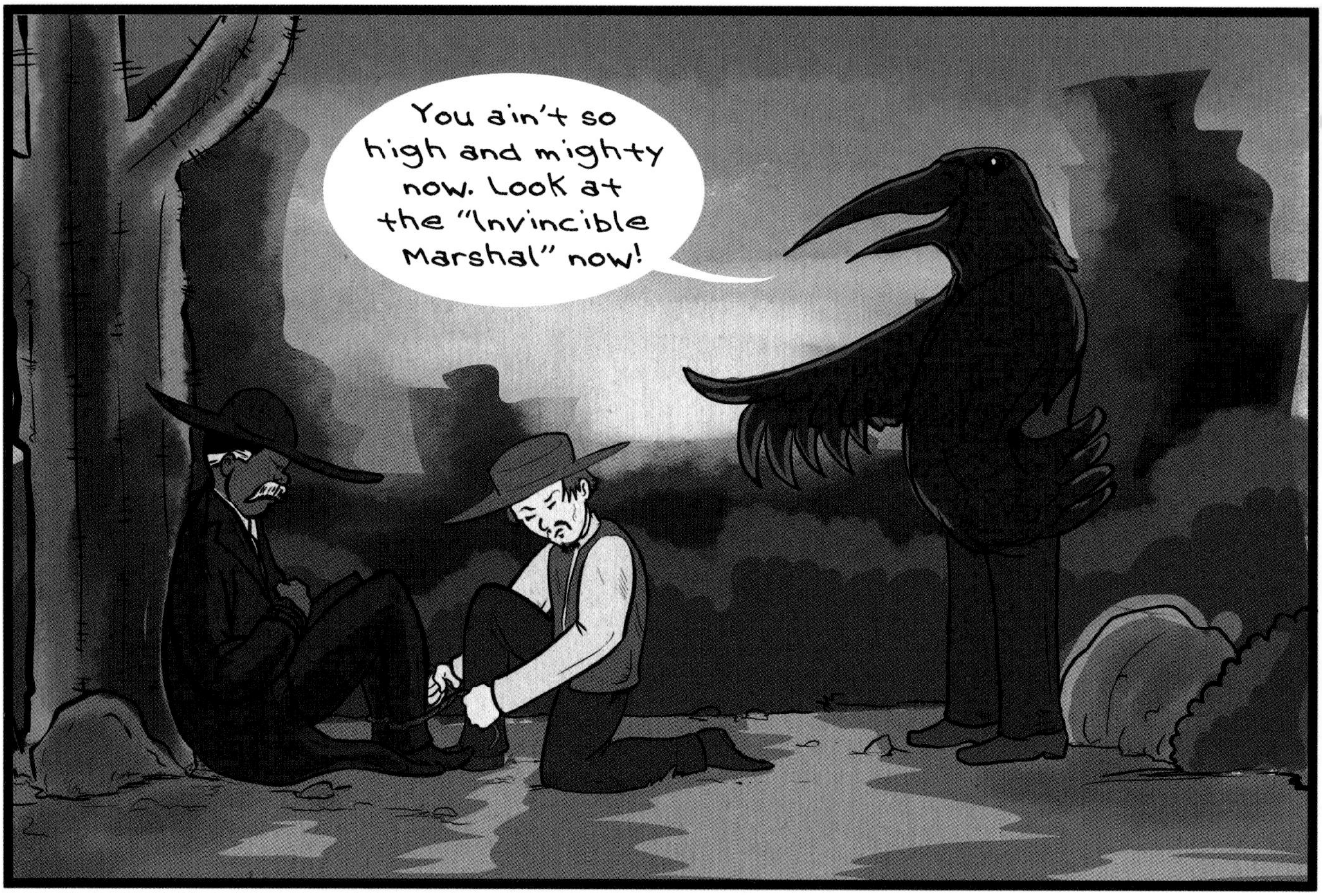
You ain't so high and mighty now. Look at the "Invincible Marshal" now!

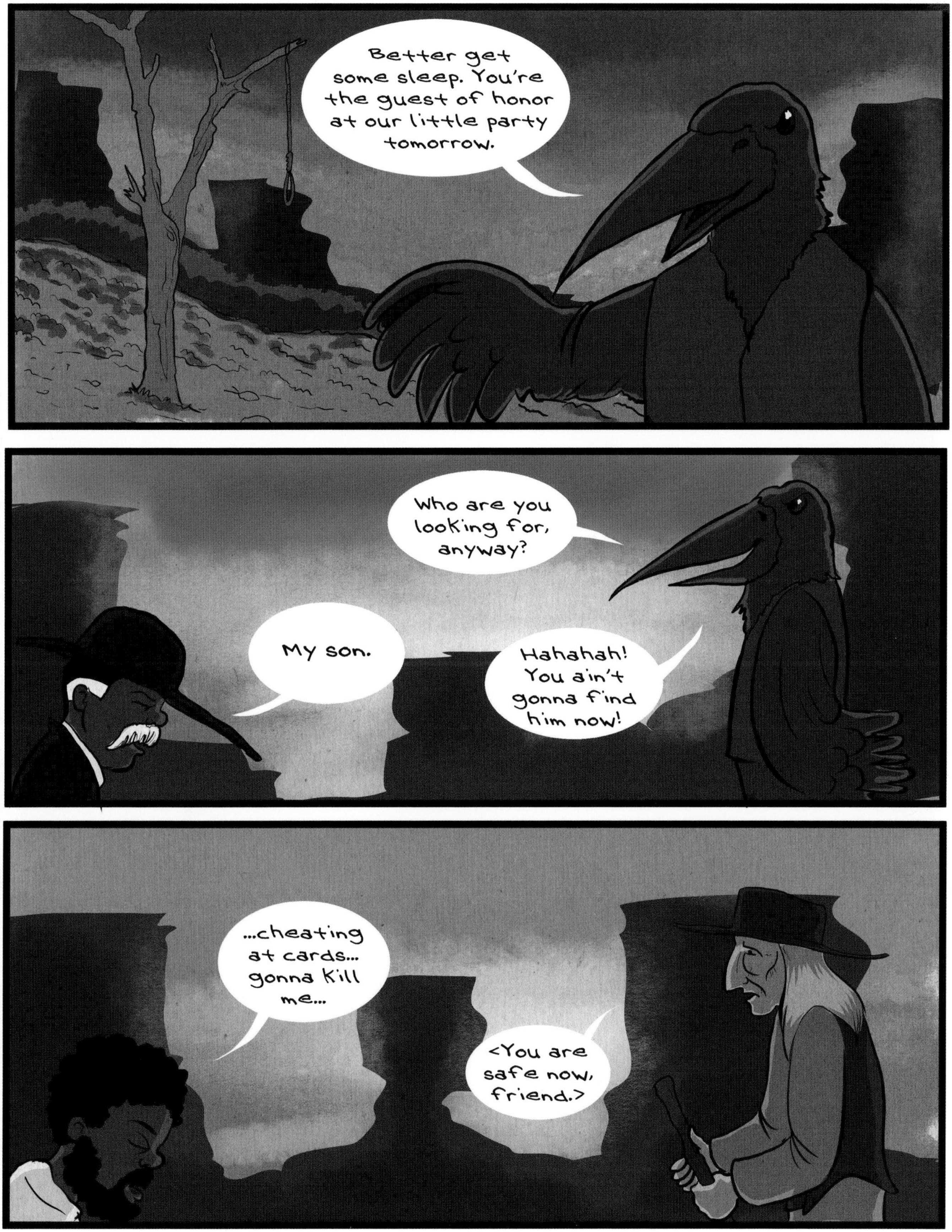
Better get some sleep. You're the guest of honor at our little party tomorrow.
Who are you looking for, anyway?
My son.
Hahahah! You ain't gonna find him now!
...cheating at cards... gonna kill me...
<You are safe now, friend.>

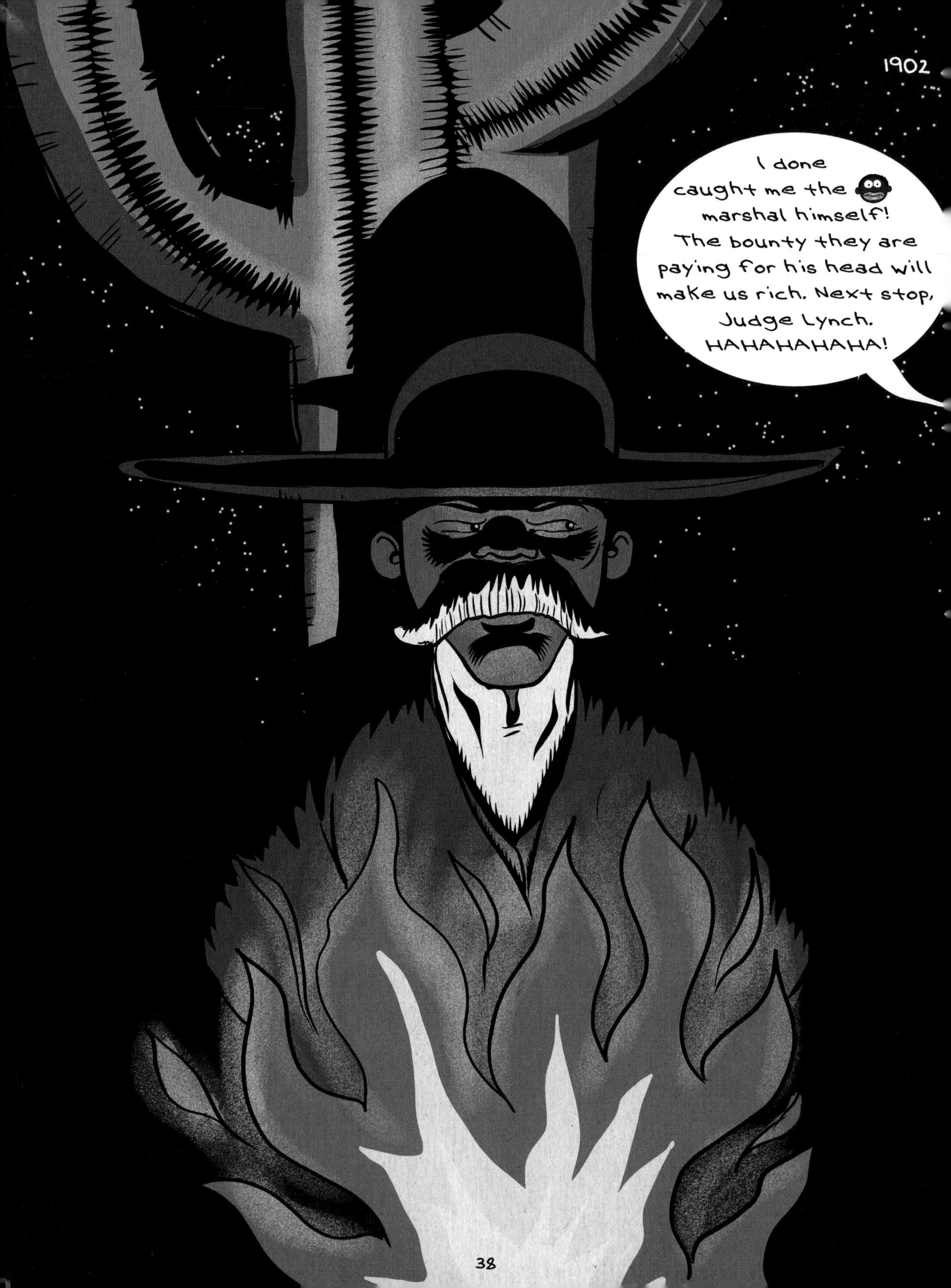
1902
I done caught me the [icon] marshal himself! The bounty they are paying for his head will make us rich. Next stop, Judge Lynch. HAHAHAHAHA!

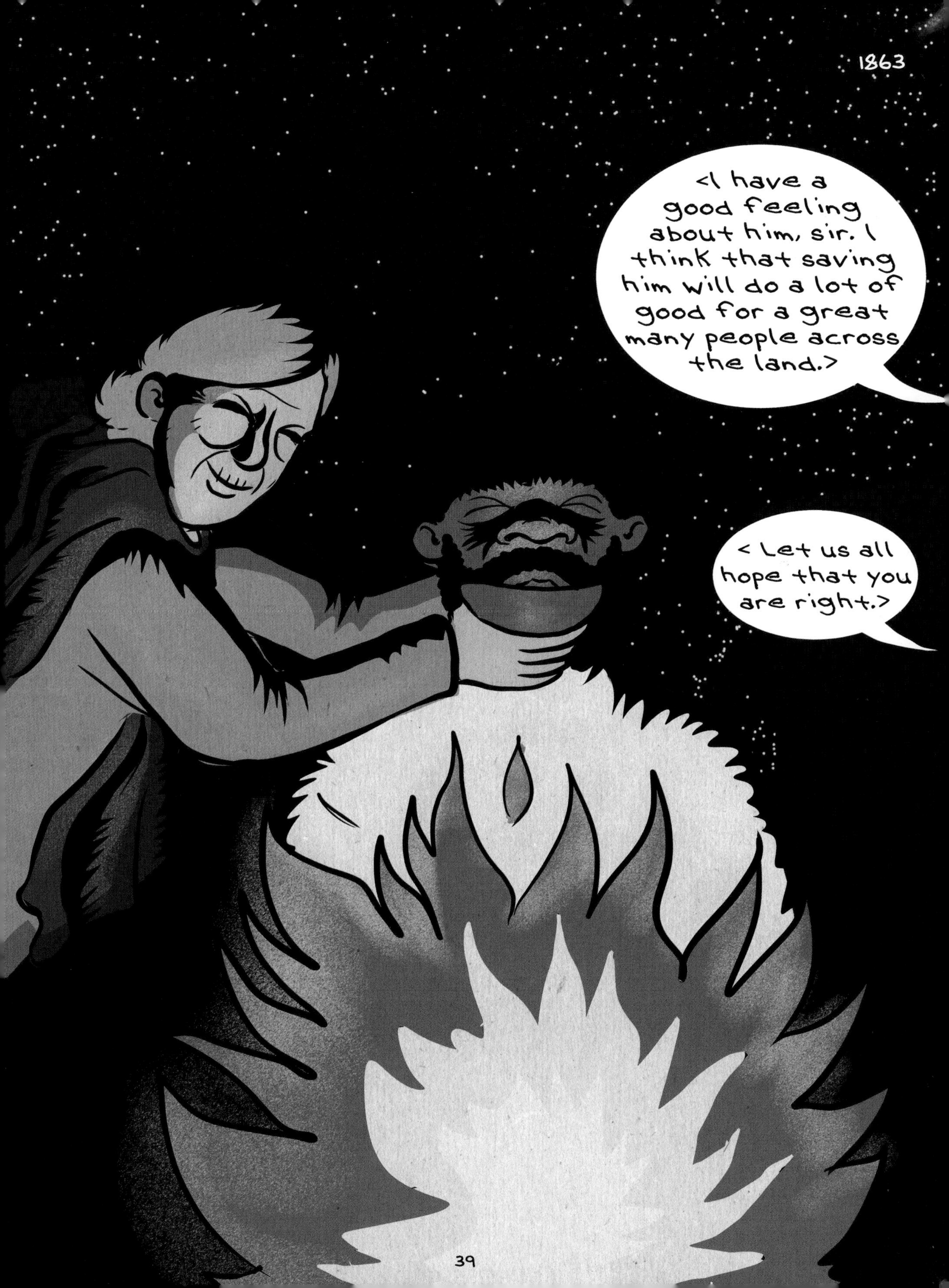
1863
<I have a good feeling about him, sir. I think that saving him will do a lot of good for a great many people across the land.>
< Let us all hope that you are right.>

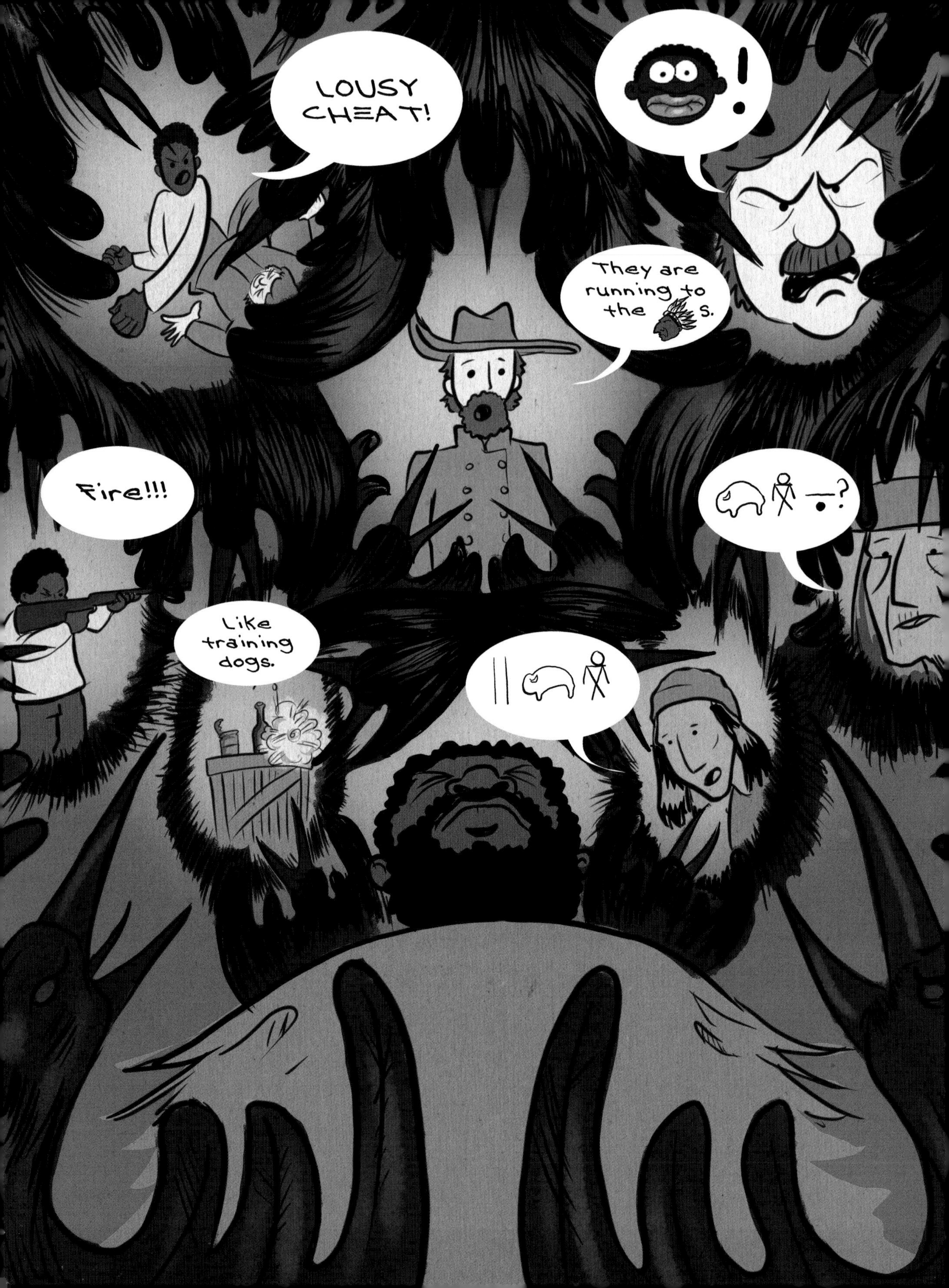
LOUSY CHEAT!
!
They are running to the s.
Fire!!!
?
Like training dogs.

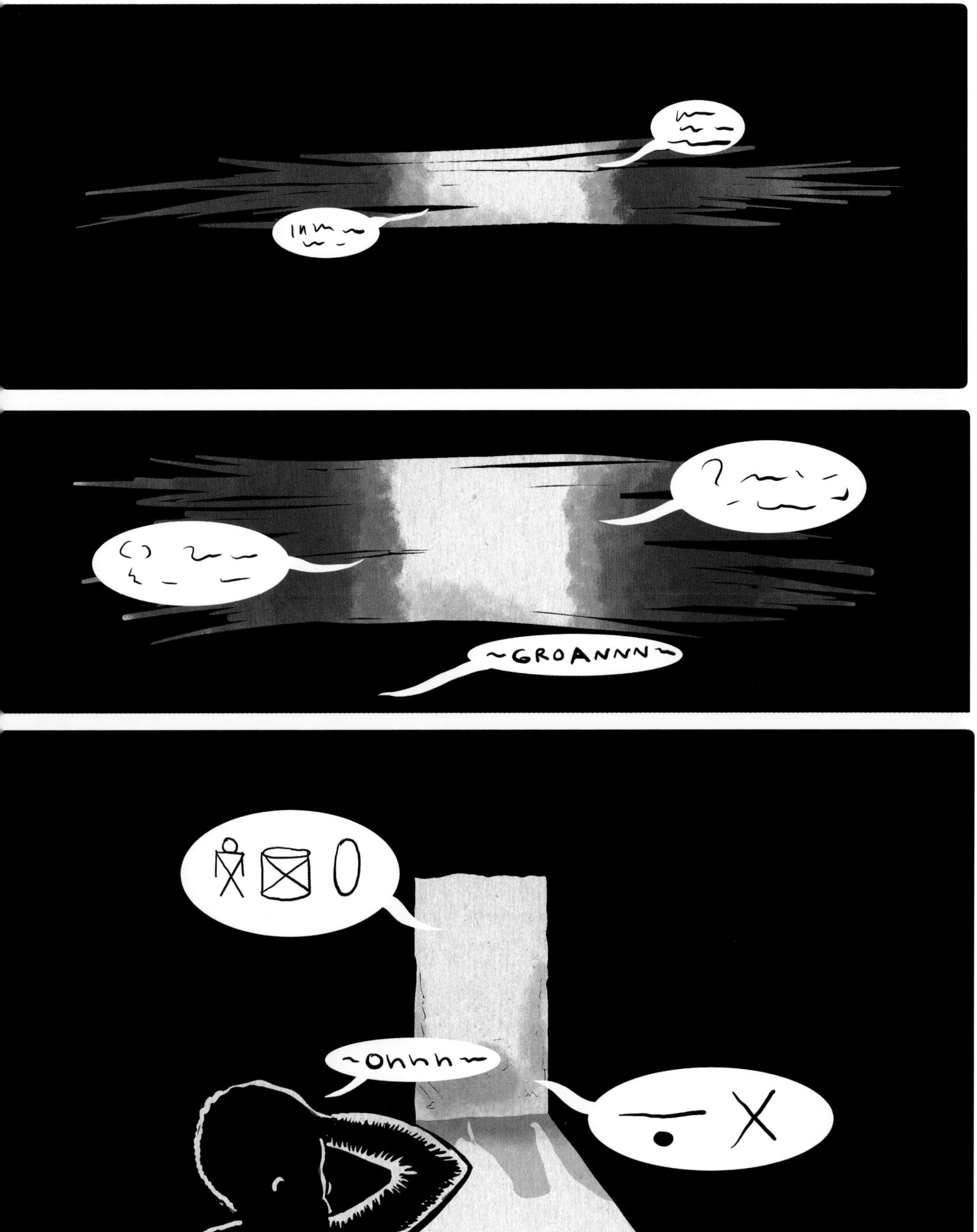
~GROANNN~
~Ohhh~

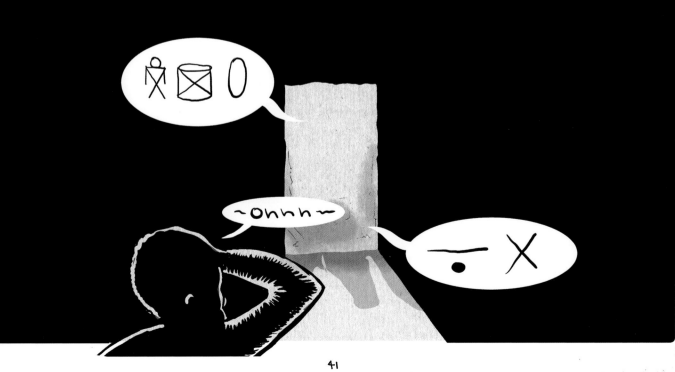

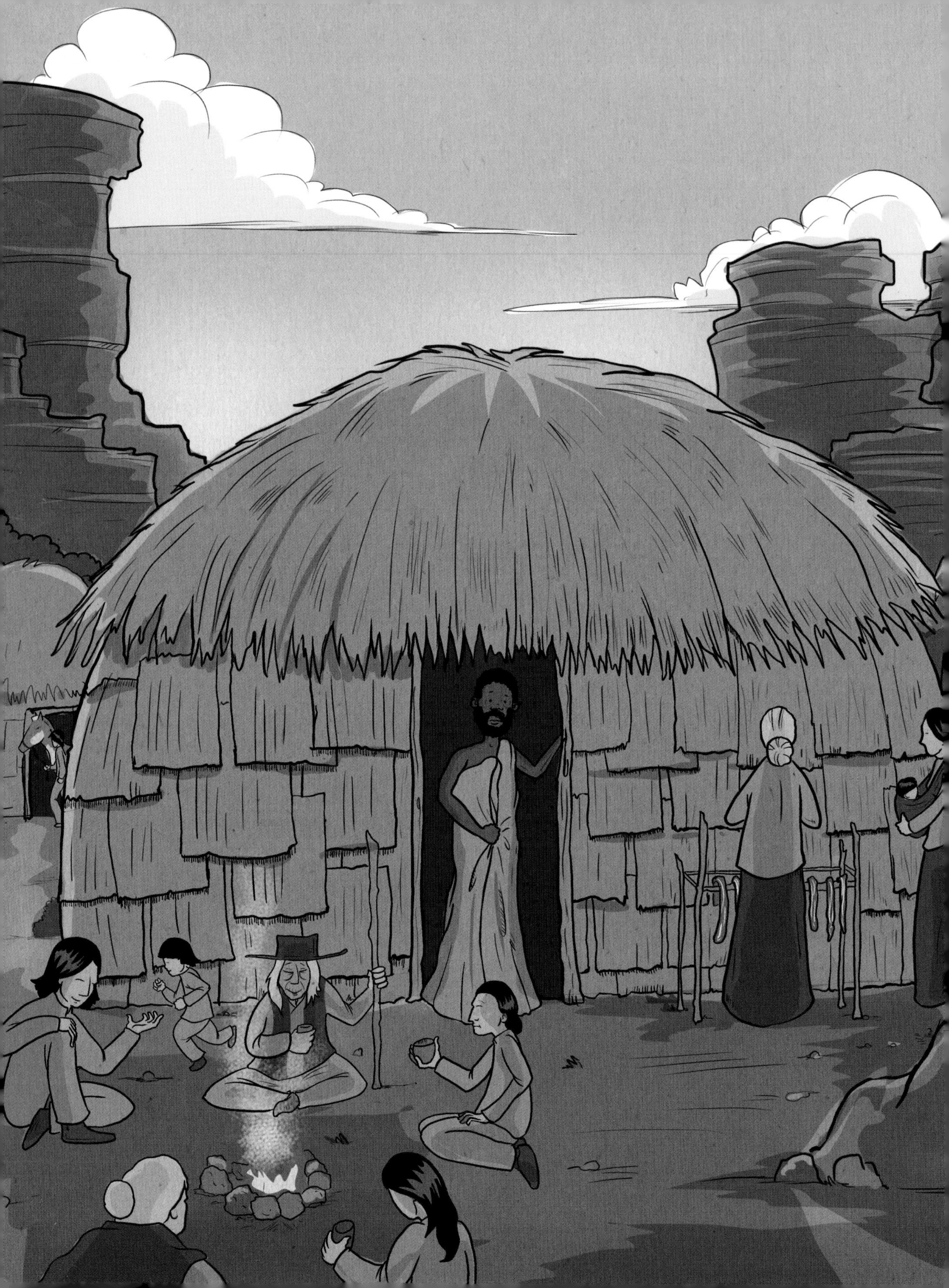

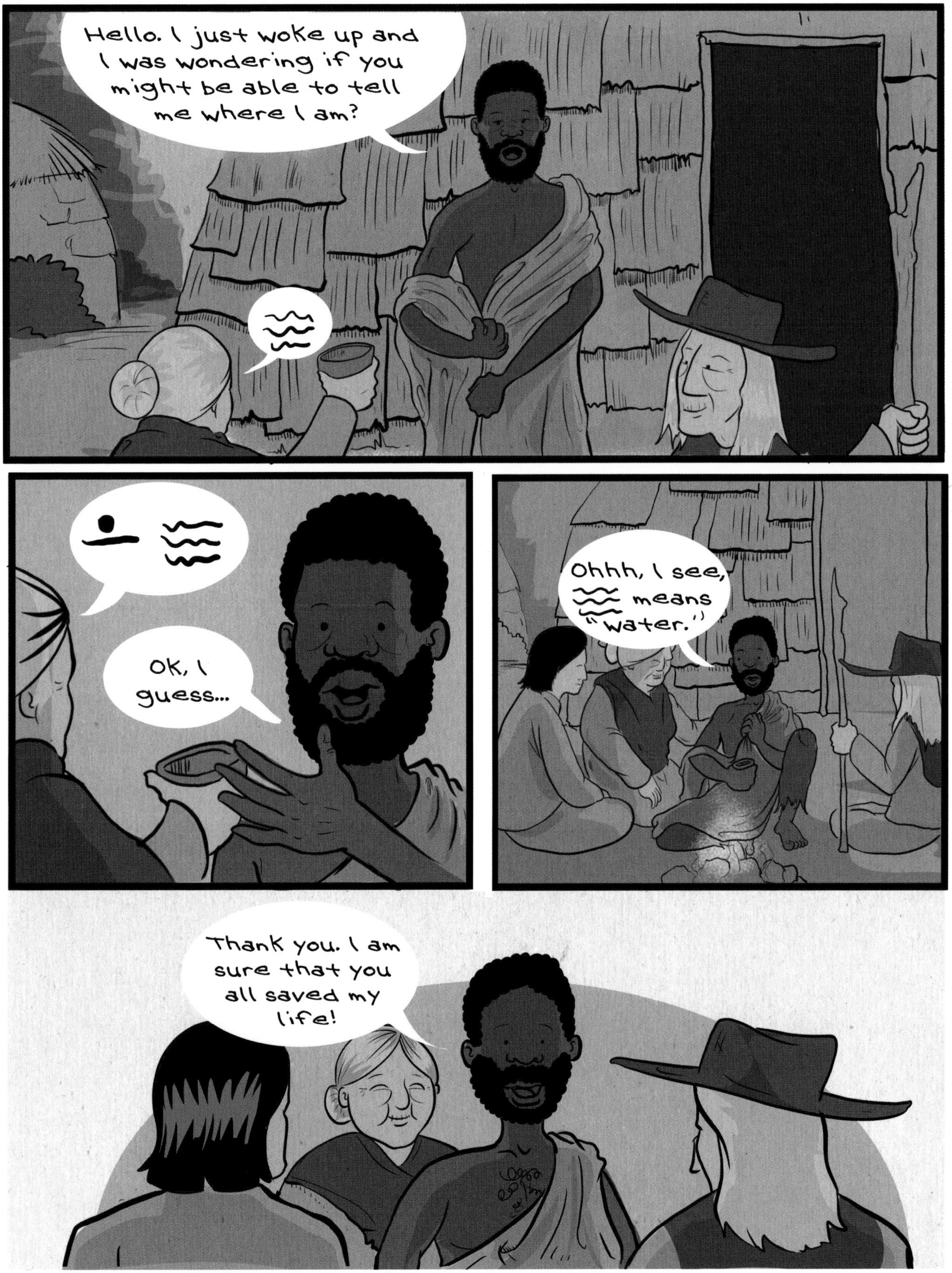
Hello. I just woke up and I was wondering if you might be able to tell me where I am?
OK, I guess...
Ohhh, I see, means "water."
Thank you. I am sure that you all saved my life!

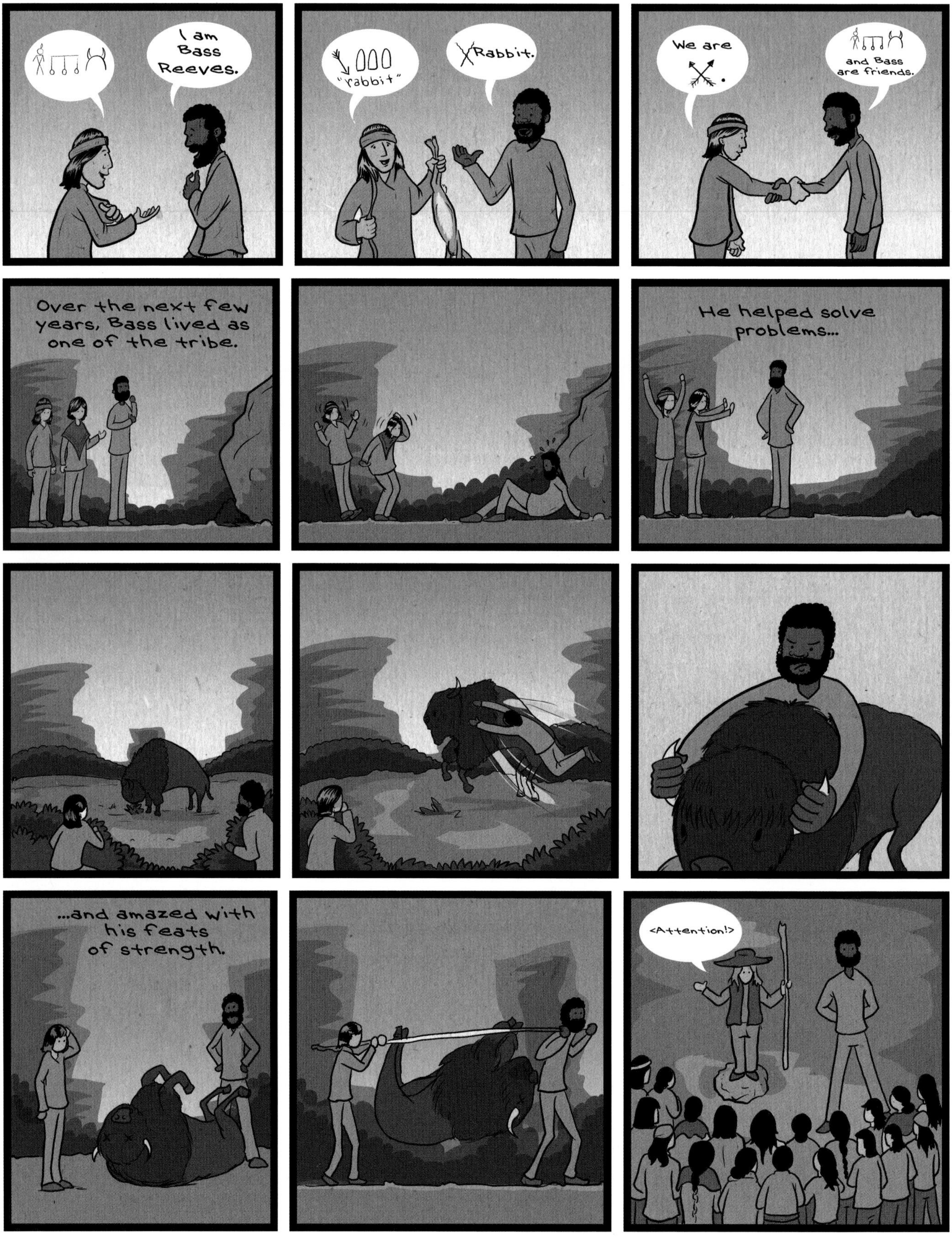
I am Bass Reeves.
"rabbit"
Rabbit.
We are
and Bass are friends.
Over the next few years, Bass lived as one of the tribe.
He helped solve problems...
...and amazed with his feats of strength.
<Attention!>

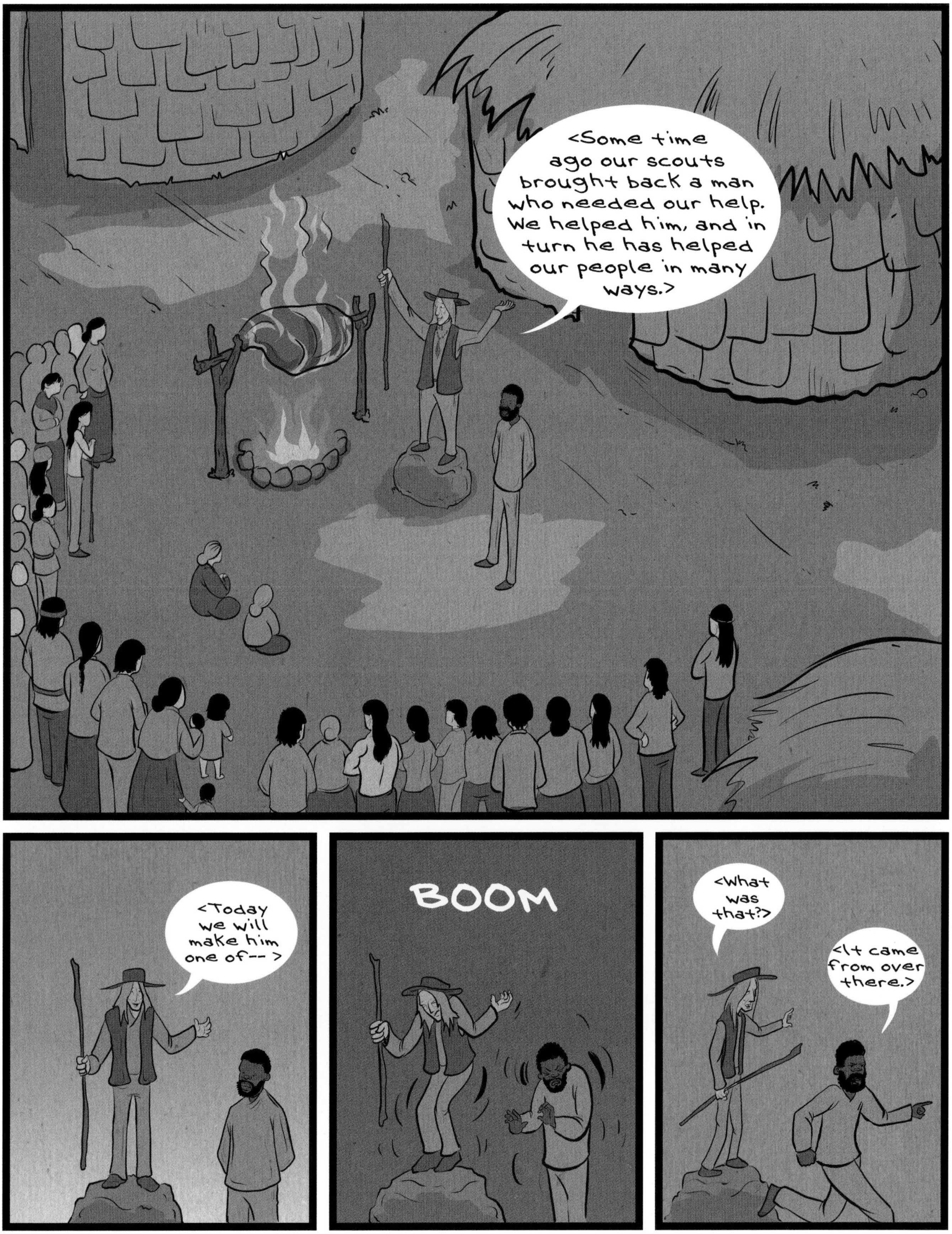
<Some time ago our scouts brought back a man who needed our help. We helped him, and in turn he has helped our people in many ways.>
<Today we will make him one of-- >
BOOM
<What was that?>
<It came from over there.>

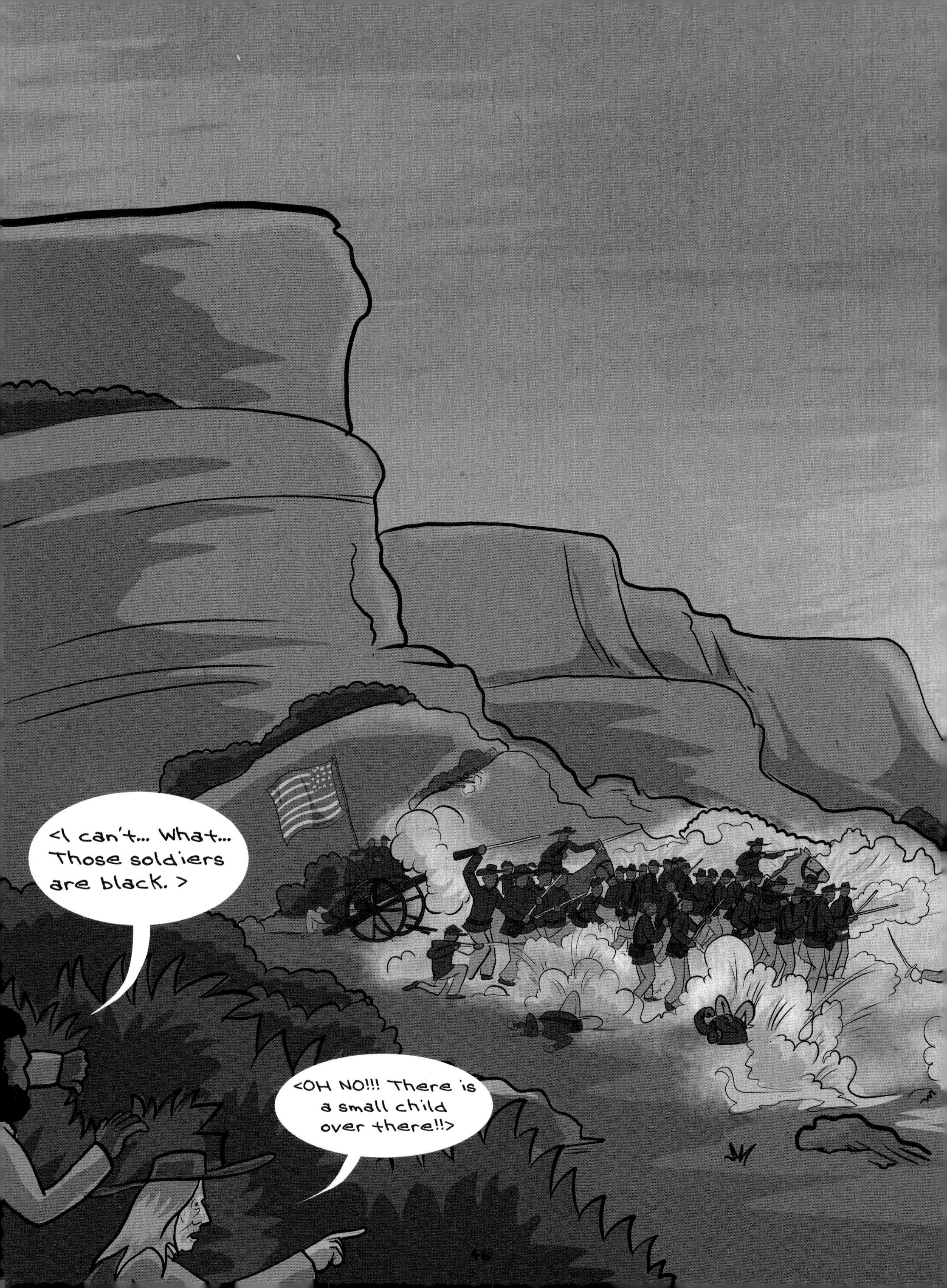
<I can't... What... Those soldiers are black. >
<OH NO!!! There is a small child over there!!>

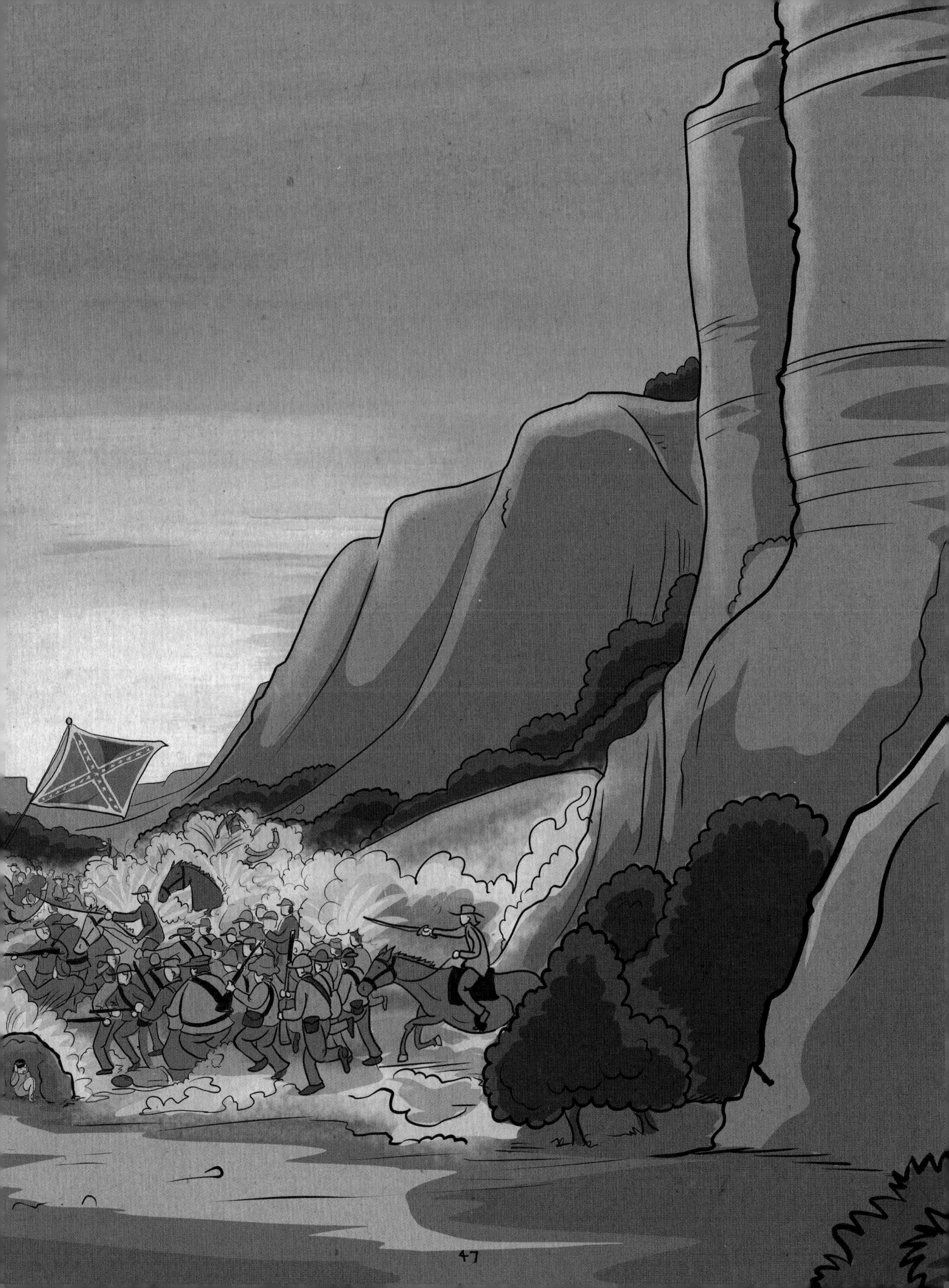

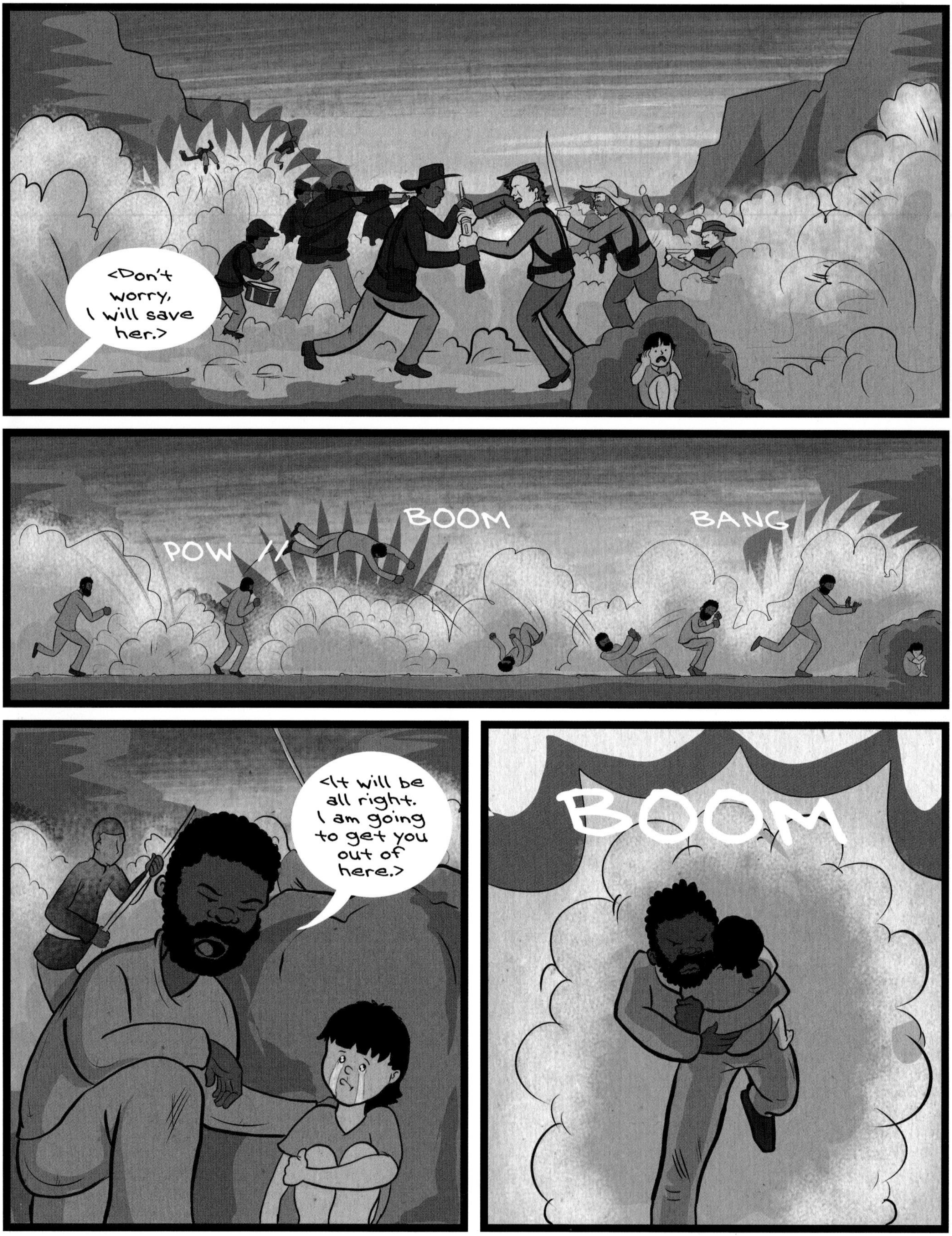
<Don't worry, I will save her.>
POW
BOOM
BANG
<It will be all right. I am going to get you out of here.>
BOOM

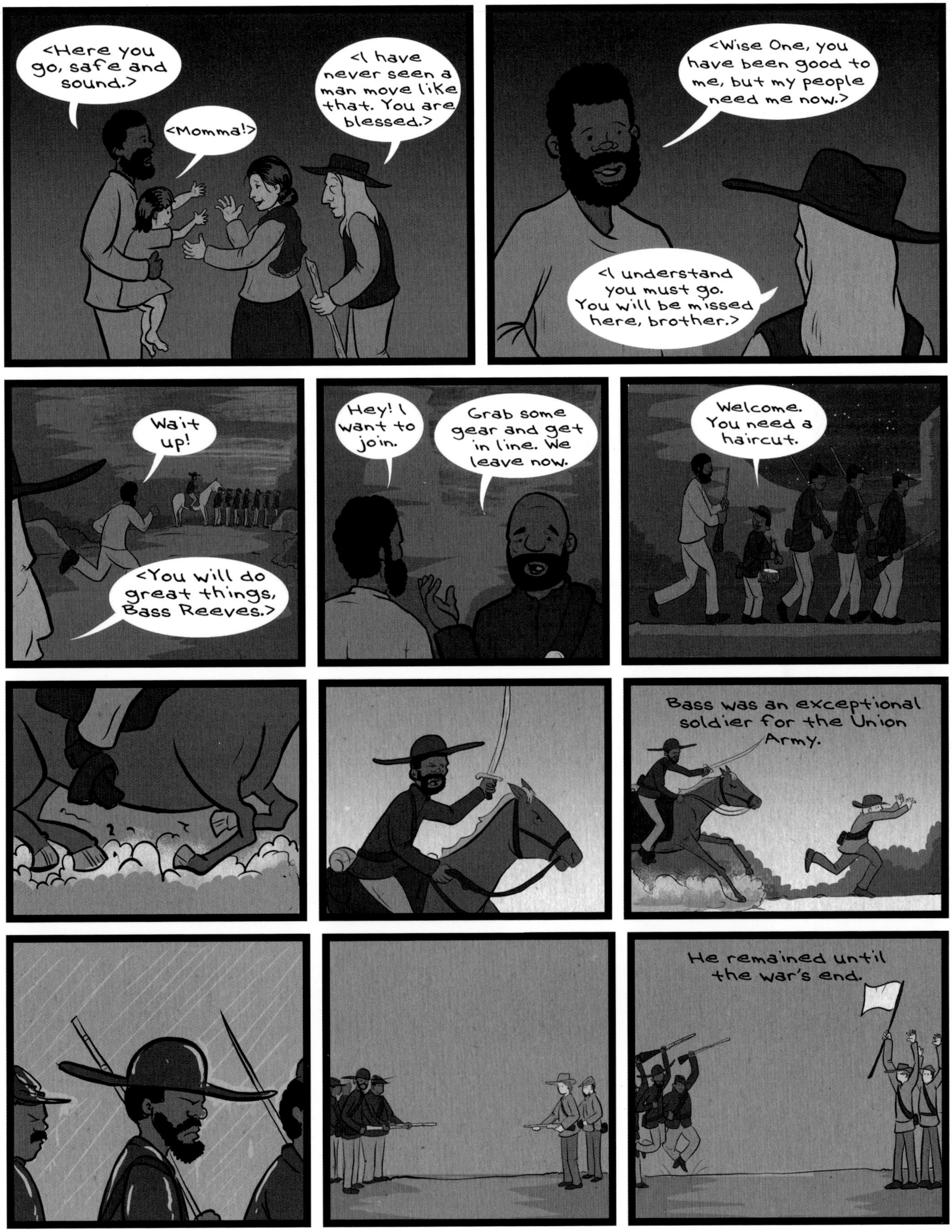
<Here you go, safe and sound.>
<Momma!>
<I have never seen a man move like that. You are blessed.>
<Wise One, you have been good to me, but my people need me now.>
<I understand you must go. You will be missed here, brother.>
Wait up!
<You will do great things, Bass Reeves.>
Hey! I want to join.
Grab some gear and get in line. We leave now.
Welcome. You need a haircut.
Bass was an exceptional soldier for the Union Army.
He remained until the war's end.

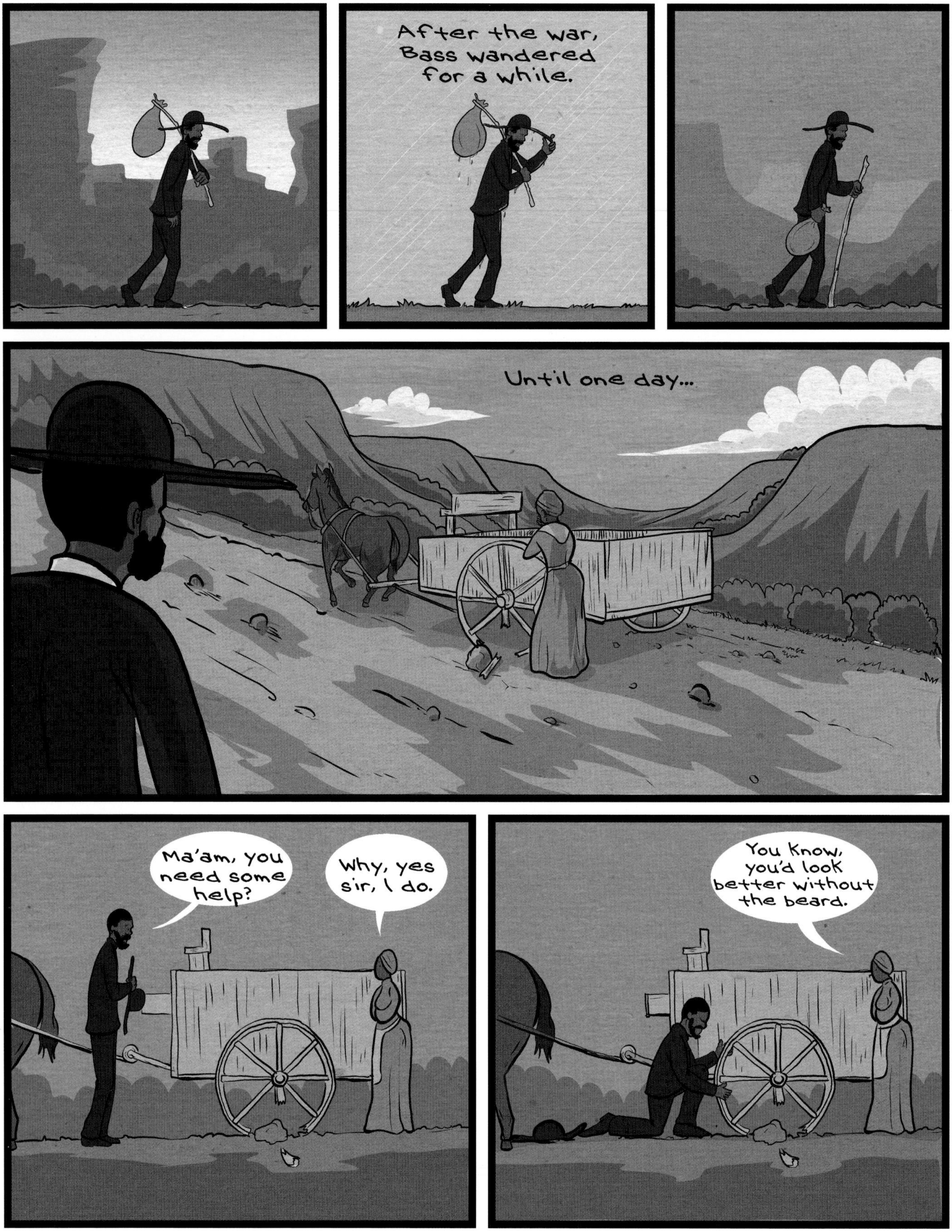
After the war, Bass wandered for a while.
Until one day...
Ma'am, you need some help?
Why, yes sir, I do.
You Know, you'd look better without the beard.

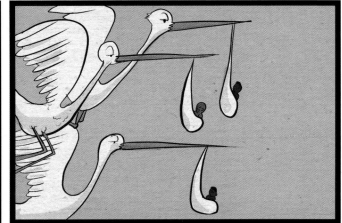

After that, Bass was able to settle down and build a quiet life... for a while.

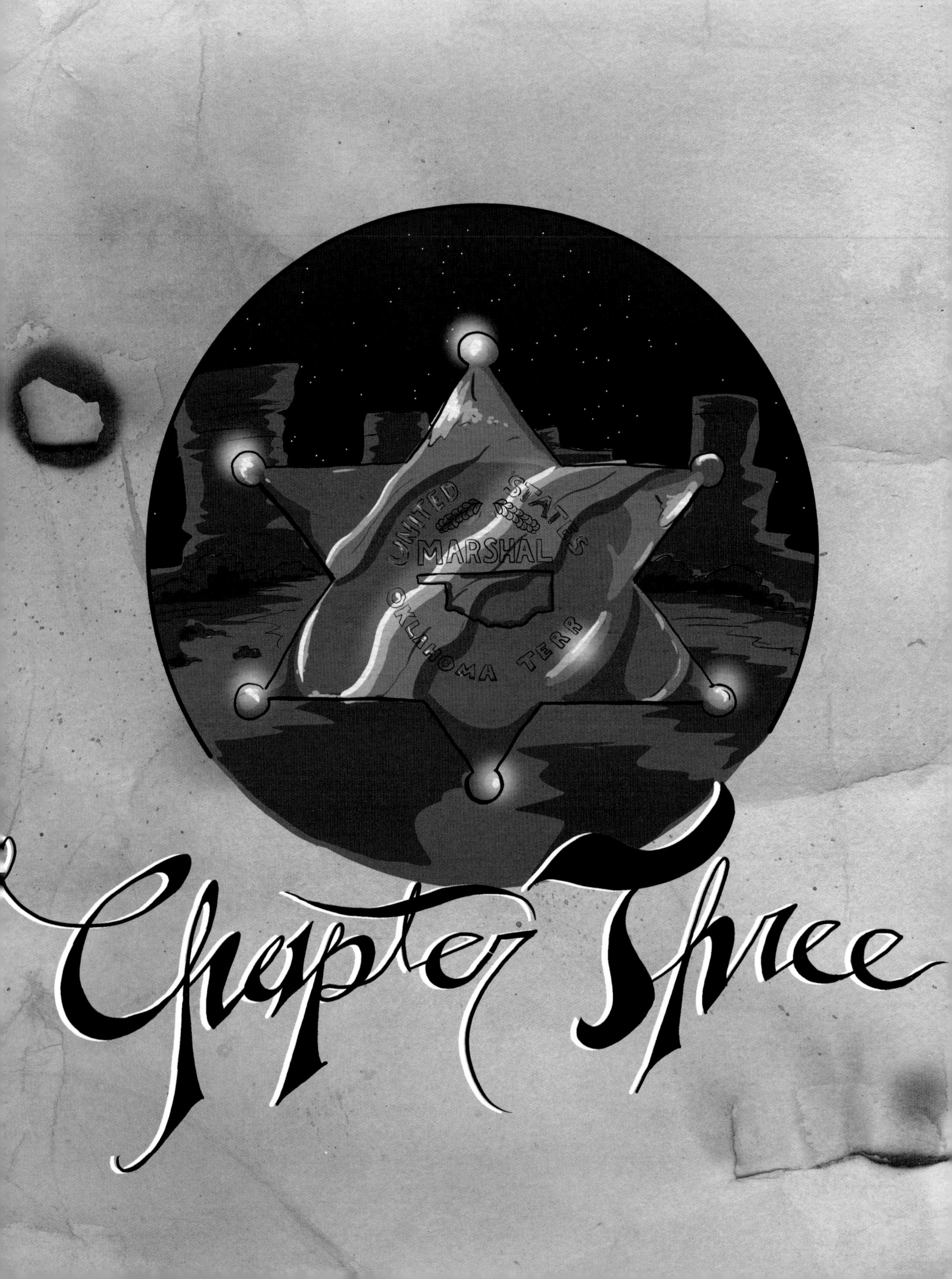
UNITED STATES
MARSHAL
OKLAHOMA TERR

Chapter Three

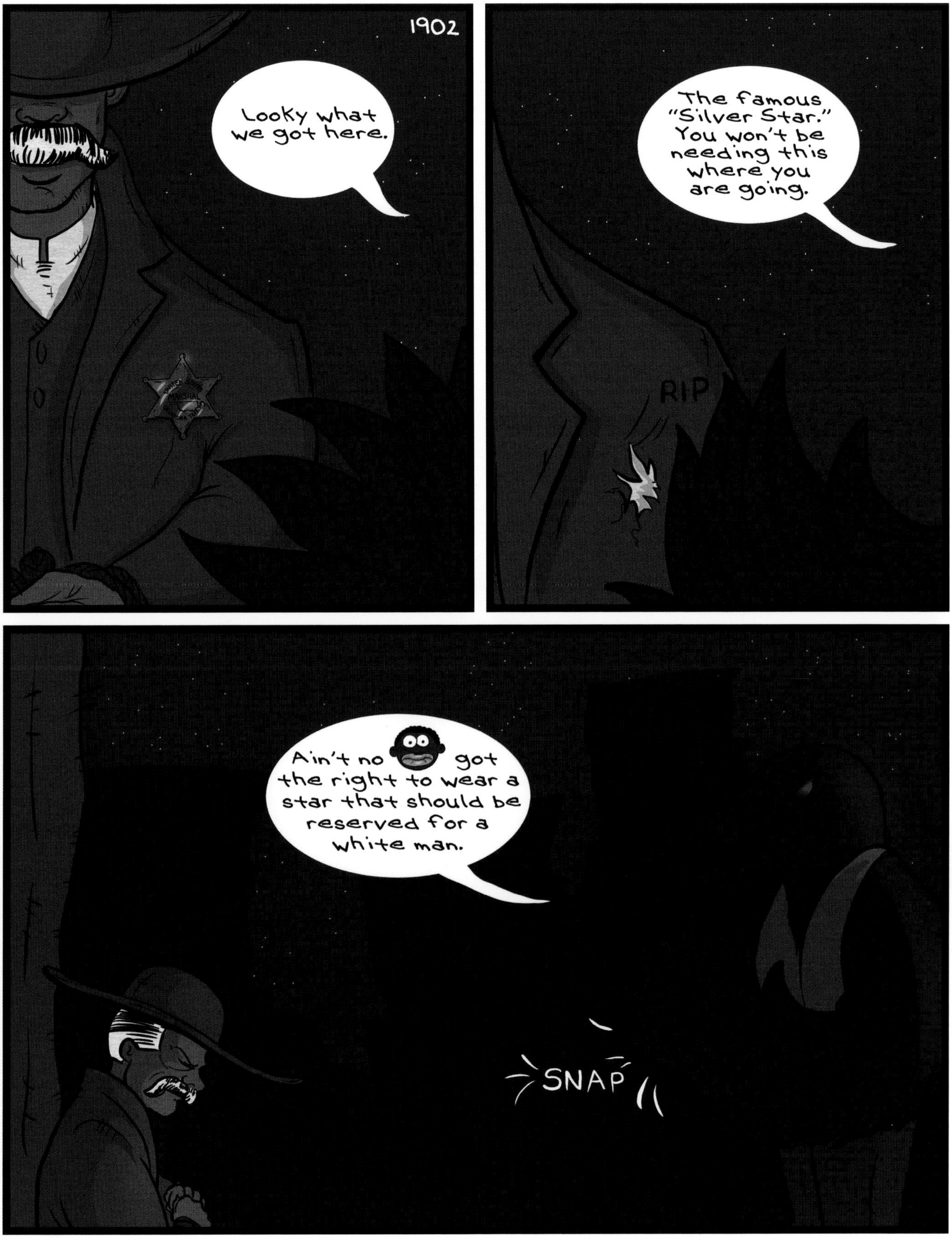
1902
Looky what we got here.
The famous "Silver Star." You won't be needing this where you are going.
RIP
Ain't no got the right to wear a star that should be reserved for a white man.
SNAP

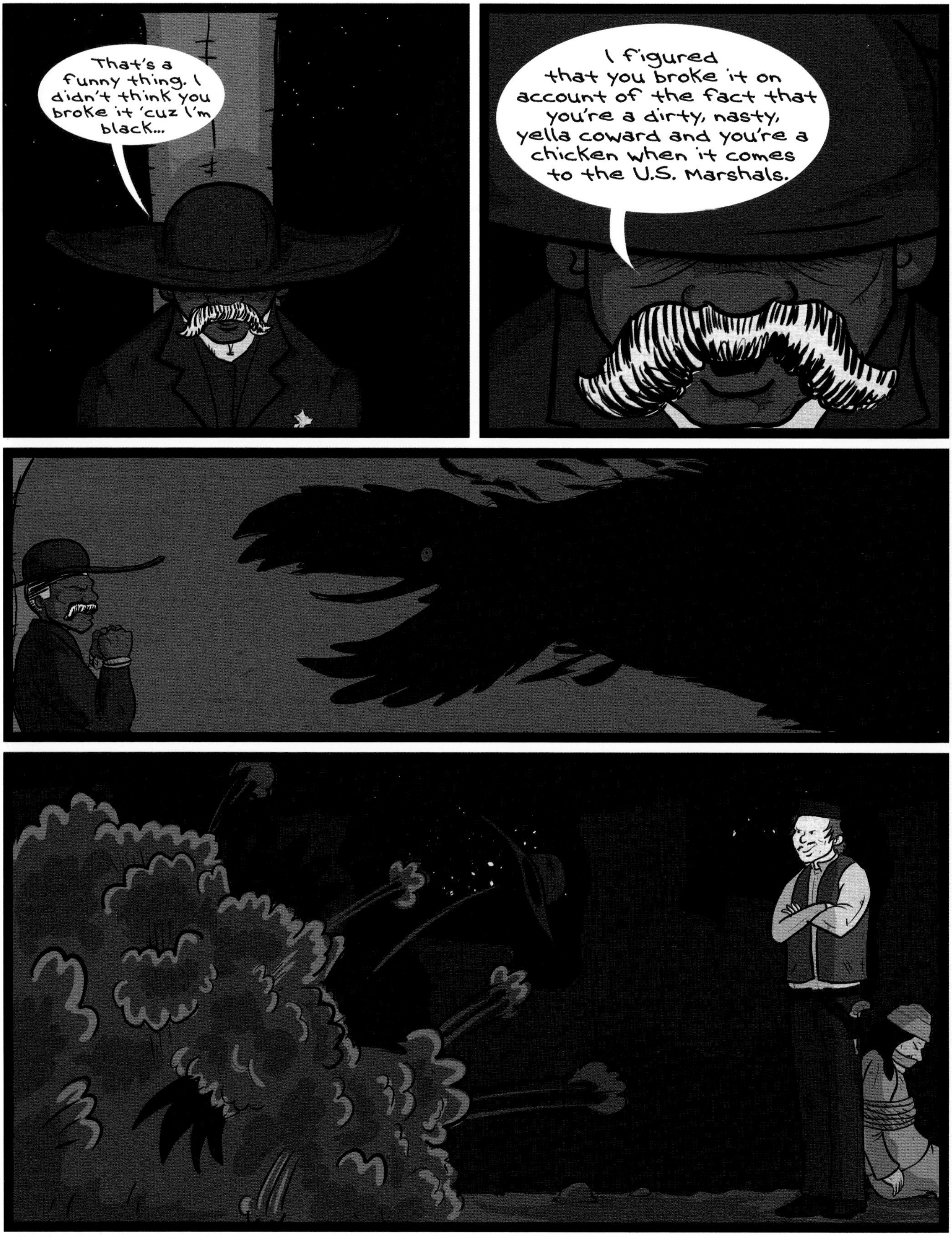
That's a funny thing. I didn't think you broke it 'cuz I'm black...
I figured that you broke it on account of the fact that you're a dirty, nasty, yella coward and you're a chicken when it comes to the U.S. Marshals.

You just keep racking up the charges. Kidnapping, two counts assault on a federal officer—that's me and my posseman—two counts horse stealing, two counts obstruction of justice, hindering an investigation, detaining federal agents, and destruction of federal property.

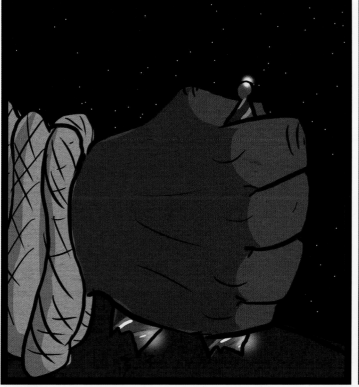

Looks like when I get out of these here ropes, you're gonna be in a world of hurt. Only one option left for you.

You better run.

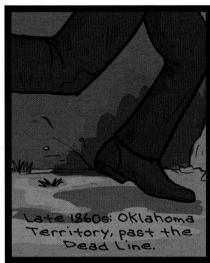

Late 1860s: Oklahoma Territory, past the Dead Line.

"When we found him he still had the warrant in his hand."

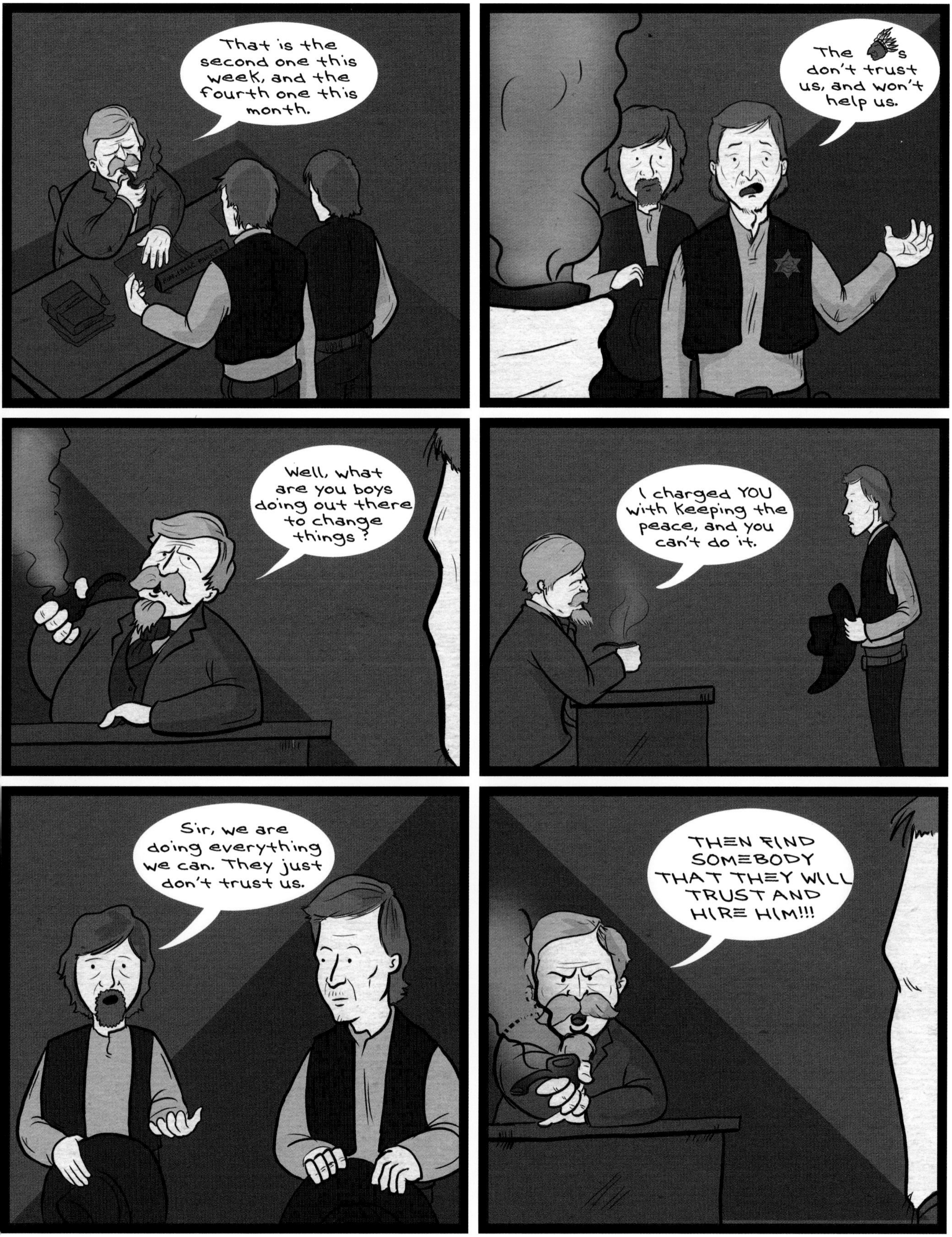
That is the second one this week, and the fourth one this month.
The s don't trust us, and won't help us.
Well, what are you boys doing out there to change things?
I charged YOU with keeping the peace, and you can't do it.
Sir, we are doing everything we can. They just don't trust us.
THEN FIND SOMEBODY THAT THEY WILL TRUST AND HIRE HIM!!!

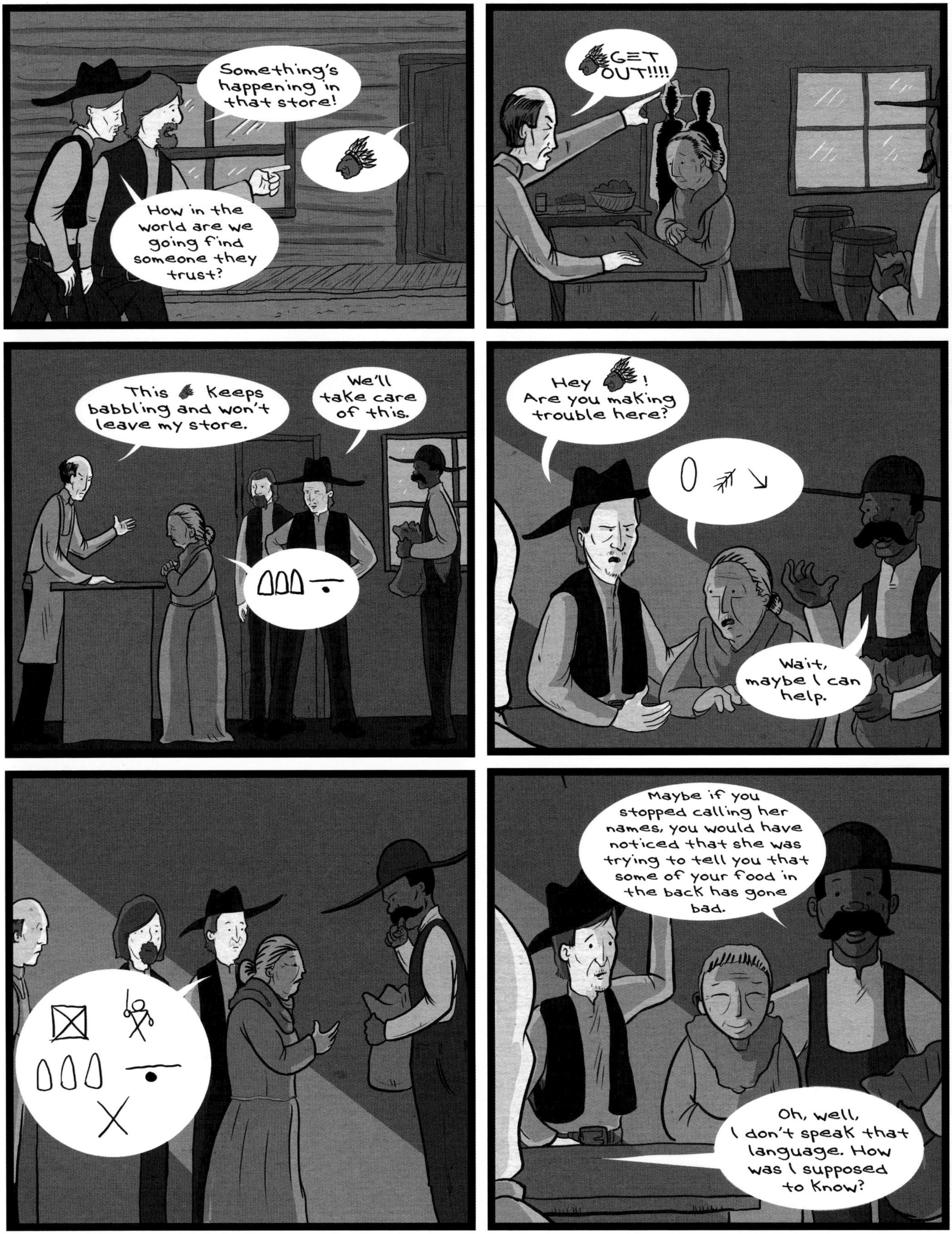
Something's happening in that store!
How in the world are we going find someone they trust?
GET OUT!!!!
This keeps babbling and won't leave my store.
We'll take care of this.
Hey !
Are you making trouble here?
Wait, maybe I can help.
Maybe if you stopped calling her names, you would have noticed that she was trying to tell you that some of your food in the back has gone bad.
Oh, well, I don't speak that language. How was I supposed to know?

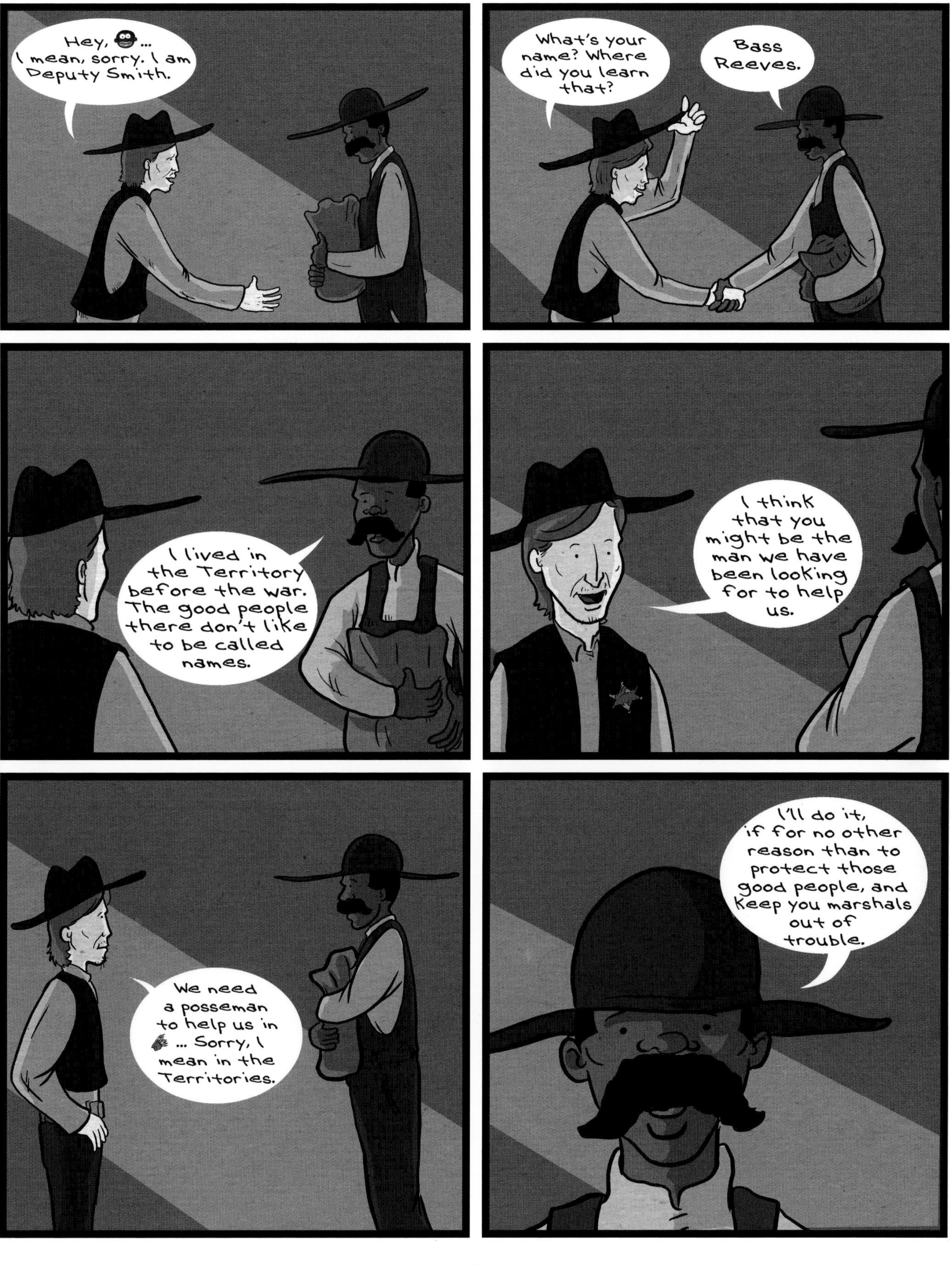
Hey, ... I mean, sorry. I am Deputy Smith.
What's your name? Where did you learn that?
Bass Reeves.
I lived in the Territory before the war. The good people there don't like to be called names.
I think that you might be the man we have been looking for to help us.
We need a posseman to help us in ... Sorry, I mean in the Territories.
I'll do it, if for no other reason than to protect those good people, and keep you marshals out of trouble.

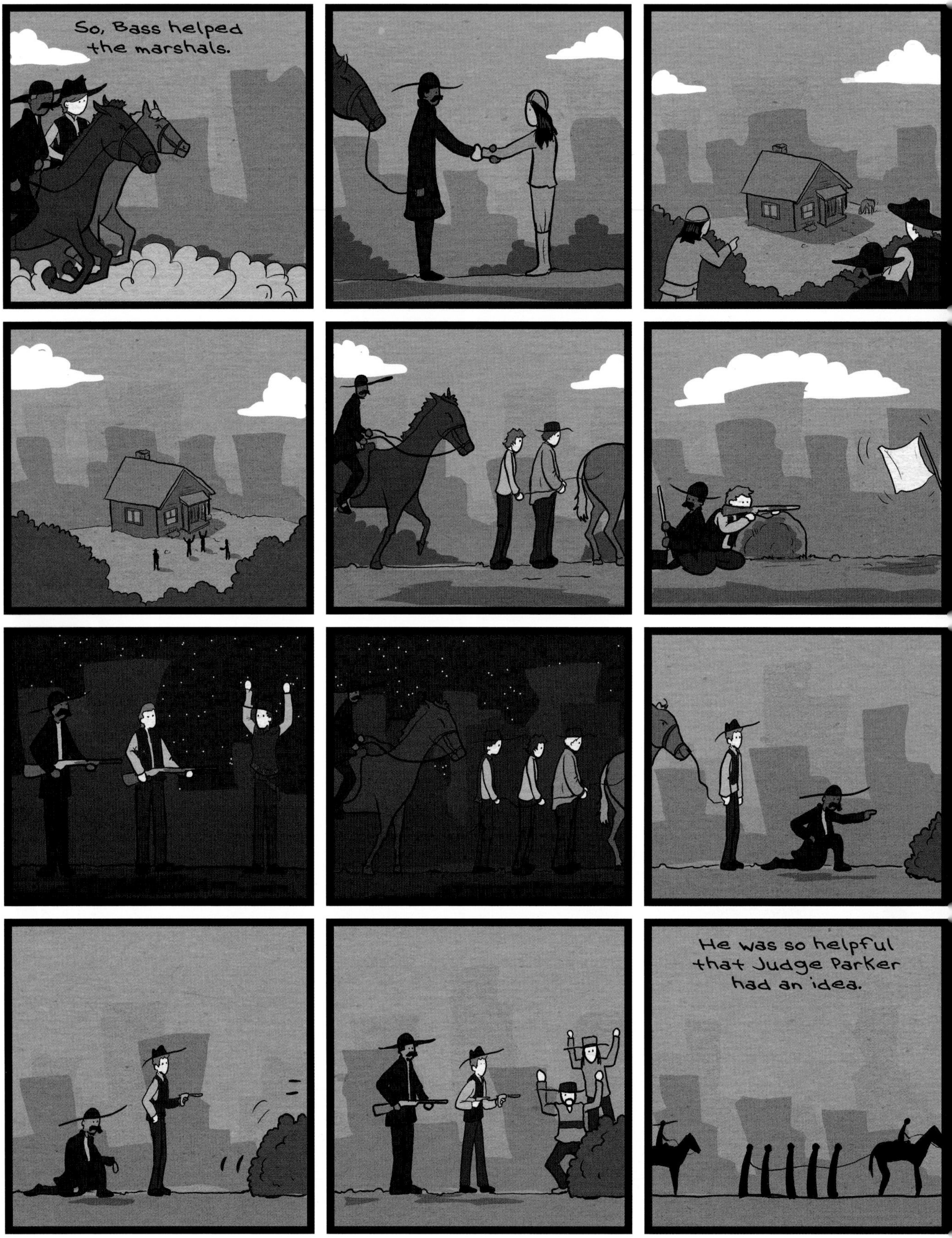
So, Bass helped the marshals.
He was so helpful that Judge Parker had an idea.

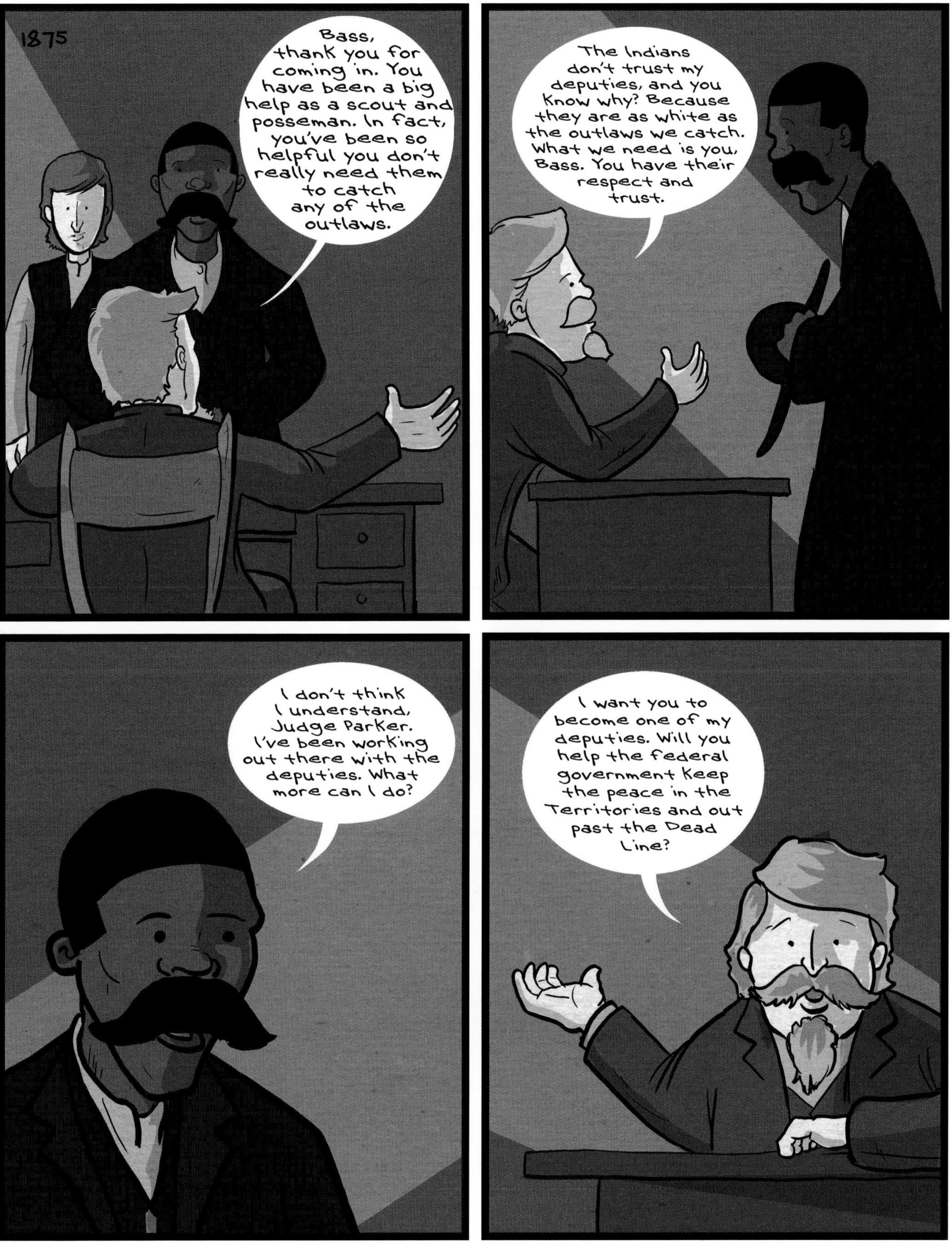
1875
Bass, thank you for coming in. You have been a big help as a scout and posseman. In fact, you've been so helpful you don't really need them to catch any of the outlaws.
The Indians don't trust my deputies, and you know why? Because they are as white as the outlaws we catch. What we need is you, Bass. You have their respect and trust.
I don't think I understand, Judge Parker. I've been working out there with the deputies. What more can I do?
I want you to become one of my deputies. Will you help the federal government keep the peace in the Territories and out past the Dead Line?

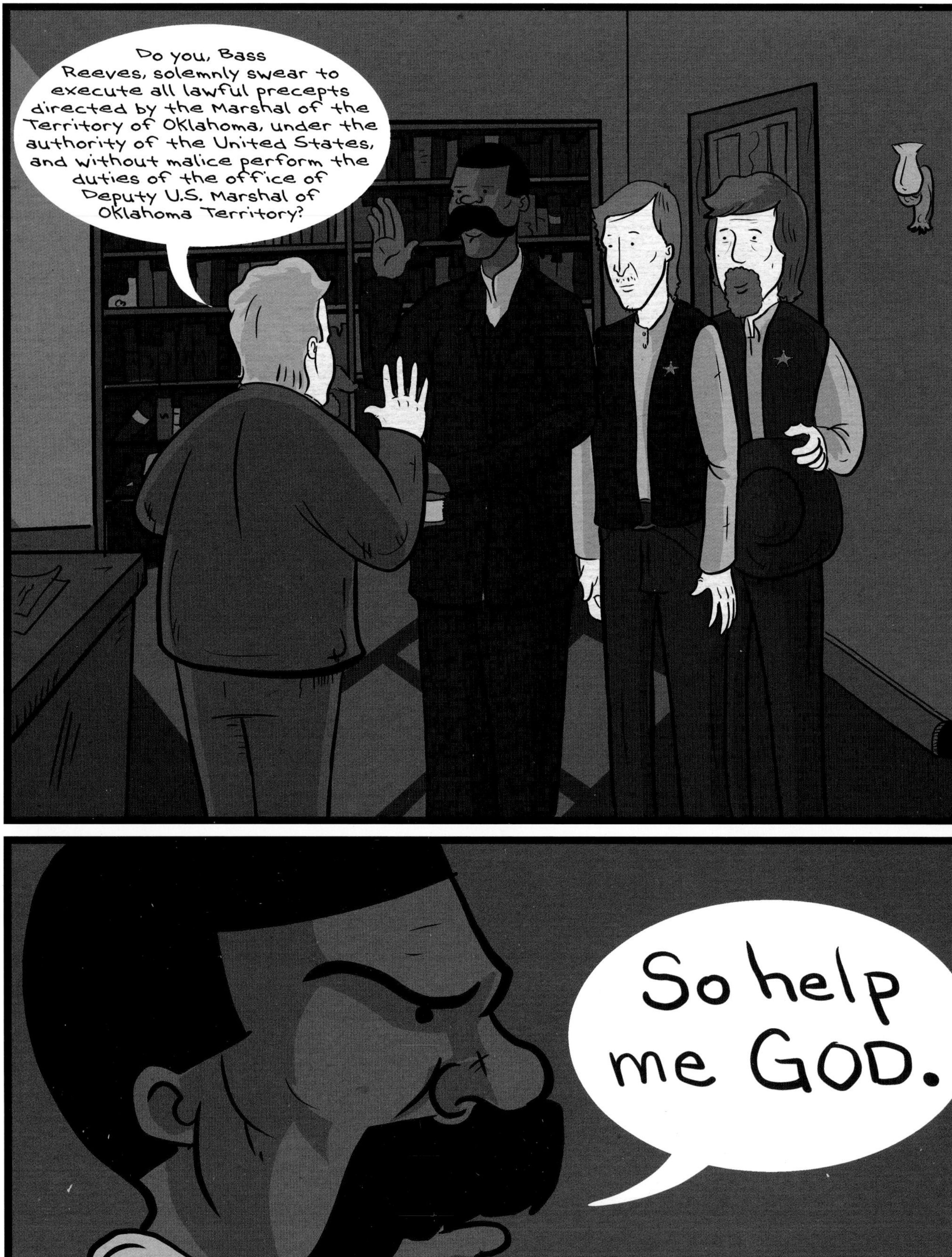
Do you, Bass Reeves, solemnly swear to execute all lawful precepts directed by the Marshal of the Territory of Oklahoma, under the authority of the United States, and without malice perform the duties of the office of Deputy U.S. Marshal of Oklahoma Territory?
So help me GOD.

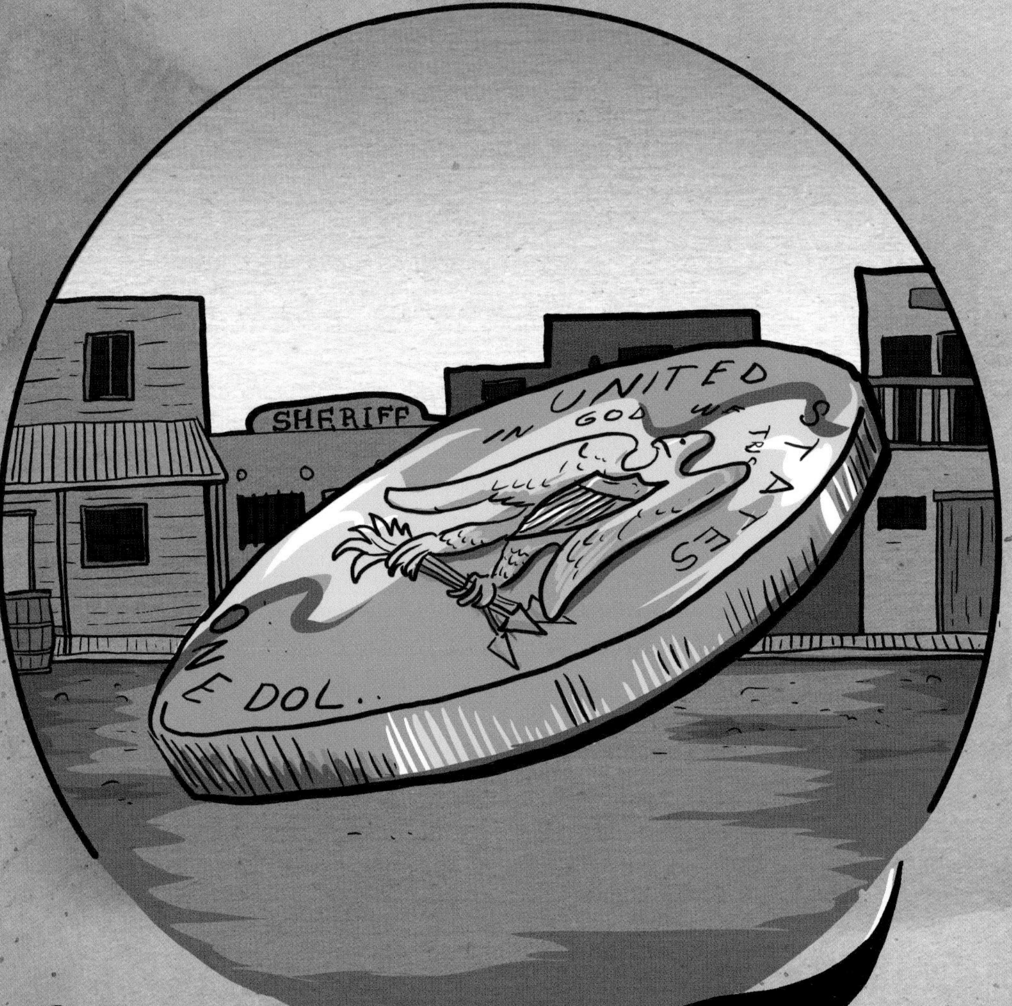
SHERIFF
UNITED STATES
IN GOD WE
ONE DOL..

Chapter Four

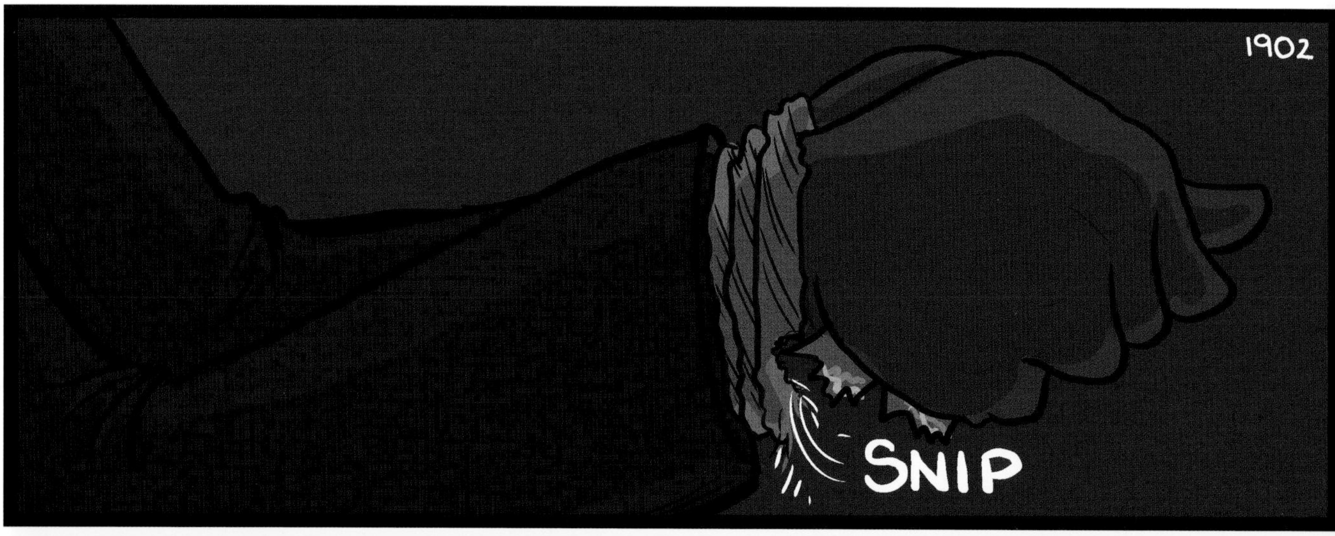
1902
SNIP

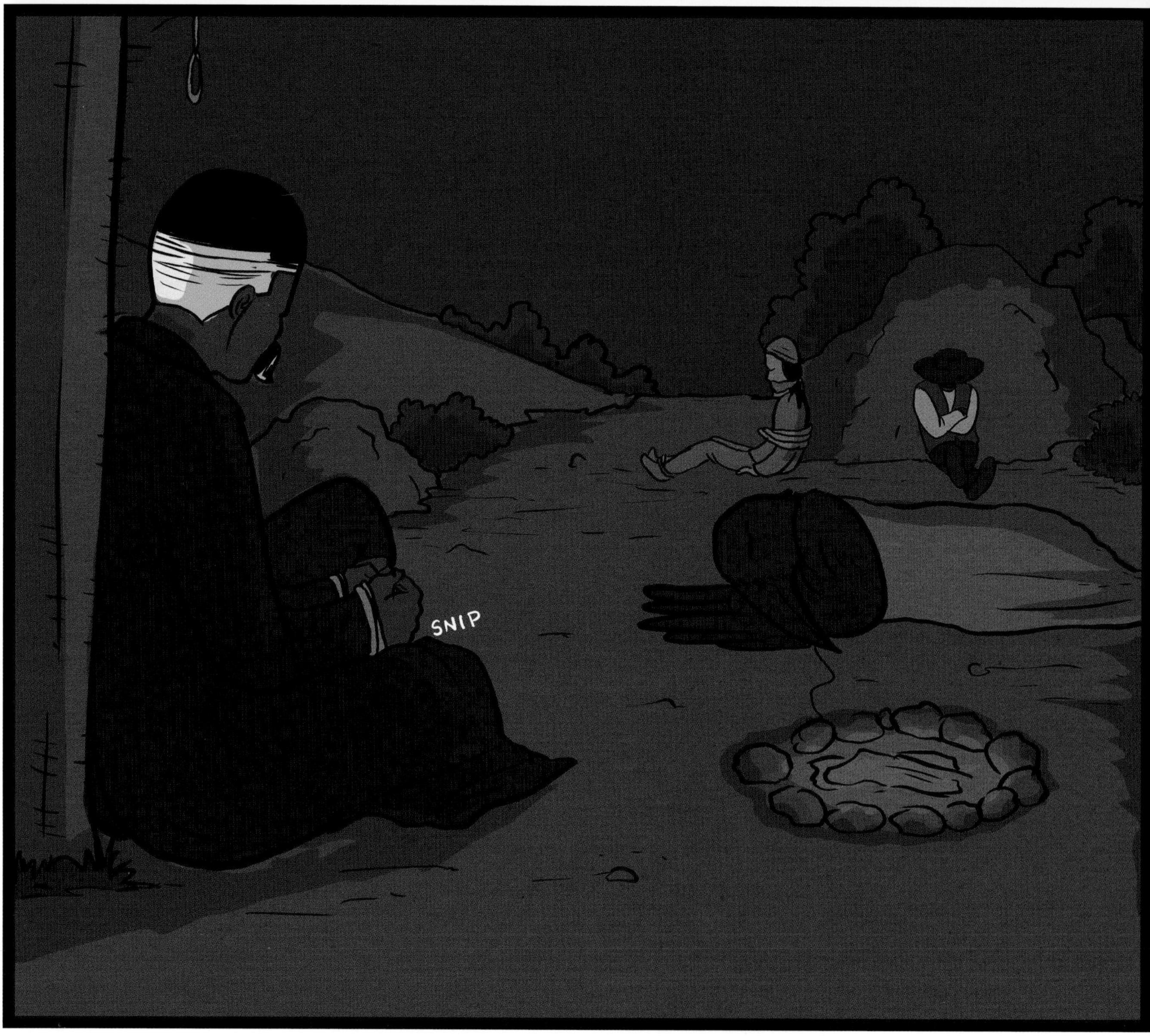
SNIP

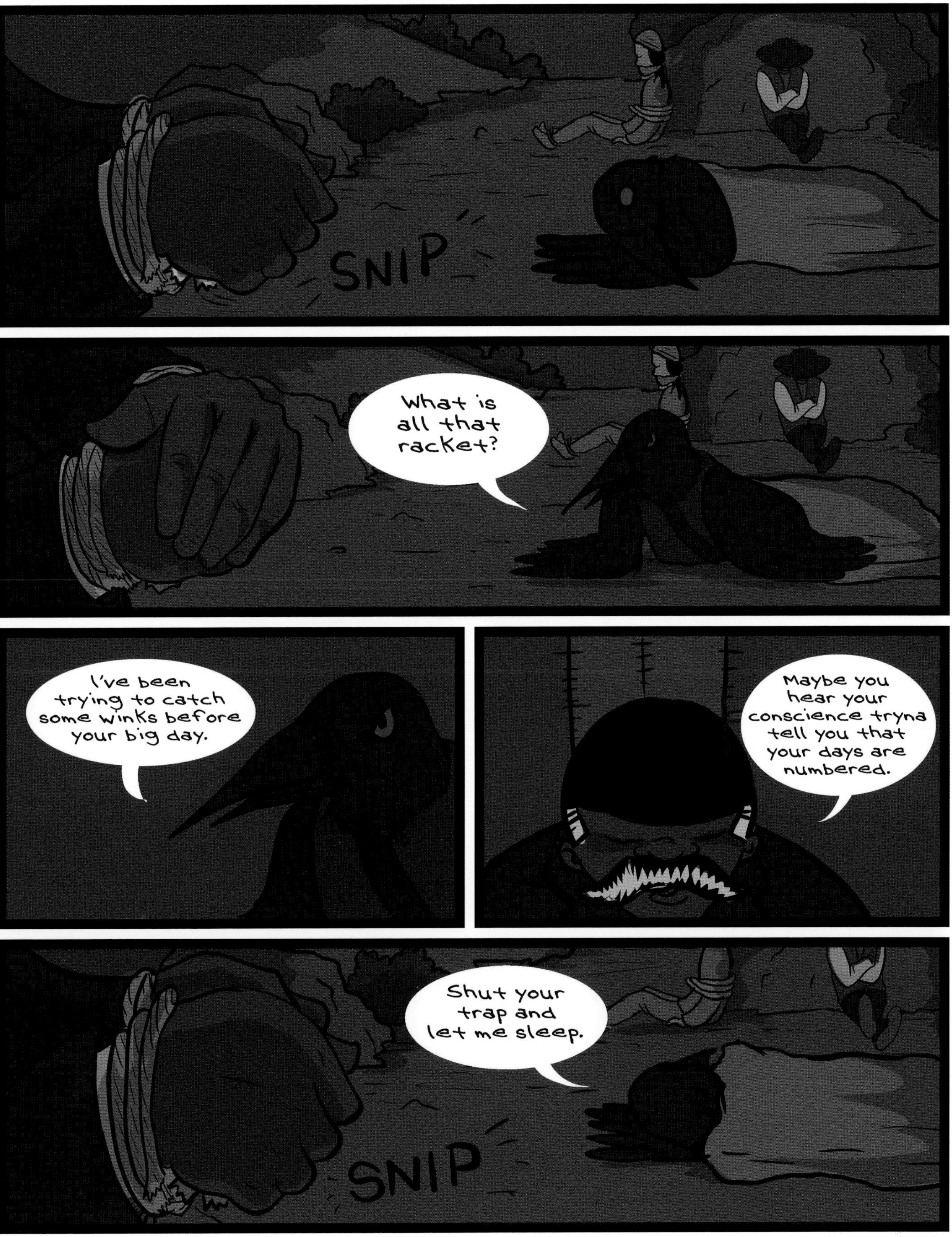
SNIP
What is all that racket?
I've been trying to catch some winks before your big day.
Maybe you hear your conscience tryna tell you that your days are numbered.
Shut your trap and let me sleep.
SNIP

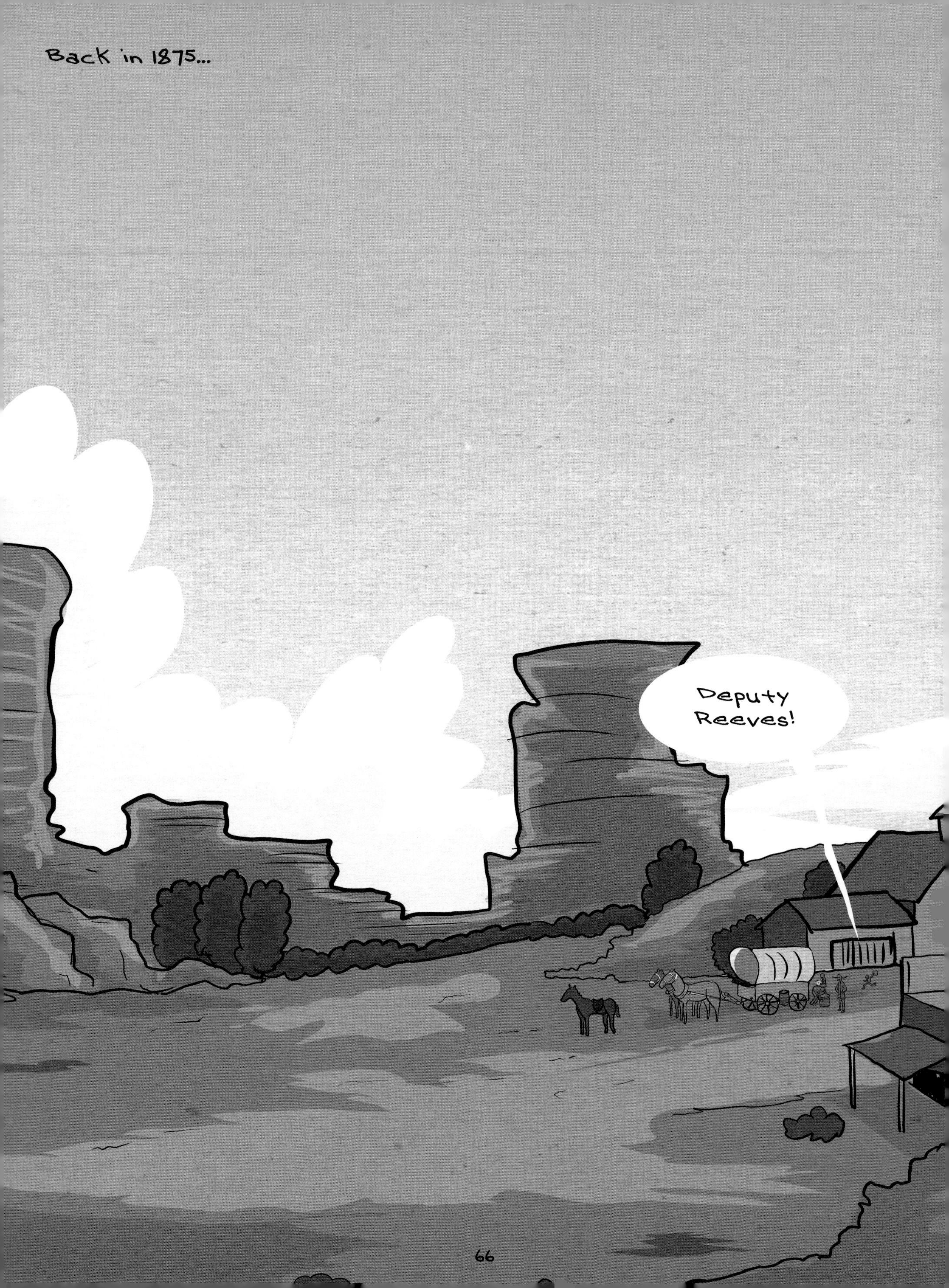
Back in 1875...
Deputy Reeves!

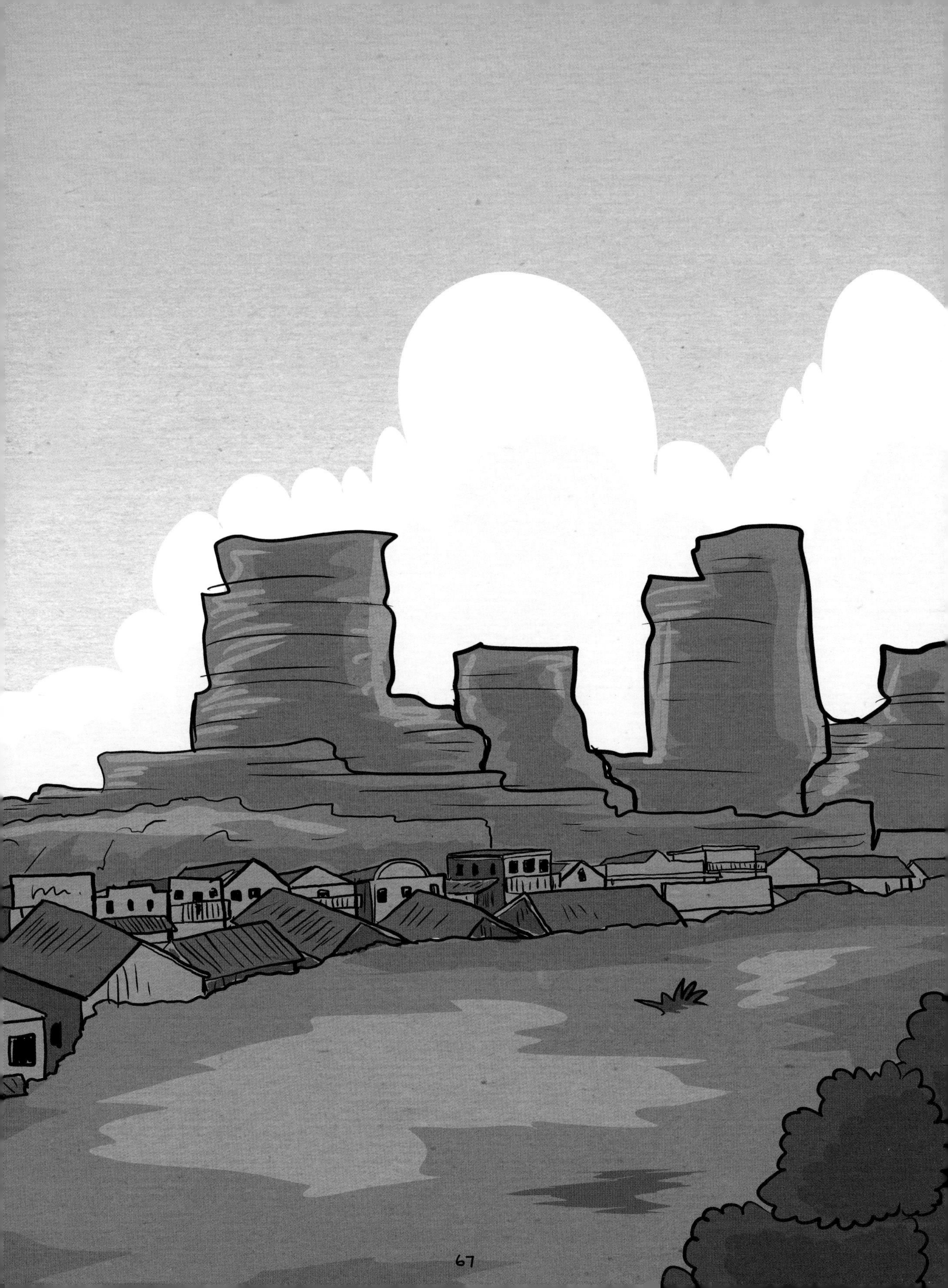

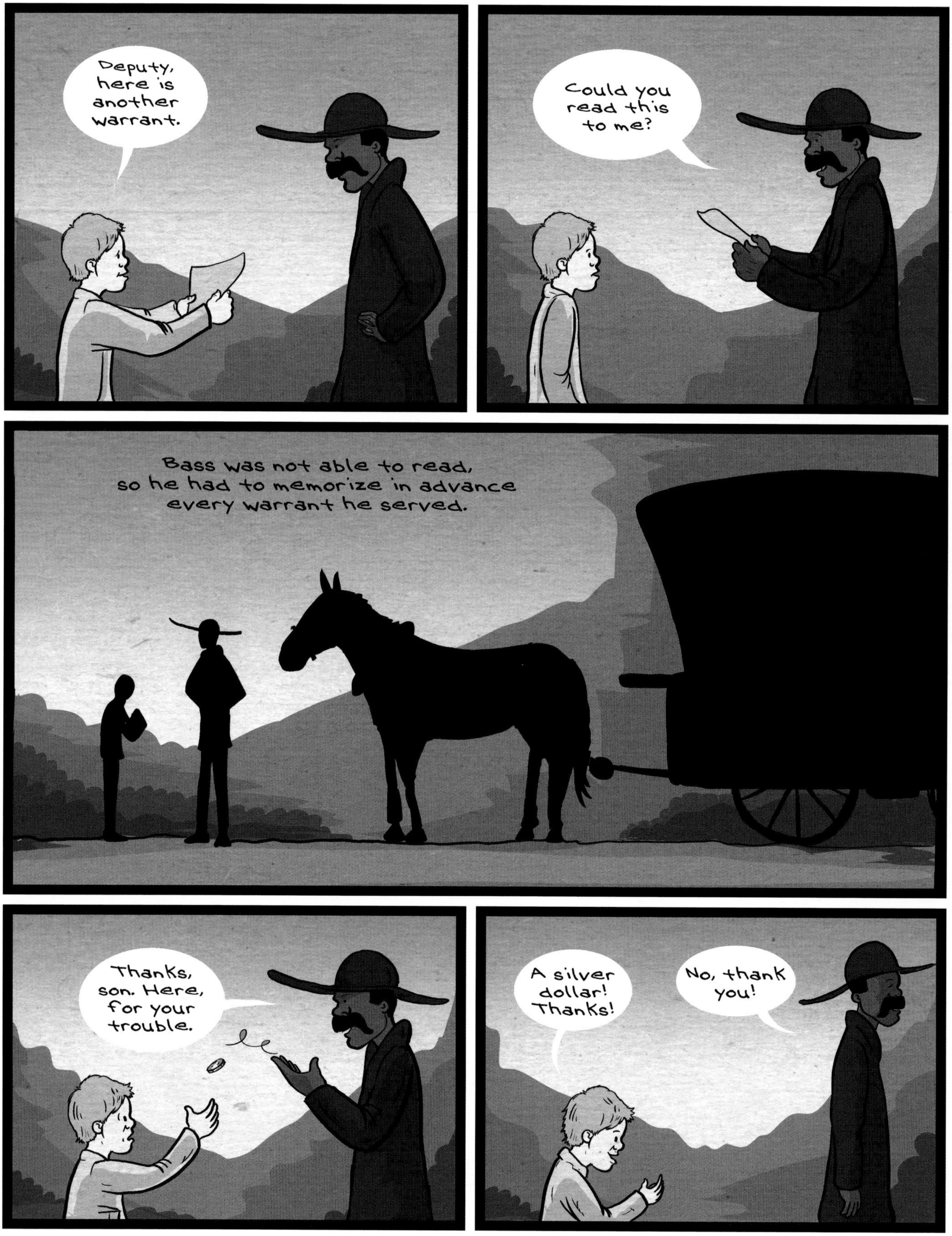
Deputy, here is another warrant.
Could you read this to me?
Bass was not able to read, so he had to memorize in advance every warrant he served.
Thanks, son. Here, for your trouble.
A silver dollar! Thanks!
No, thank you!

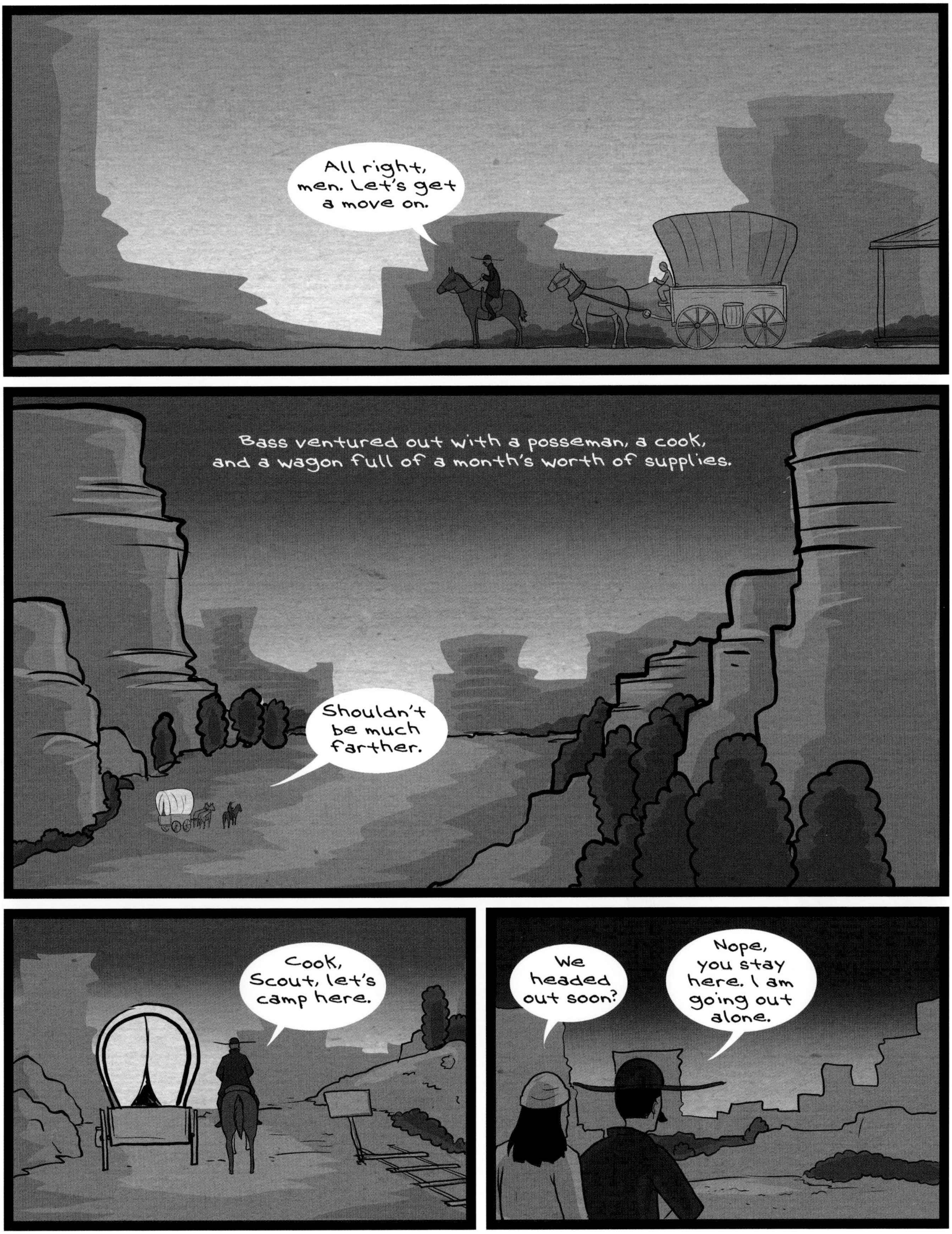
All right, men. Let's get a move on.
Bass ventured out with a posseman, a cook, and a wagon full of a month's worth of supplies.
Shouldn't be much farther.
Cook, Scout, let's camp here.
We headed out soon?
Nope, you stay here. I am going out alone.

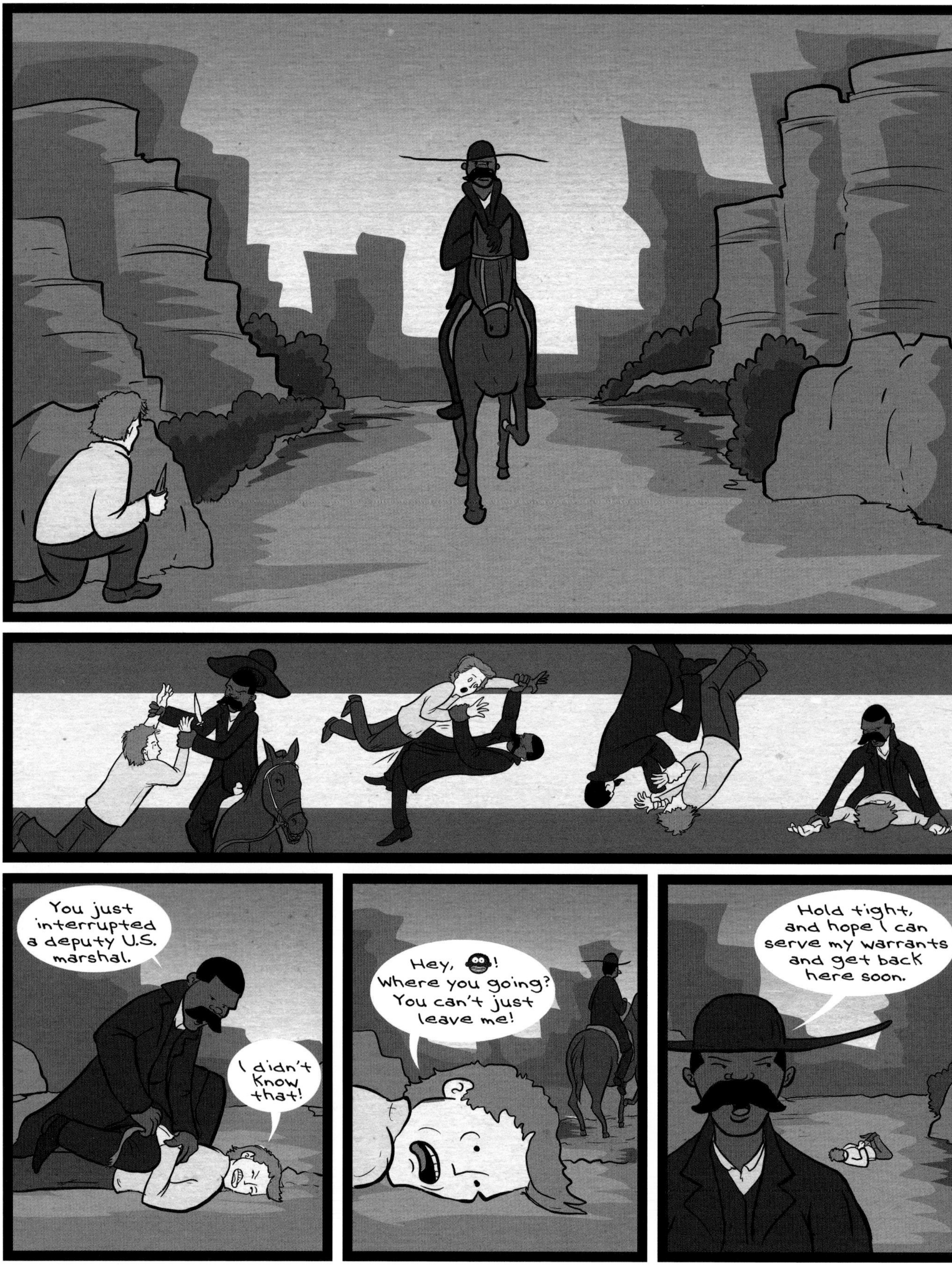
You just interrupted a deputy U.S. marshal.
I didn't know that!
Hey, !
Where you going? You can't just leave me!
Hold tight, and hope I can serve my warrants and get back here soon.

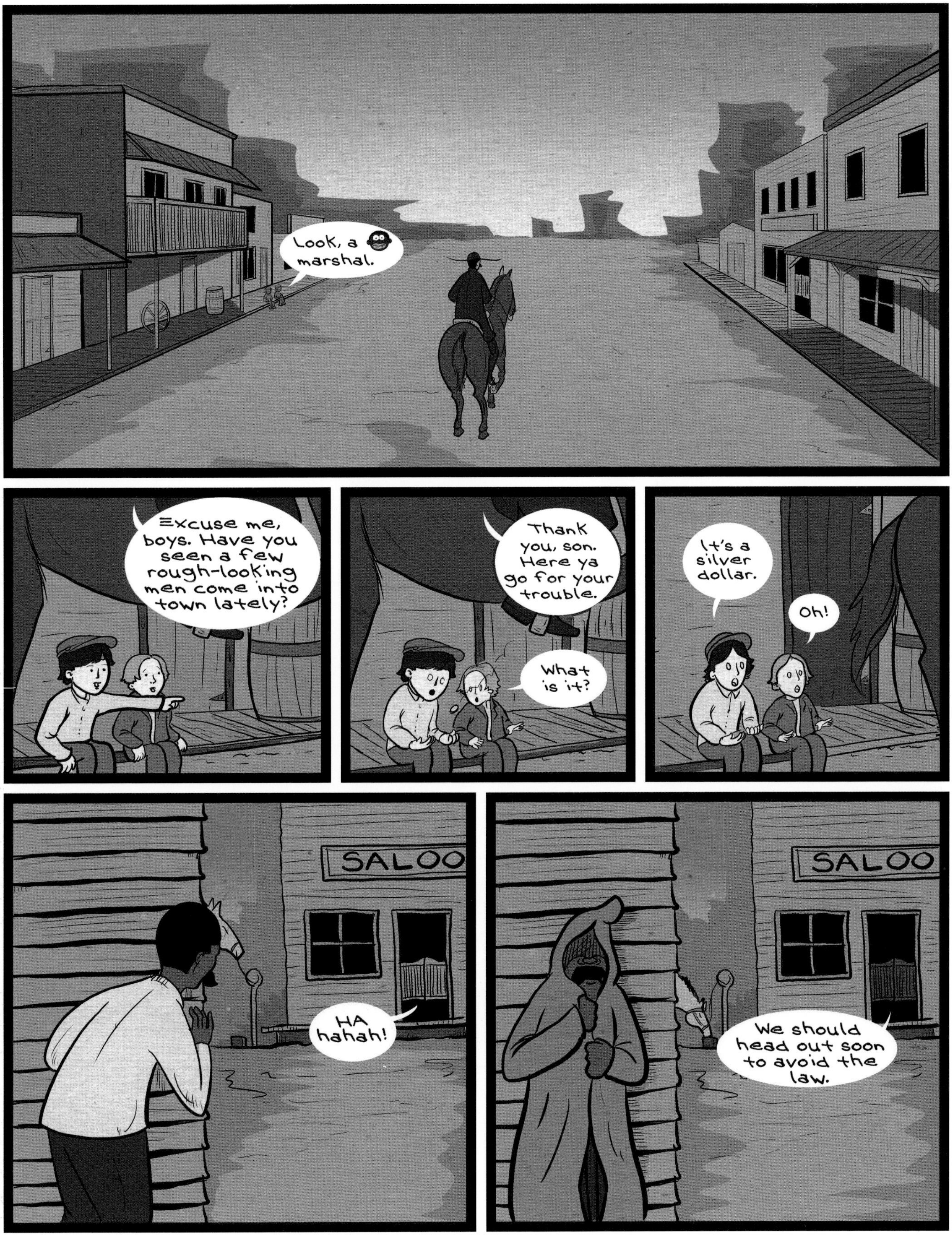
Look, a marshal.
Excuse me, boys. Have you seen a few rough-looking men come into town lately?
Thank you, son. Here ya go for your trouble.
What is it?
It's a silver dollar.
Oh!
SALOO
HA hahah!
SALOO
We should head out soon to avoid the law.

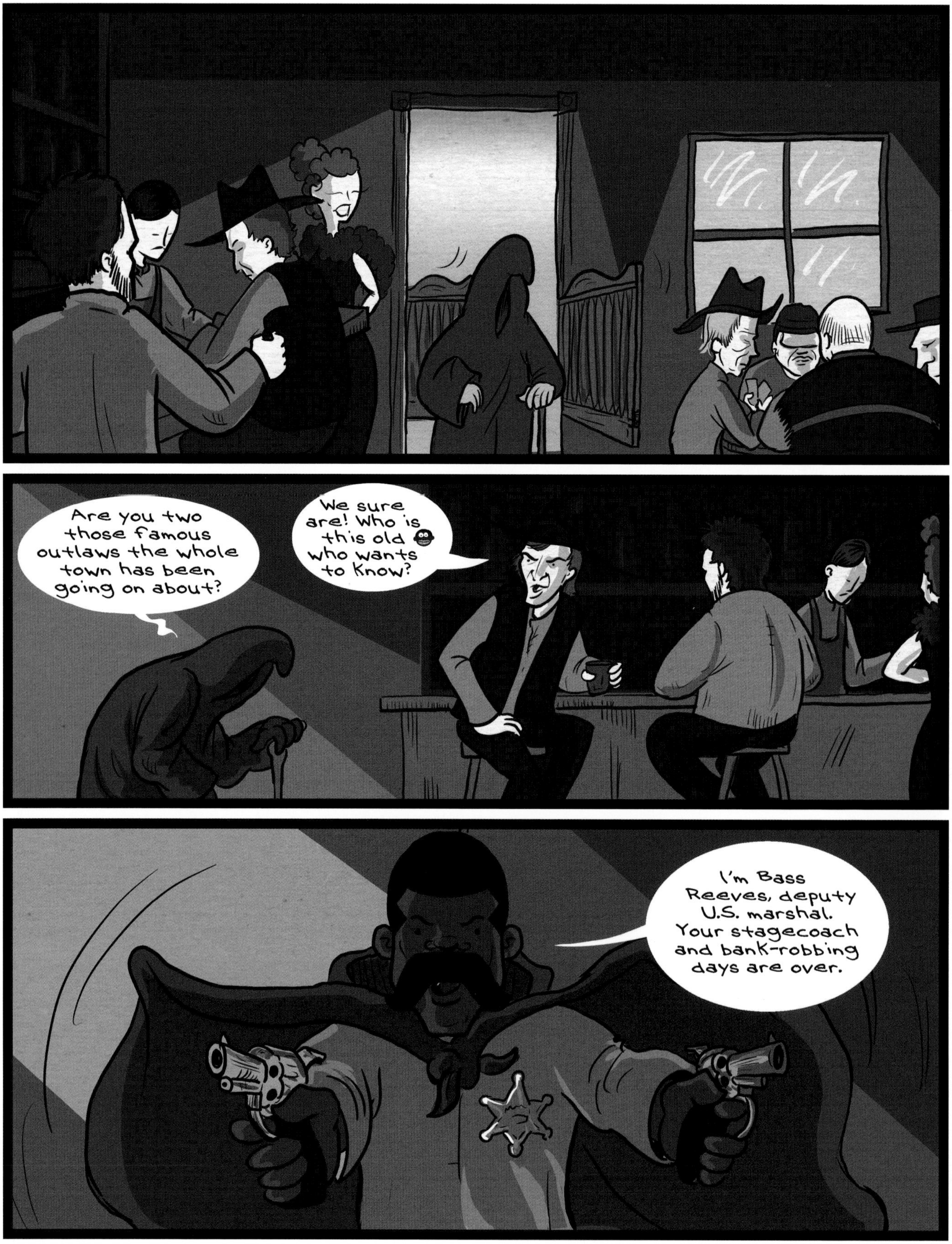
Are you two those famous outlaws the whole town has been going on about?
We sure are! Who is this old who wants to know?
I'm Bass Reeves, deputy U.S. marshal. Your stagecoach and bank-robbing days are over.

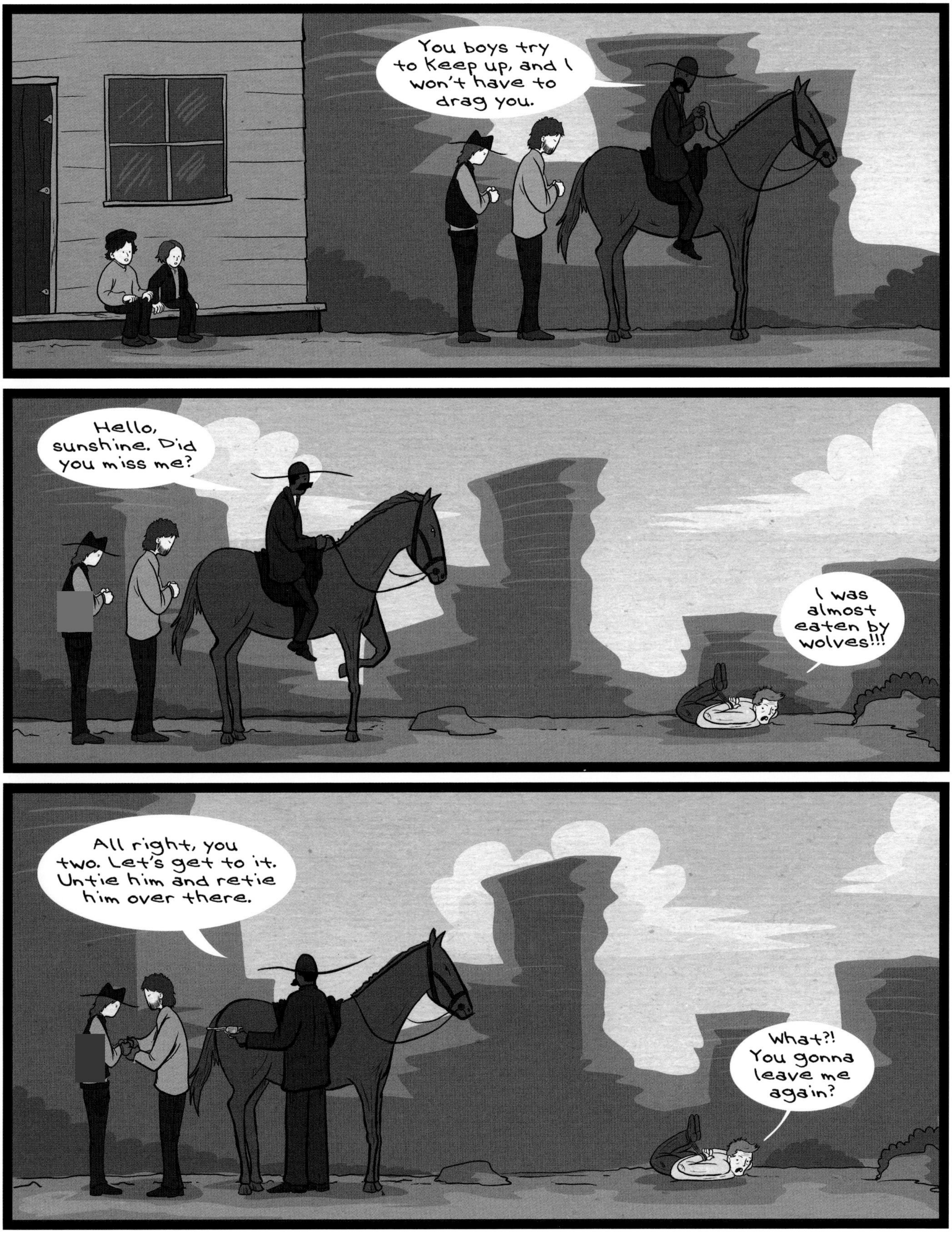
You boys try to keep up, and I won't have to drag you.
Hello, sunshine. Did you miss me?
I was almost eaten by wolves!!!
All right, you two. Let's get to it. Untie him and retie him over there.
What?! You gonna leave me again?

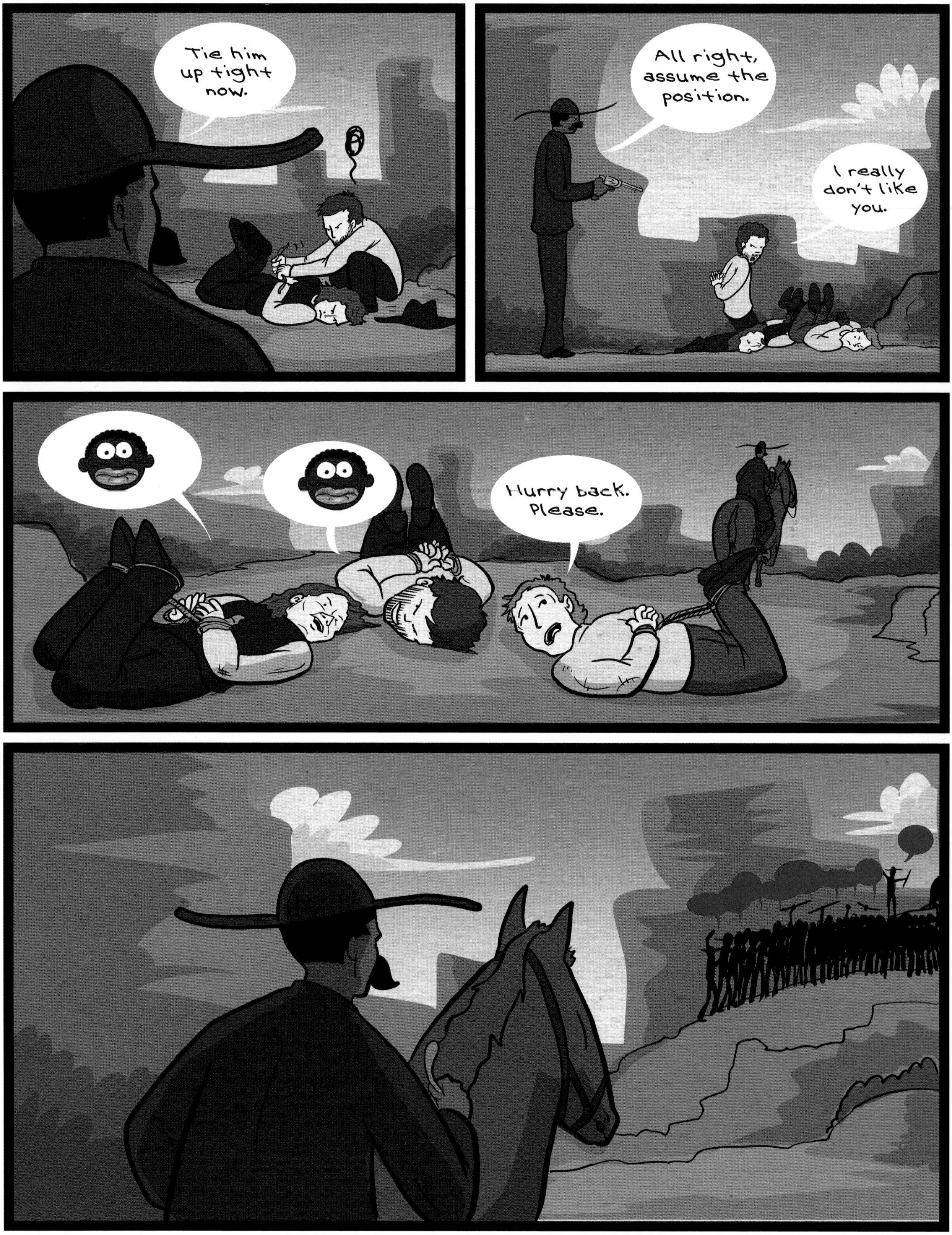
Tie him up tight now.
All right, assume the position.
I really don't like you.
Hurry back. Please.

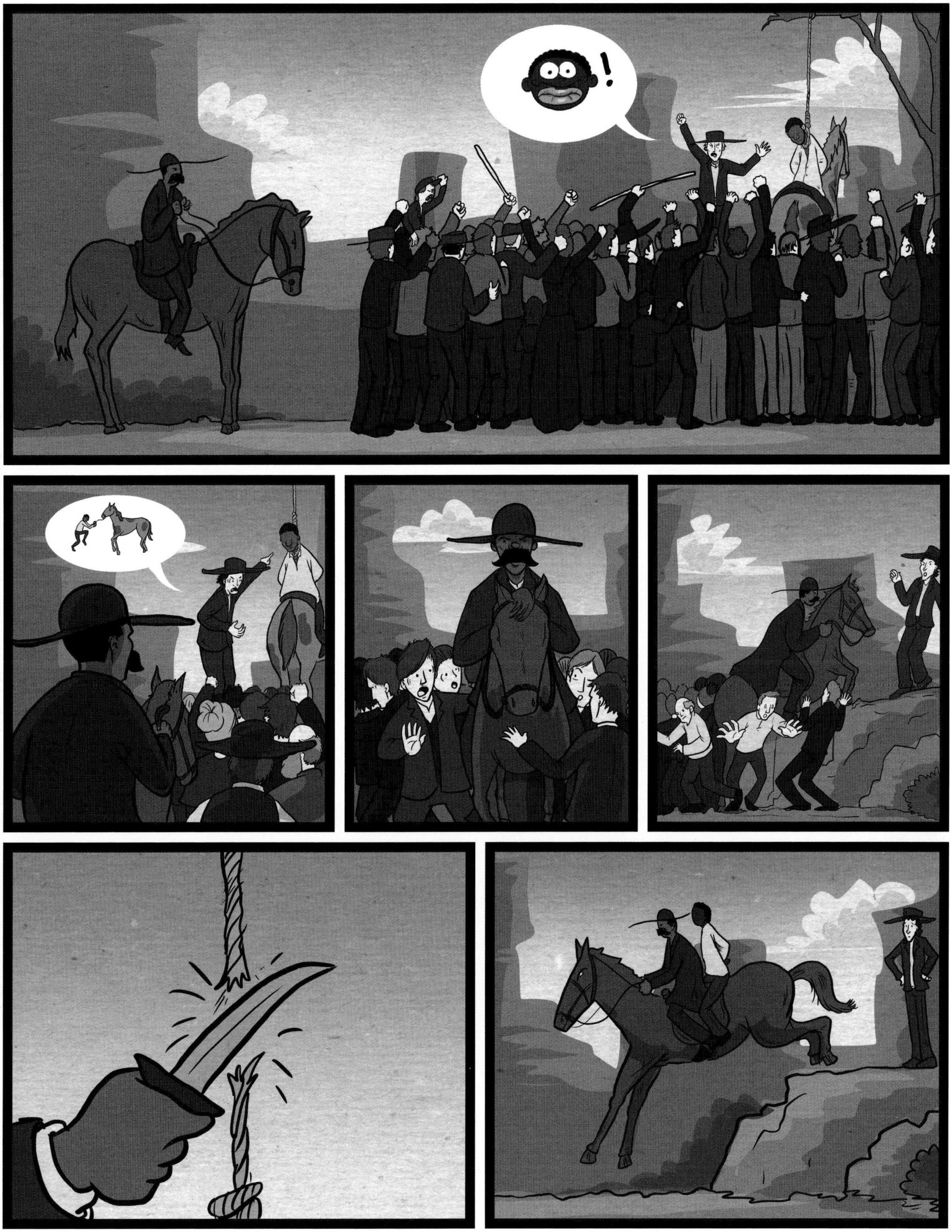
!

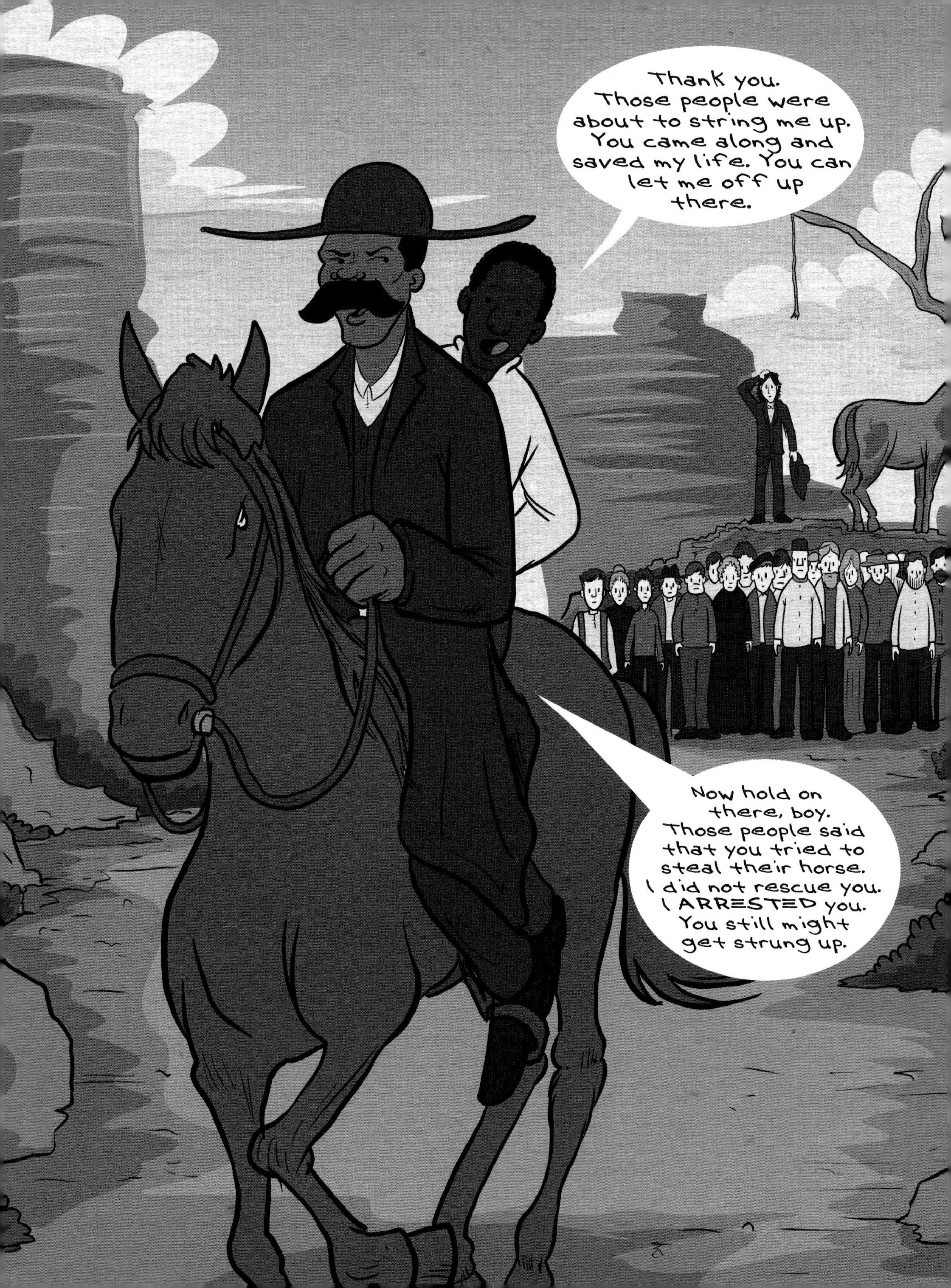
Thank you. Those people were about to string me up. You came along and saved my life. You can let me off up there.
Now hold on there, boy. Those people said that you tried to steal their horse. I did not rescue you. I ARRESTED you. You still might get strung up.

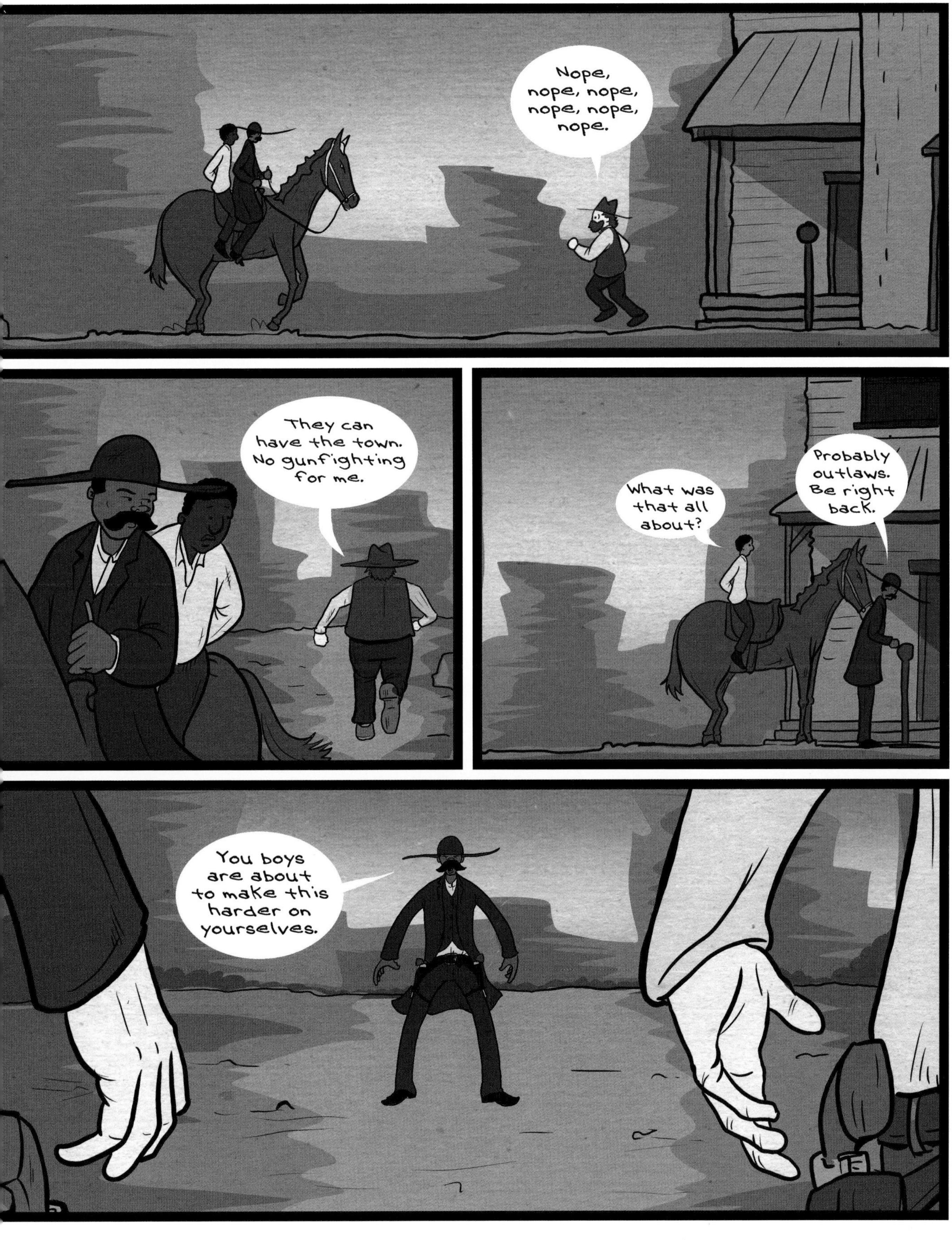
Nope, nope, nope, nope, nope, nope.
They can have the town. No gunfighting for me.
What was that all about?
Probably outlaws. Be right back.
You boys are about to make this harder on yourselves.

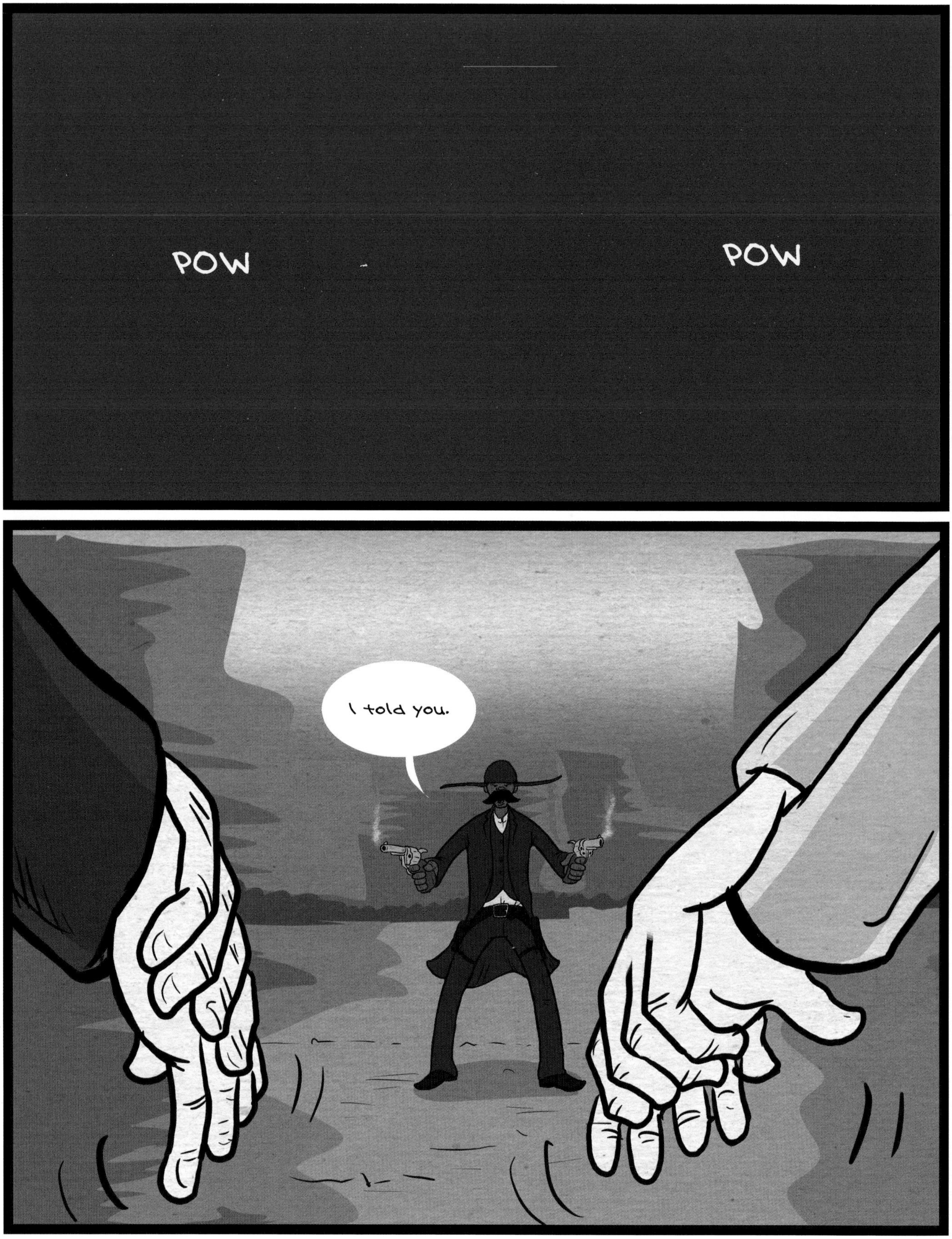
POW
POW
I told you.

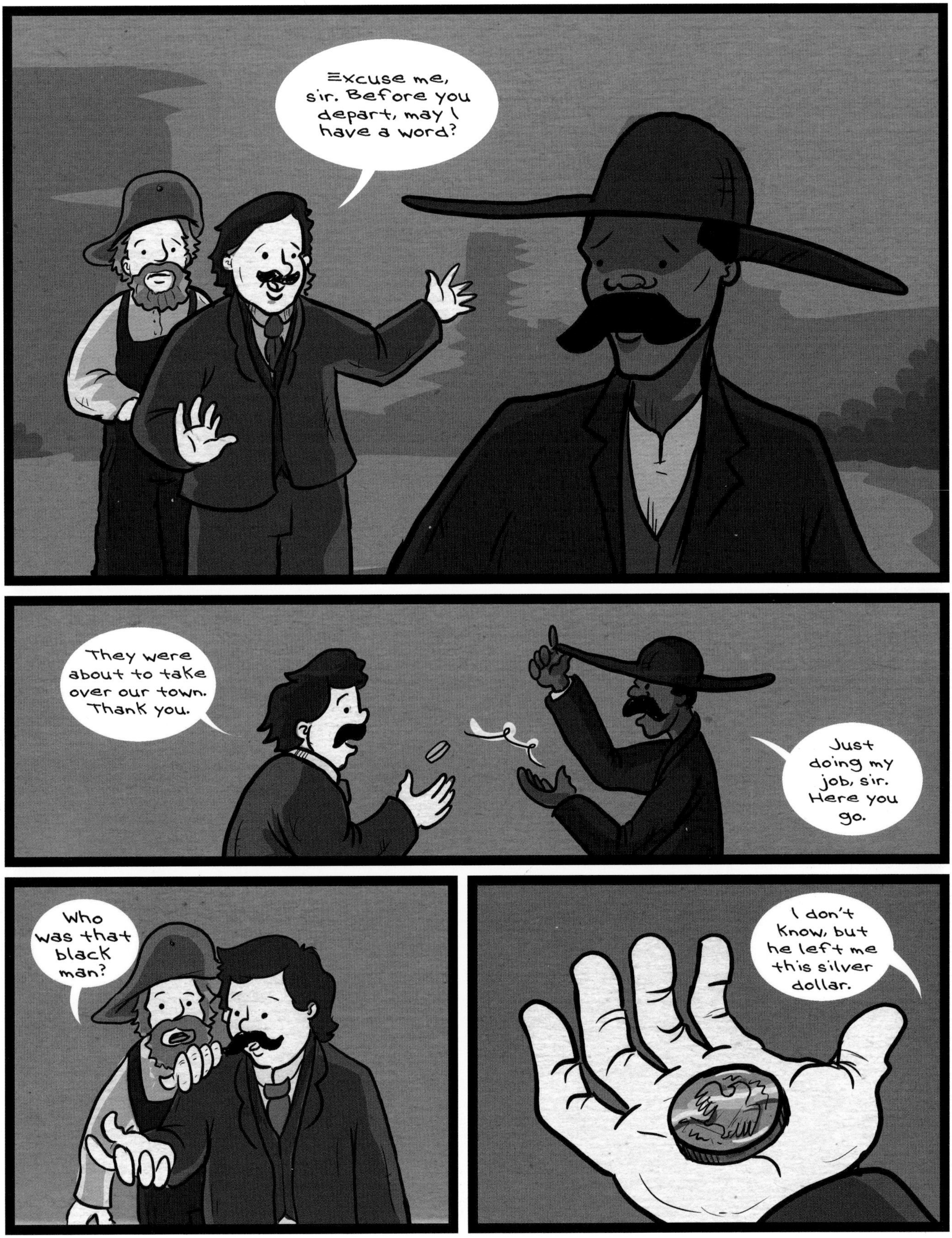
Excuse me, sir. Before you depart, may I have a word?
They were about to take over our town. Thank you.
Just doing my job, sir. Here you go.
Who was that black man?
I don't know, but he left me this silver dollar.

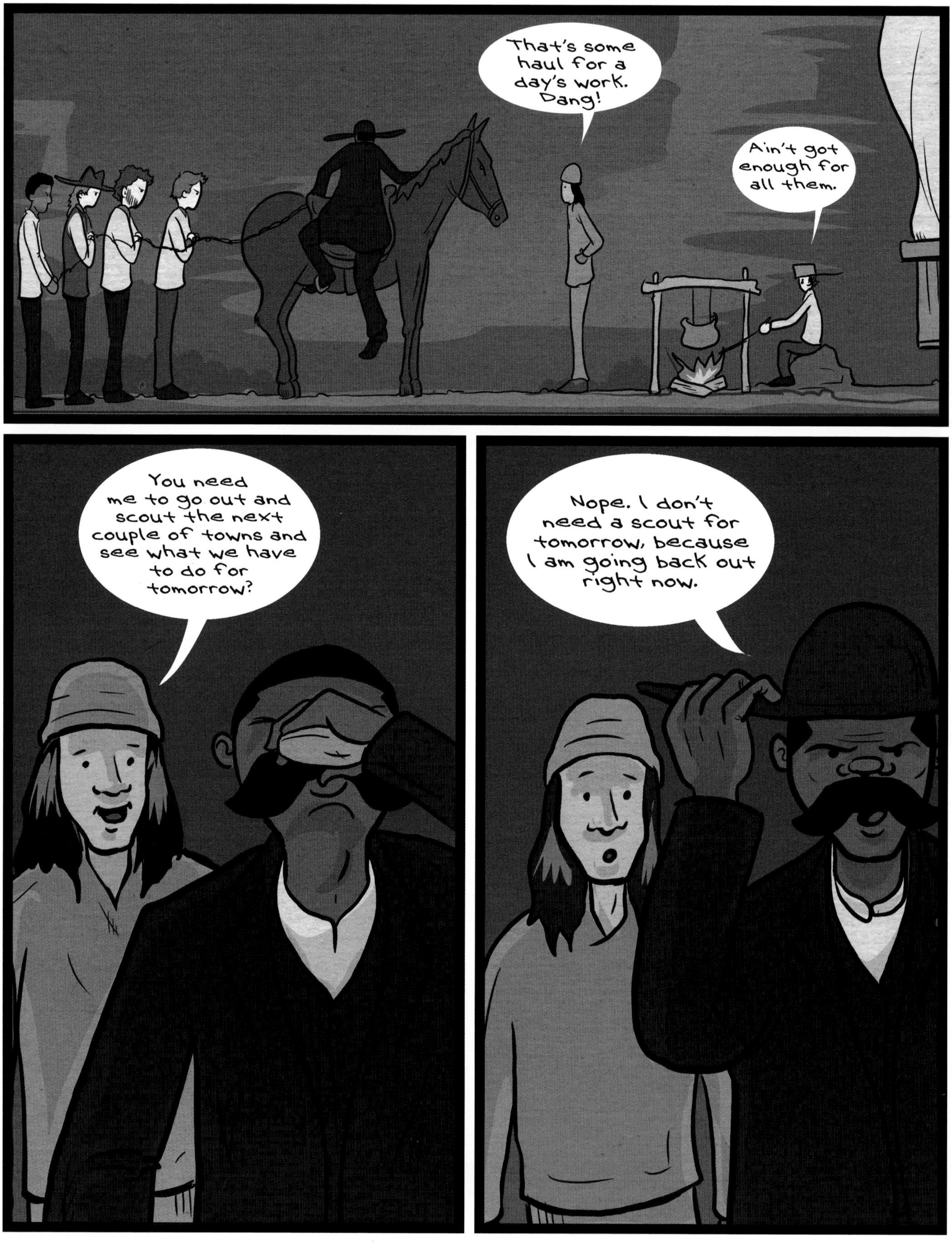
That's some haul for a day's work. Dang!
Ain't got enough for all them.
You need me to go out and scout the next couple of towns and see what we have to do for tomorrow?
Nope. I don't need a scout for tomorrow, because I am going back out right now.

SNAP

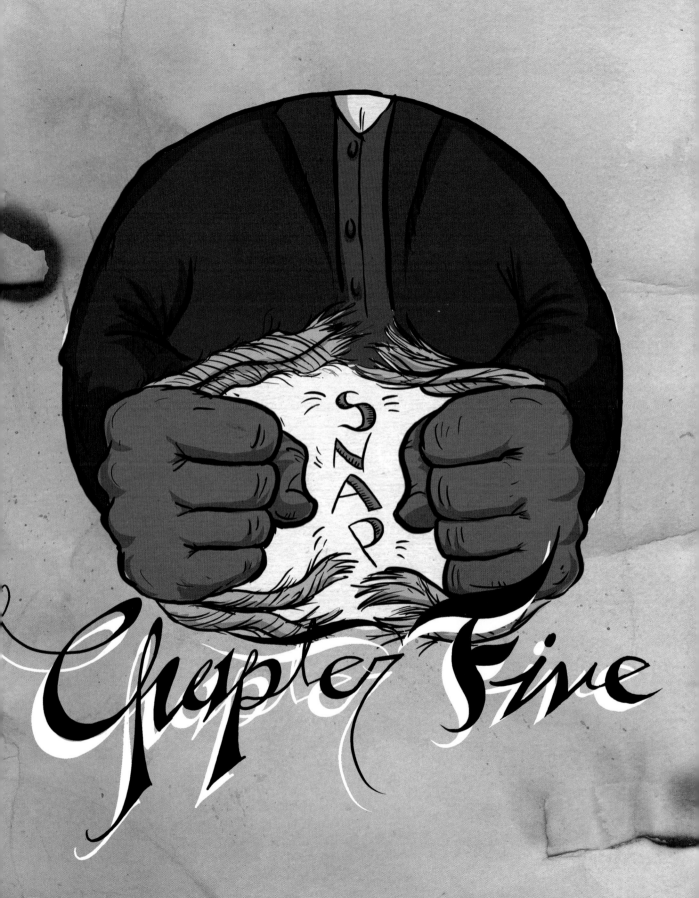

Chapter Five

1902
Time to wake up...

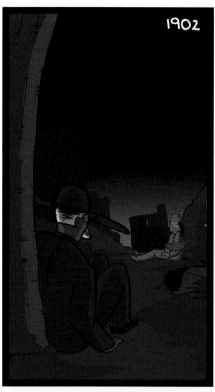

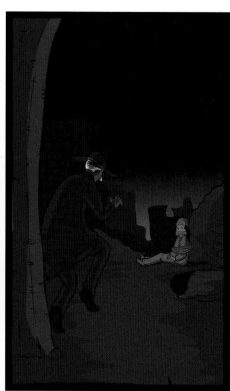

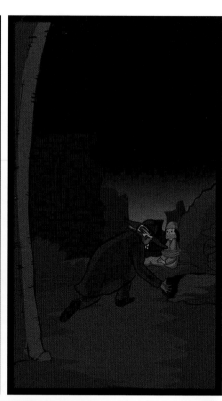

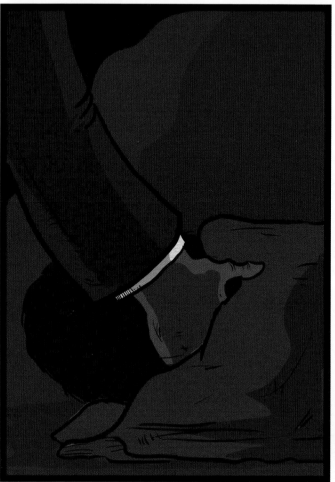

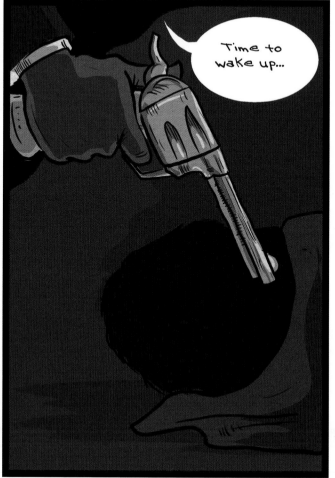

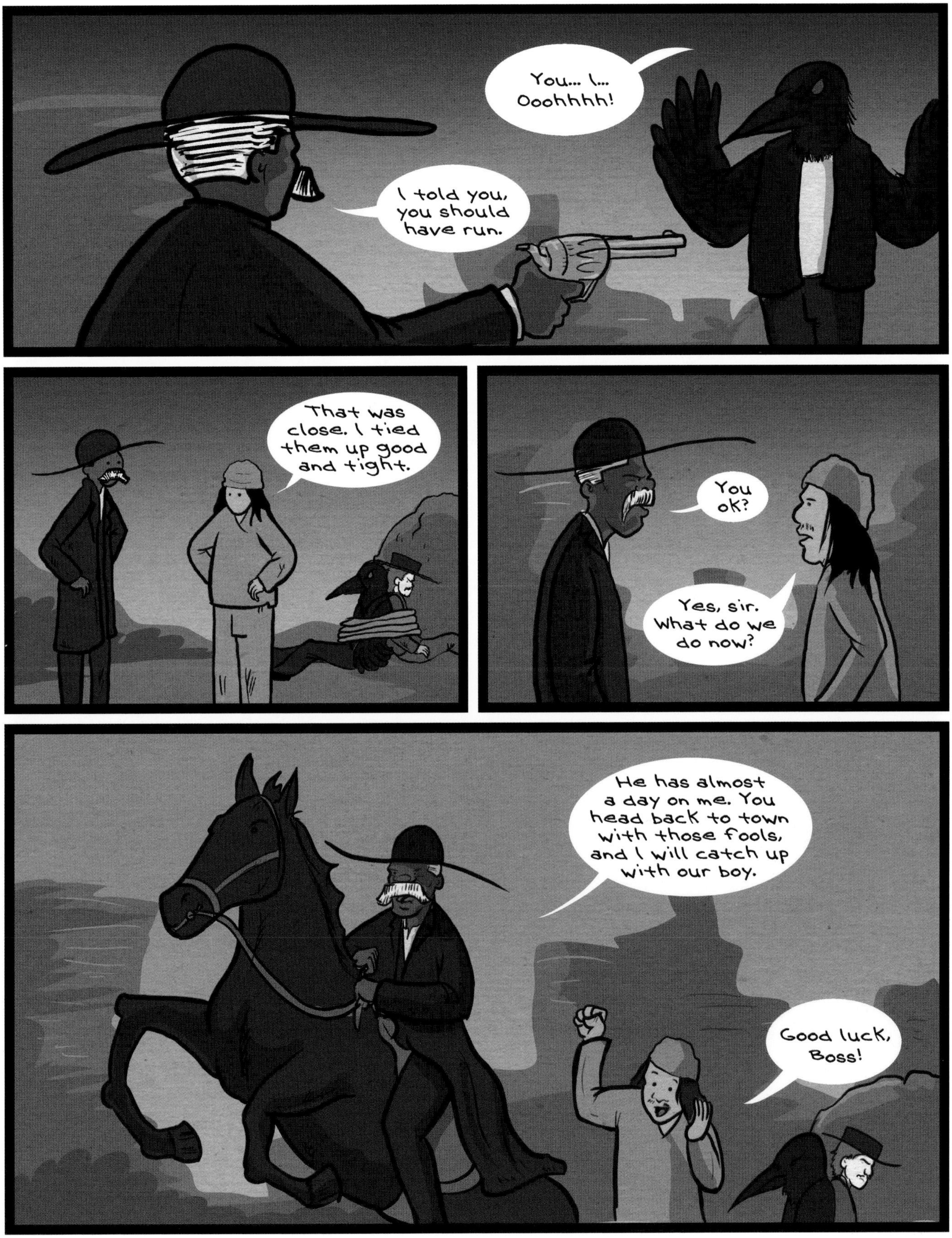
You... I...
Ooohhhh!
I told you, you should have run.
That was close. I tied them up good and tight.
You ok?
Yes, sir. What do we do now?
He has almost a day on me. You head back to town with those fools, and I will catch up with our boy.
Good luck, Boss!

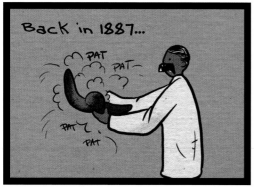

Back in 1887...

PAT
PAT
PAT
PAT

PAT   PAT

POW

How do
I look?

Terrible.

Good.

He is
crazy, going
out there.

He is not
crazy. He is
the Invincible
Marshal...

...and 27 miles is not that
far away for him when it comes
to enforcing the law.

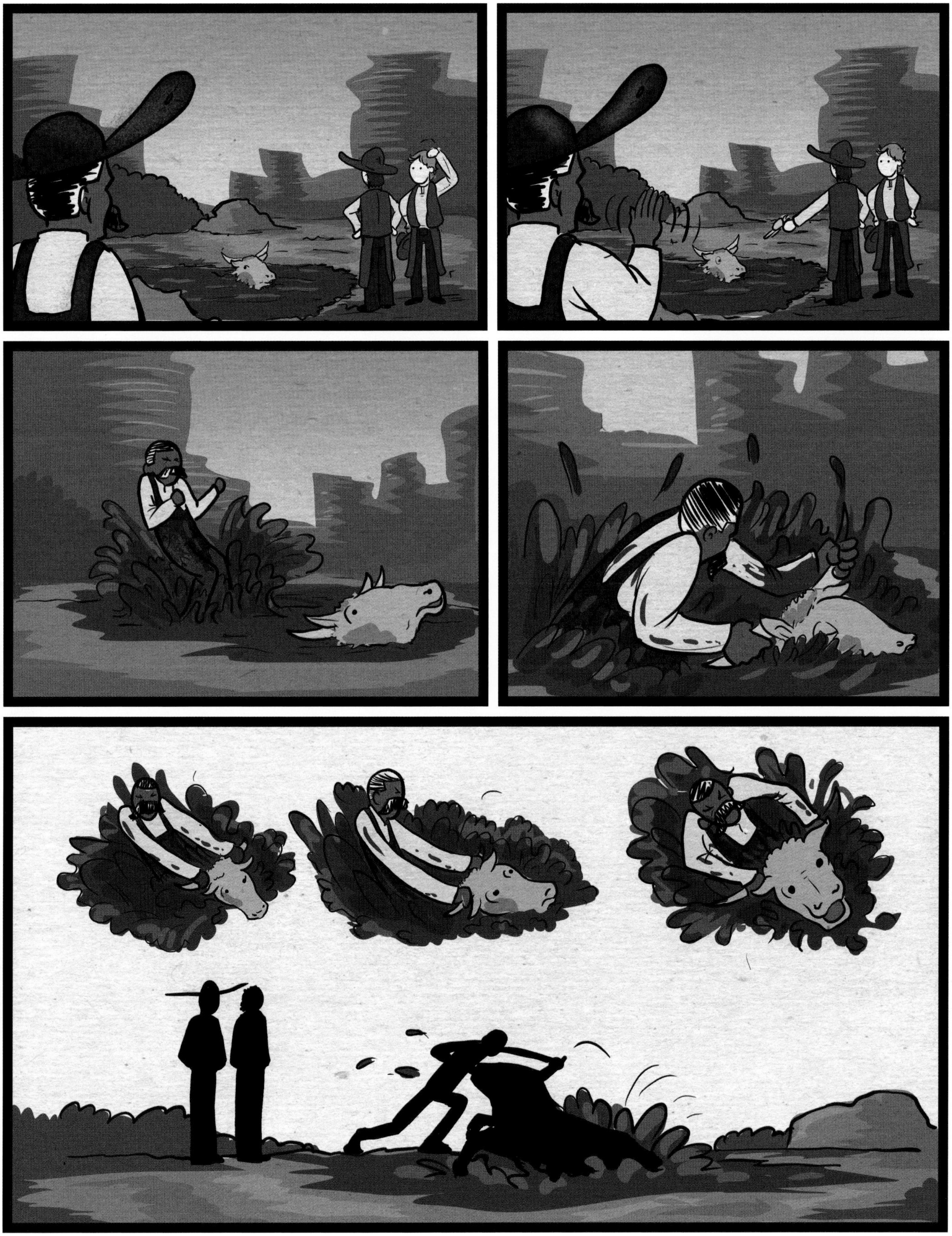

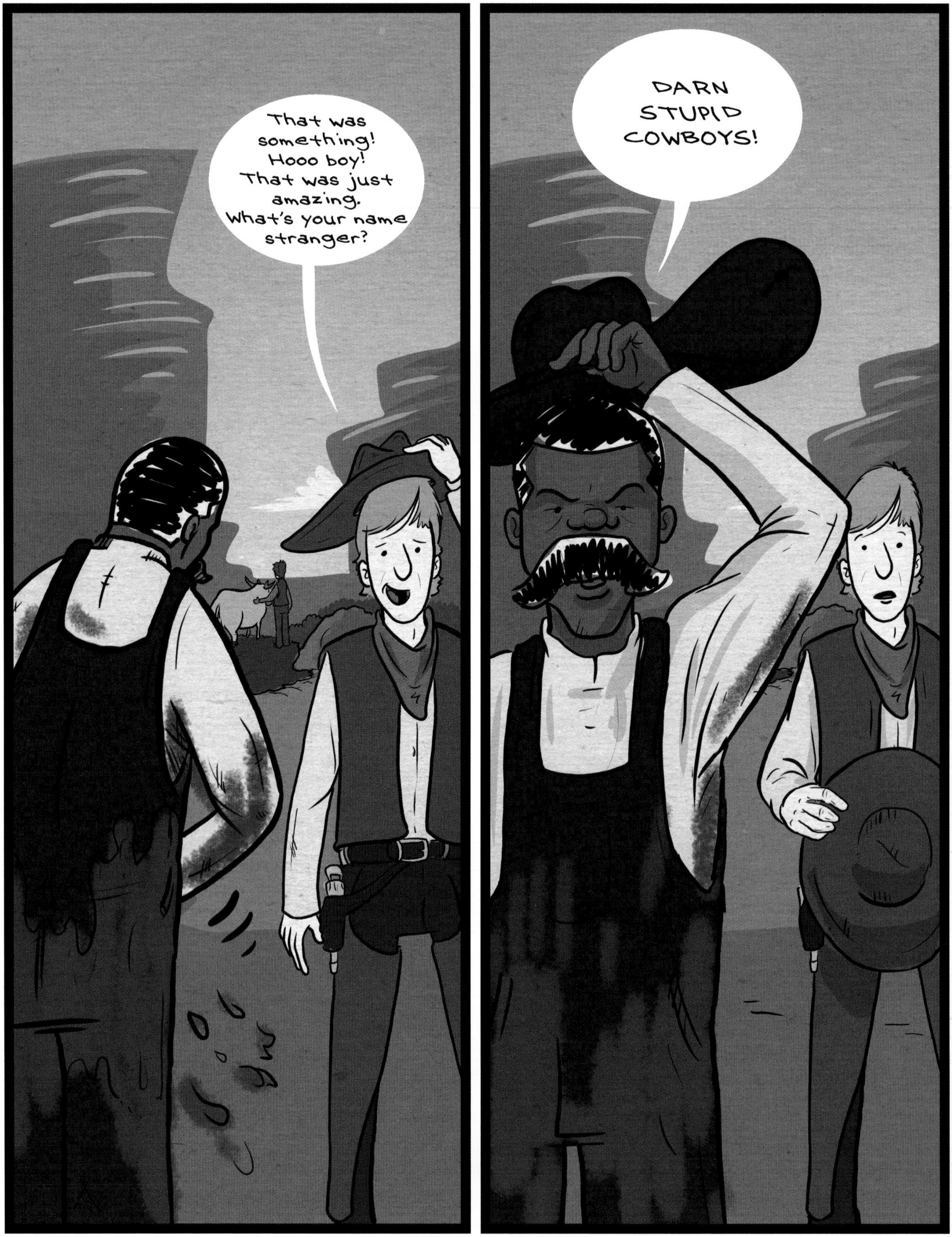
That was something! Hooo boy! That was just amazing. What's your name stranger?
DARN STUPID COWBOYS!

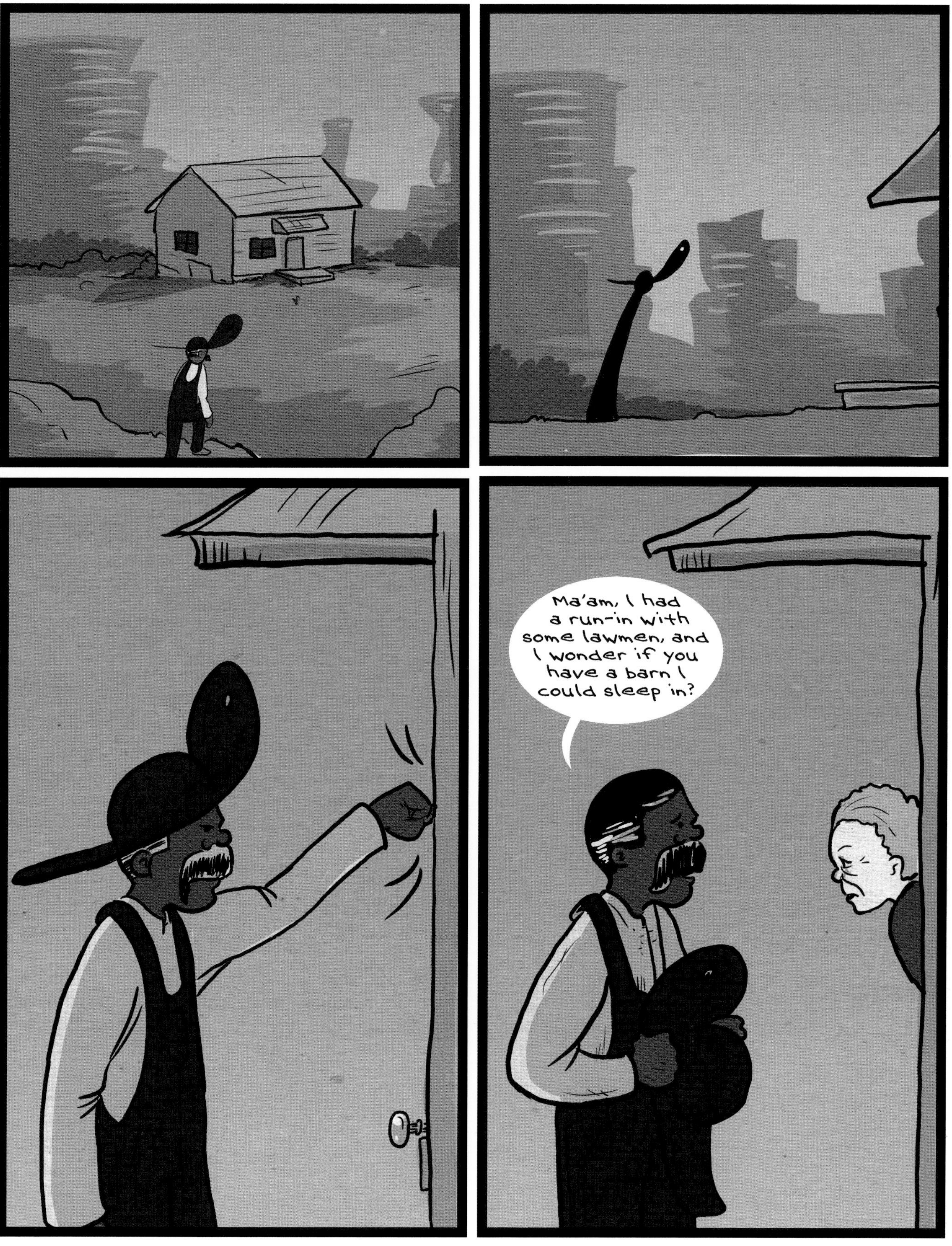
Ma'am, I had a run-in with some lawmen, and I wonder if you have a barn I could sleep in?

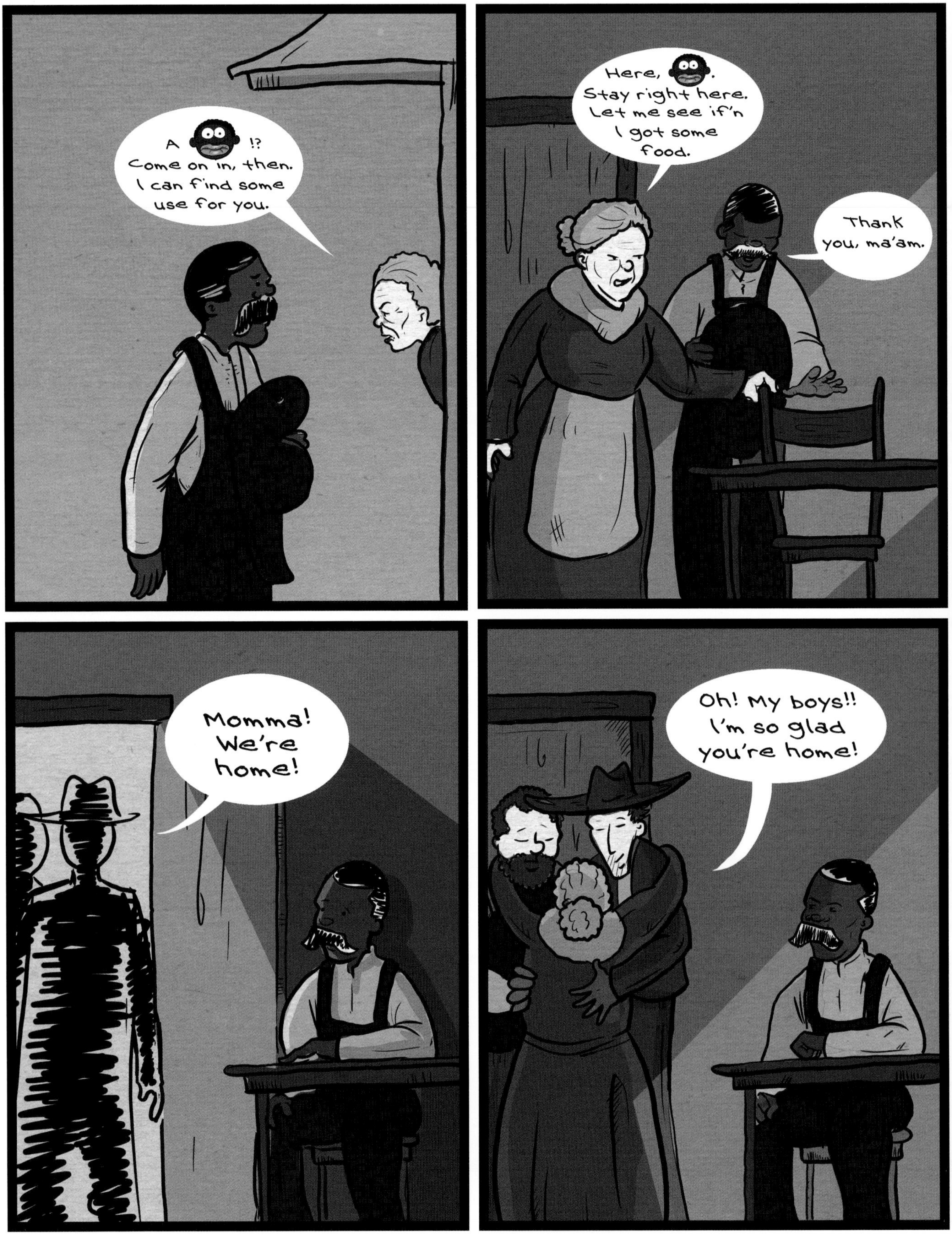
A !? Come on in, then. I can find some use for you.
Here, . Stay right here. Let me see if'n I got some food.
Thank you, ma'am.
Momma! We're home!
Oh! My boys!! I'm so glad you're home!

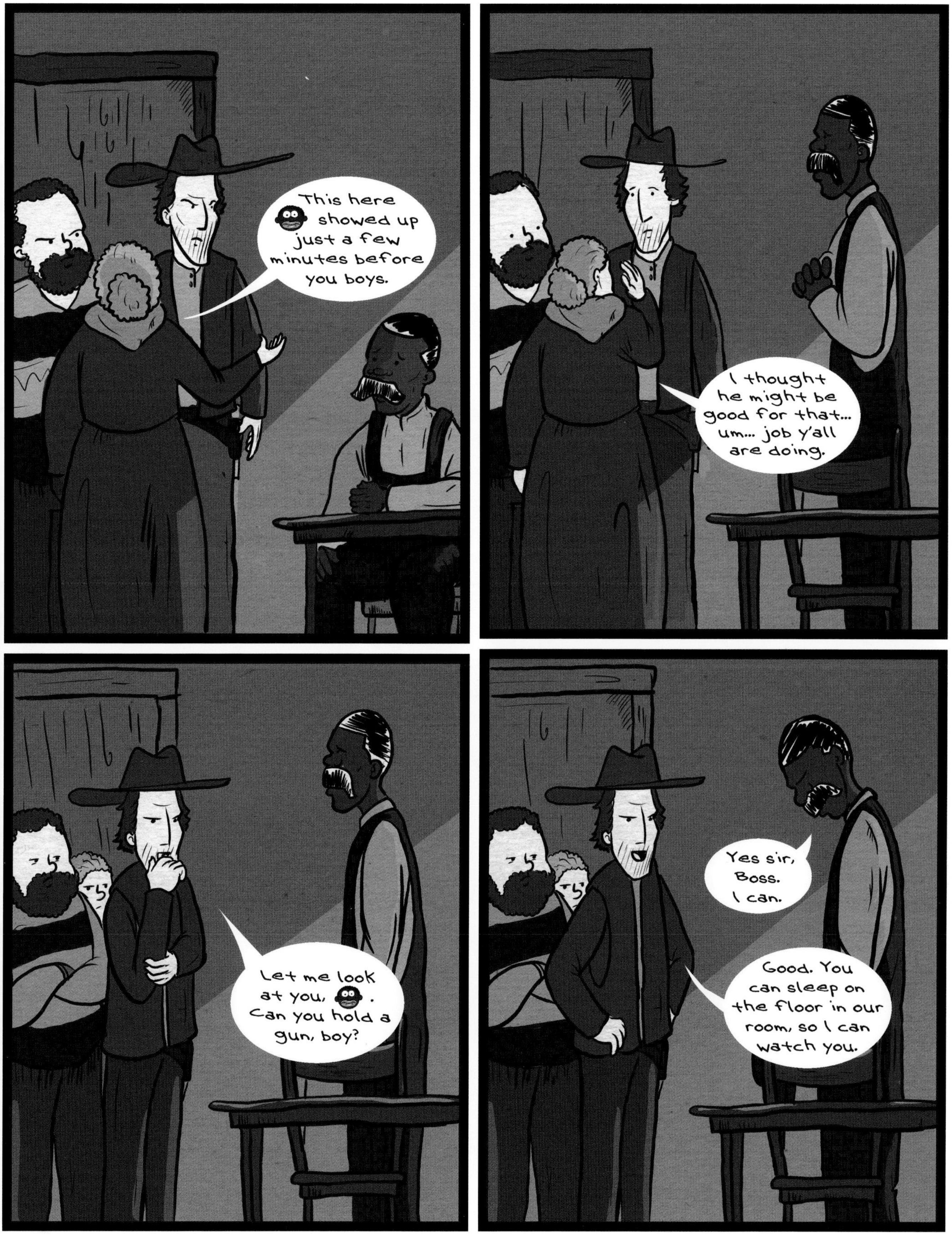
This here showed up just a few minutes before you boys.
I thought he might be good for that... um... job y'all are doing.
Let me look at you, . Can you hold a gun, boy?
Yes sir, Boss. I can.
Good. You can sleep on the floor in our room, so I can watch you.

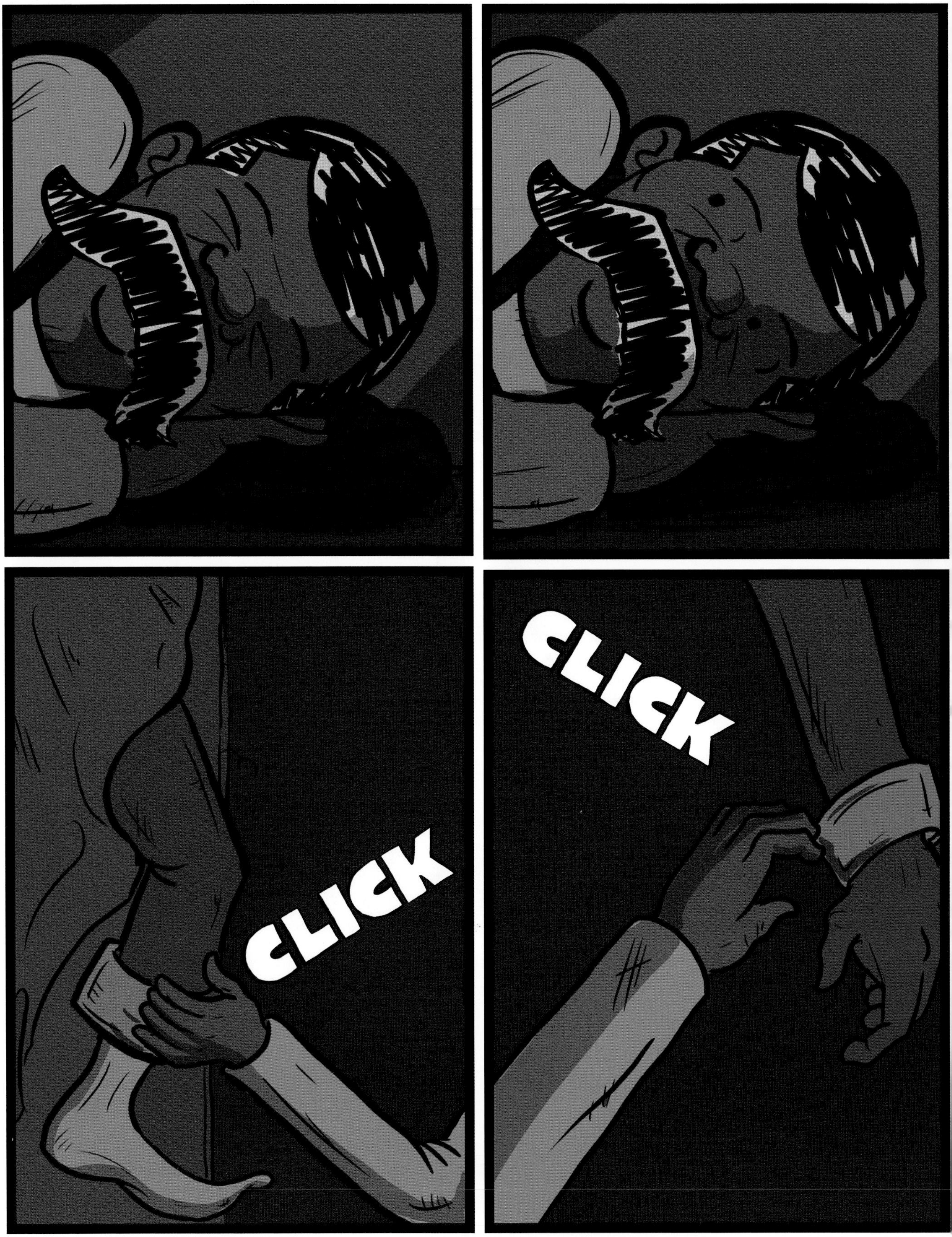
CLICK
CLICK

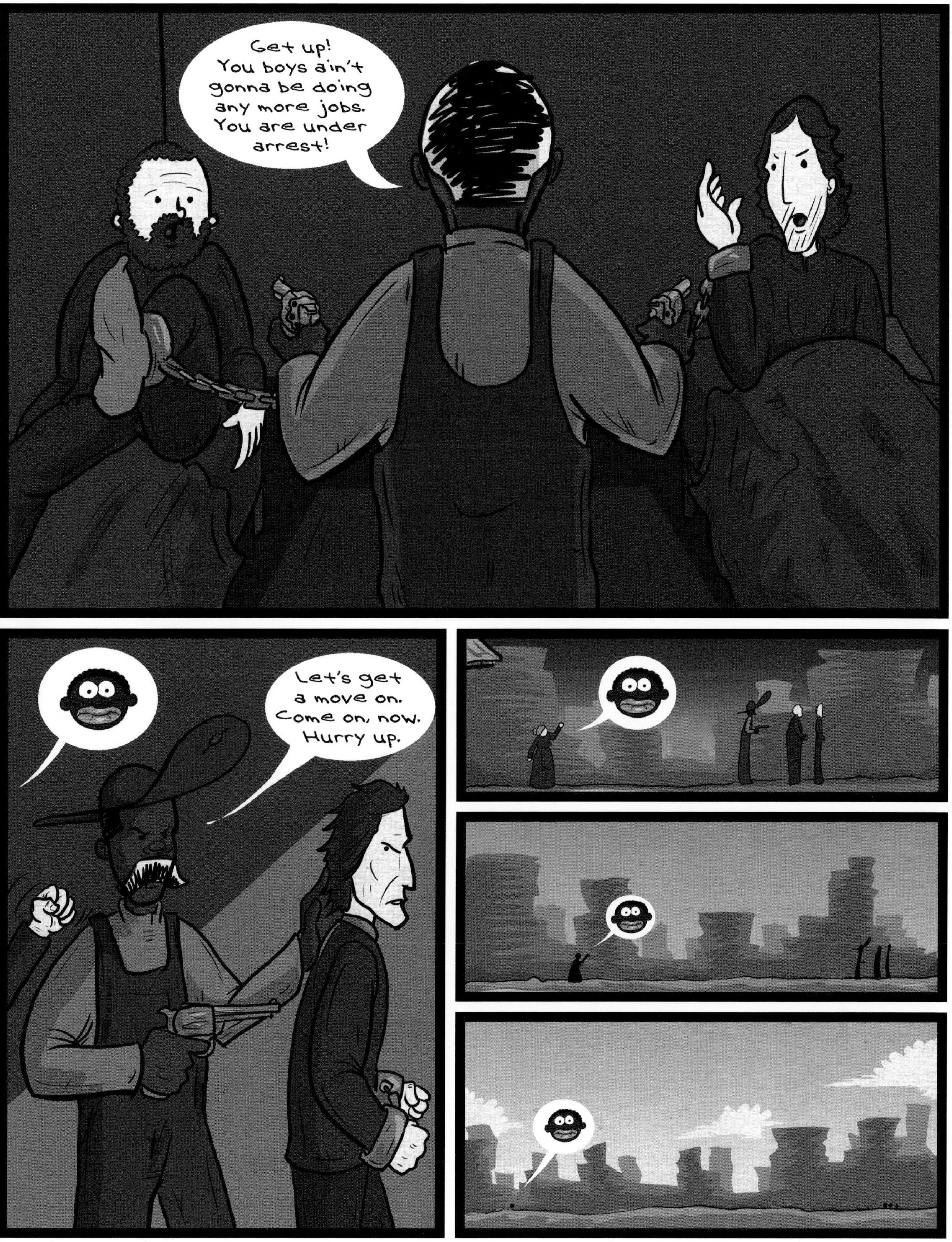
Get up! You boys ain't gonna be doing any more jobs. You are under arrest!
Let's get a move on. Come on, now. Hurry up.

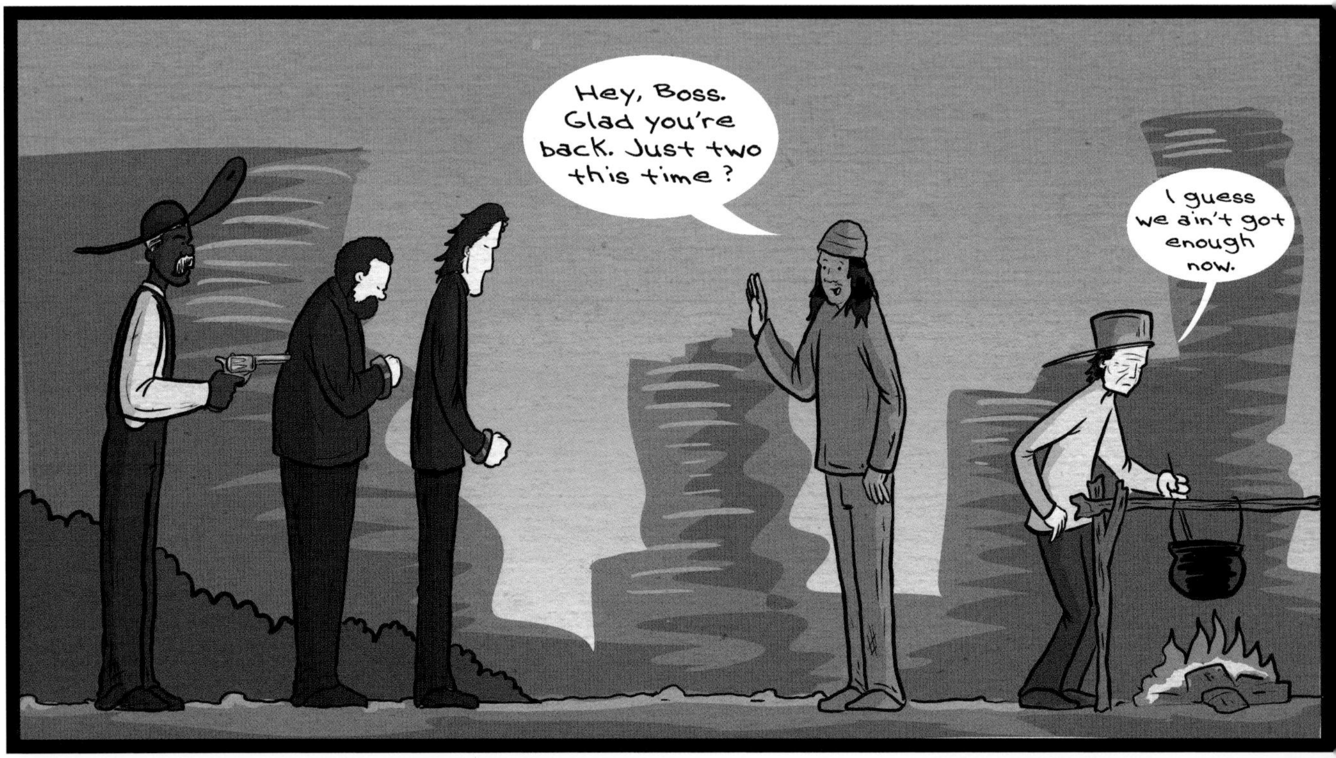
Hey, Boss. Glad you're back. Just two this time ?
I guess we ain't got enough now.

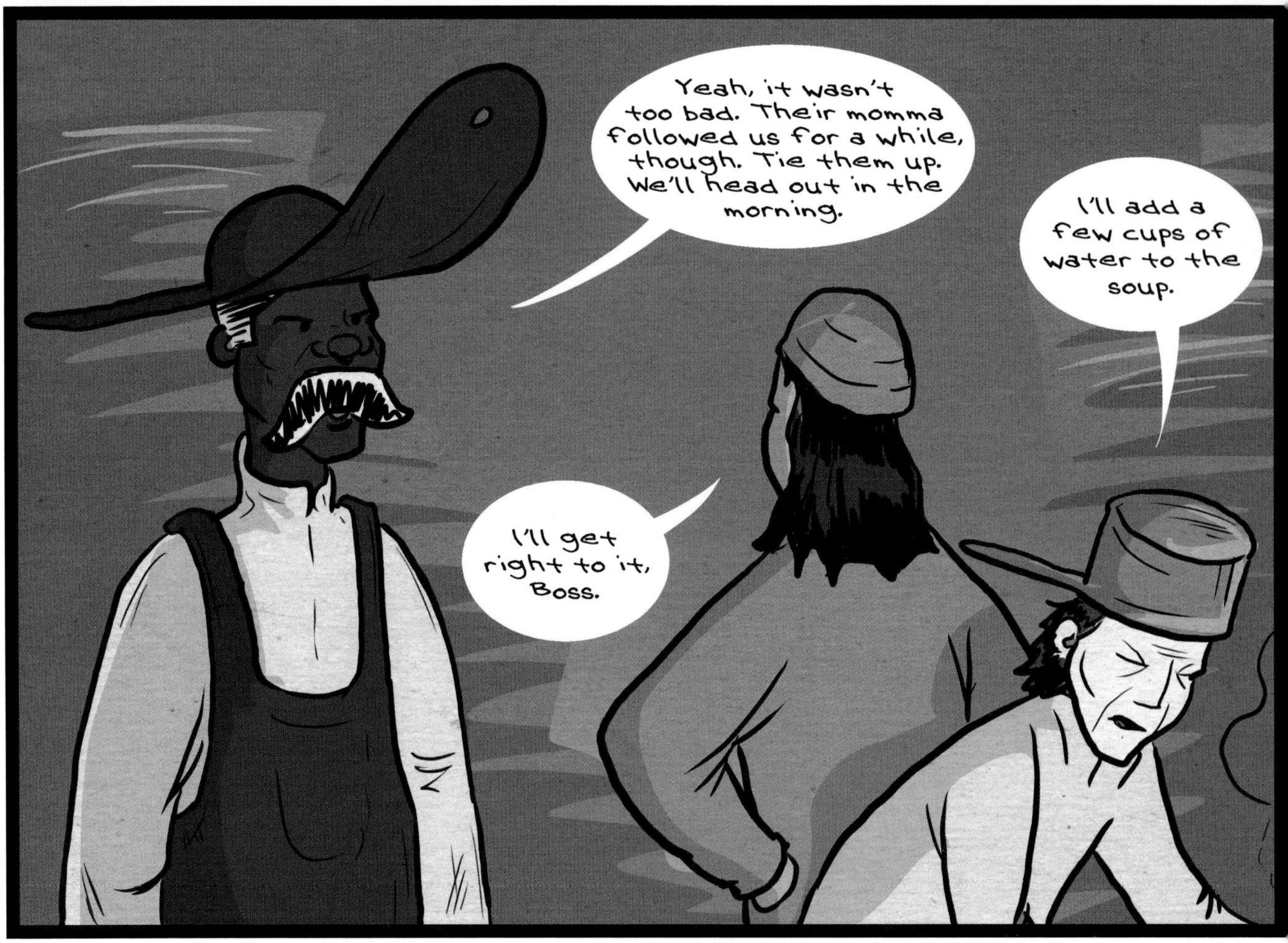
Yeah, it wasn't too bad. Their momma followed us for a while, though. Tie them up. We'll head out in the morning.
I'll add a few cups of water to the soup.
I'll get right to it, Boss.

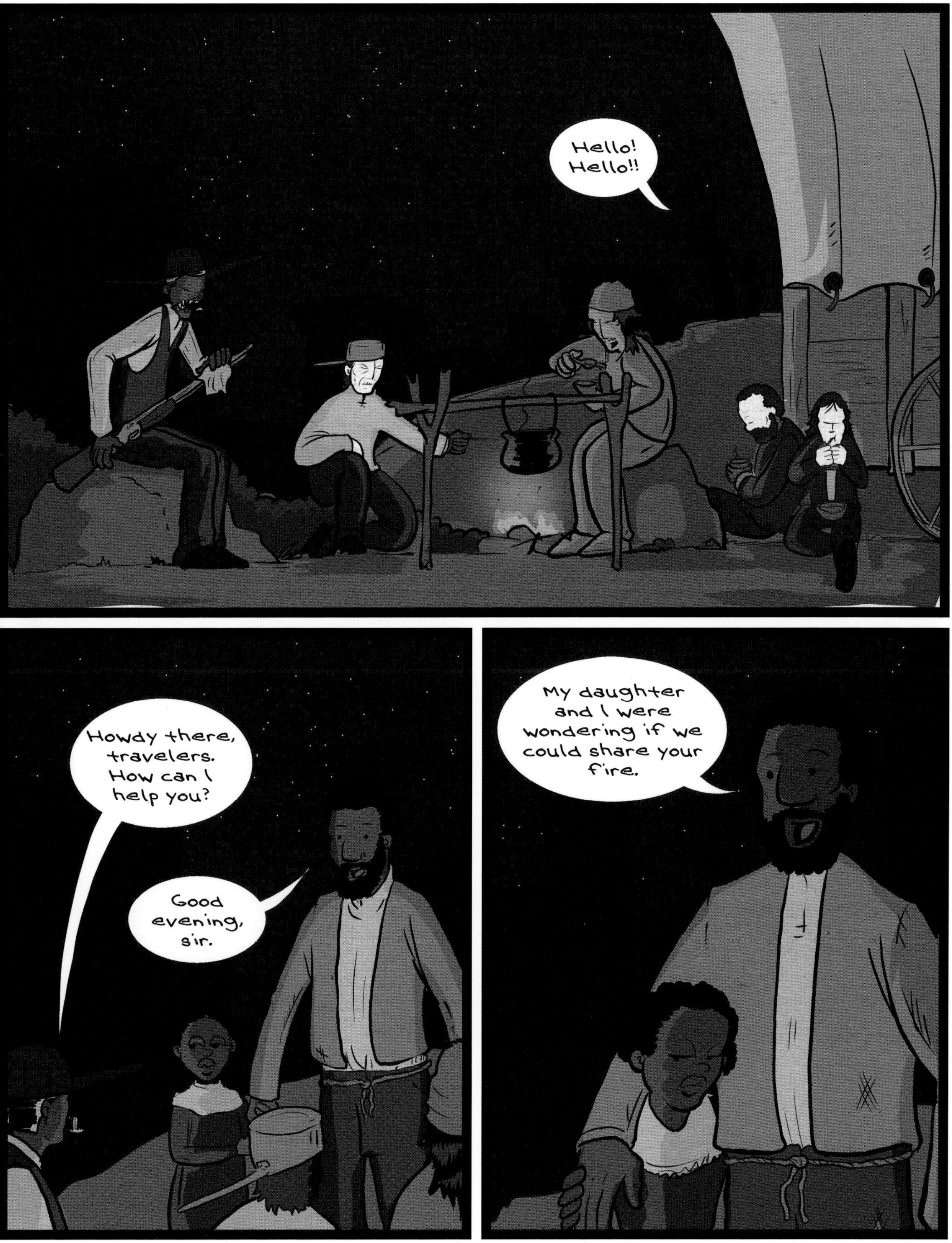
Hello!
Hello!!
Howdy there, travelers. How can I help you?
Good evening, sir.
My daughter and I were wondering if we could share your fire.

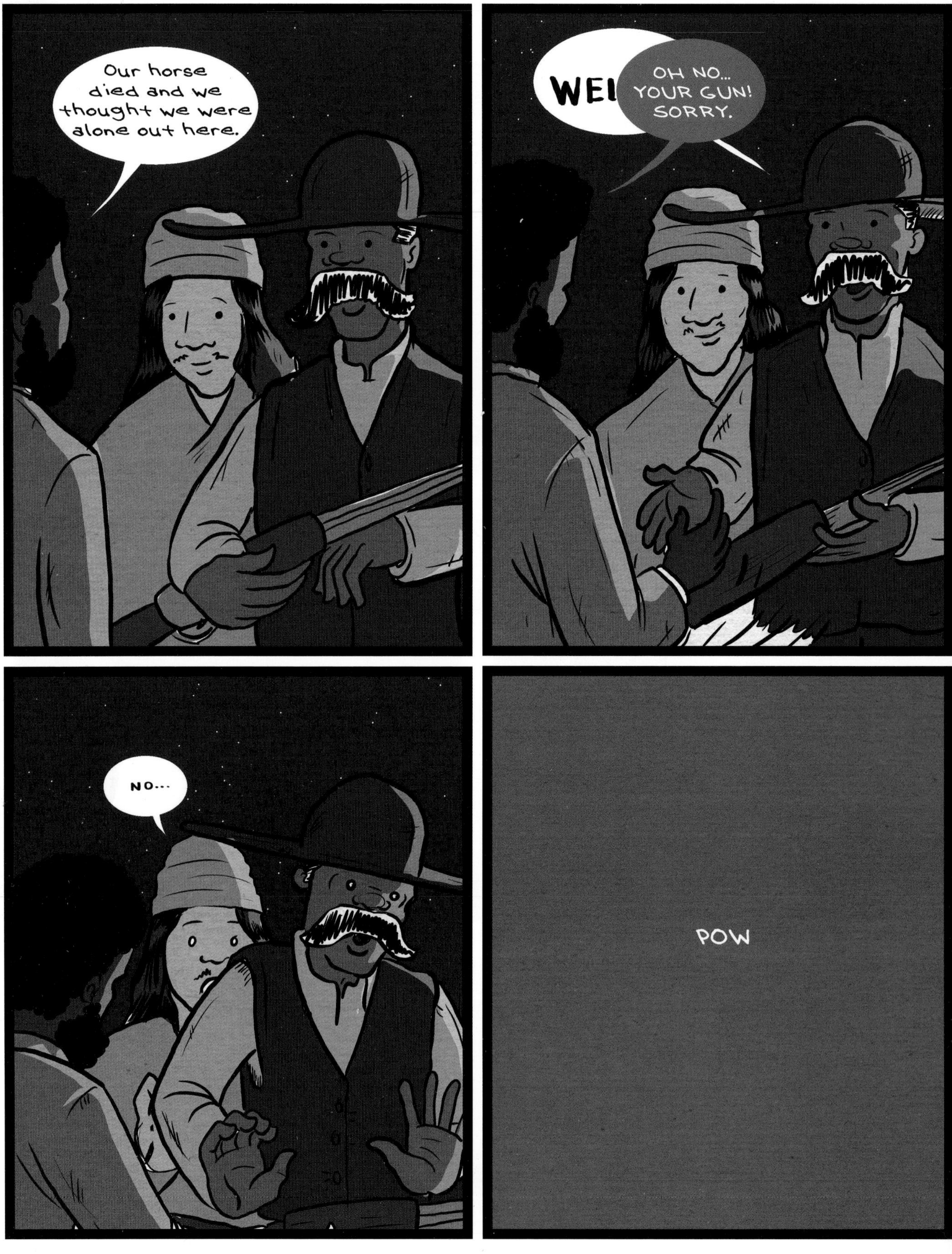

Our horse died and we thought we were alone out here.
WEI
OH NO... YOUR GUN! SORRY.
NO...
POW

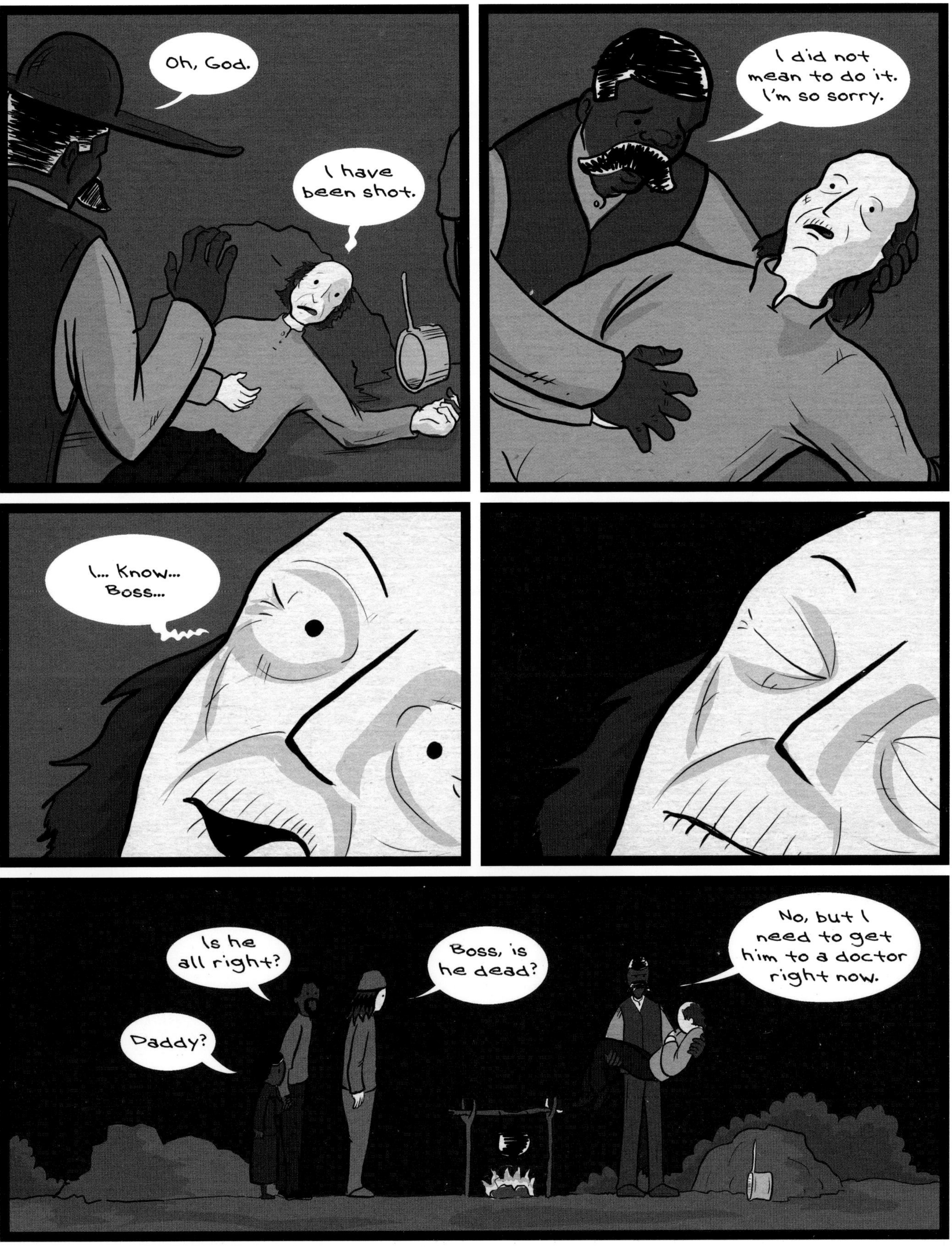
Oh, God.
I have been shot.
I did not mean to do it. I'm so sorry.
I... Know... Boss...
Is he all right?
Daddy?
Boss, is he dead?
No, but I need to get him to a doctor right now.

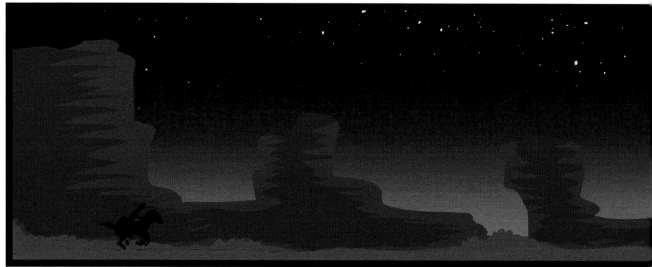

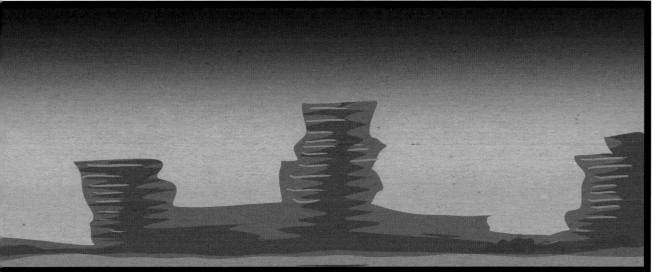

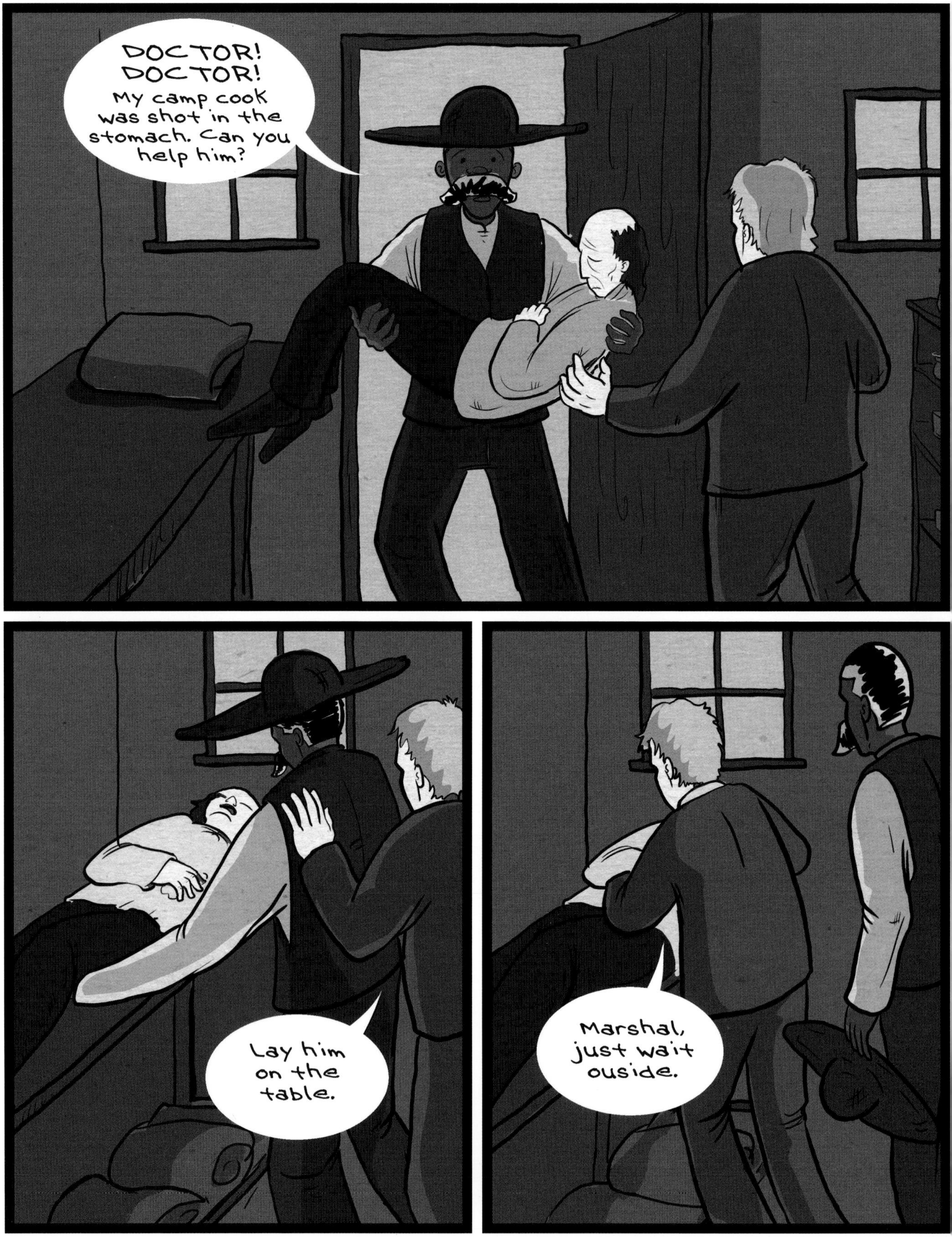
DOCTOR! DOCTOR! My camp cook was shot in the stomach. Can you help him?
Lay him on the table.
Marshal, just wait ouside.

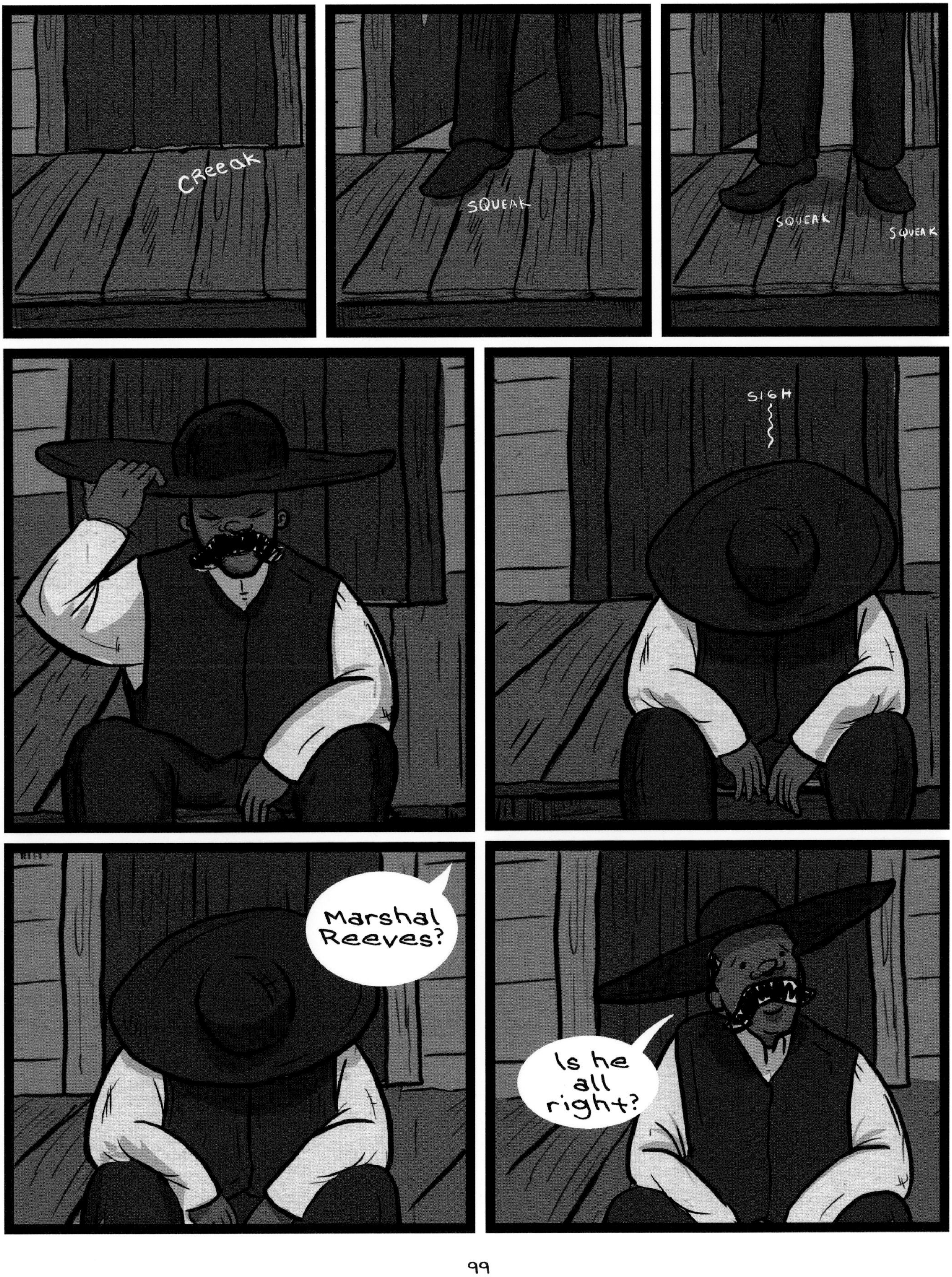
CReeak
SQUEAK
SQUEAK
SQUEAK
SIGH
Marshal Reeves?
Is he all right?

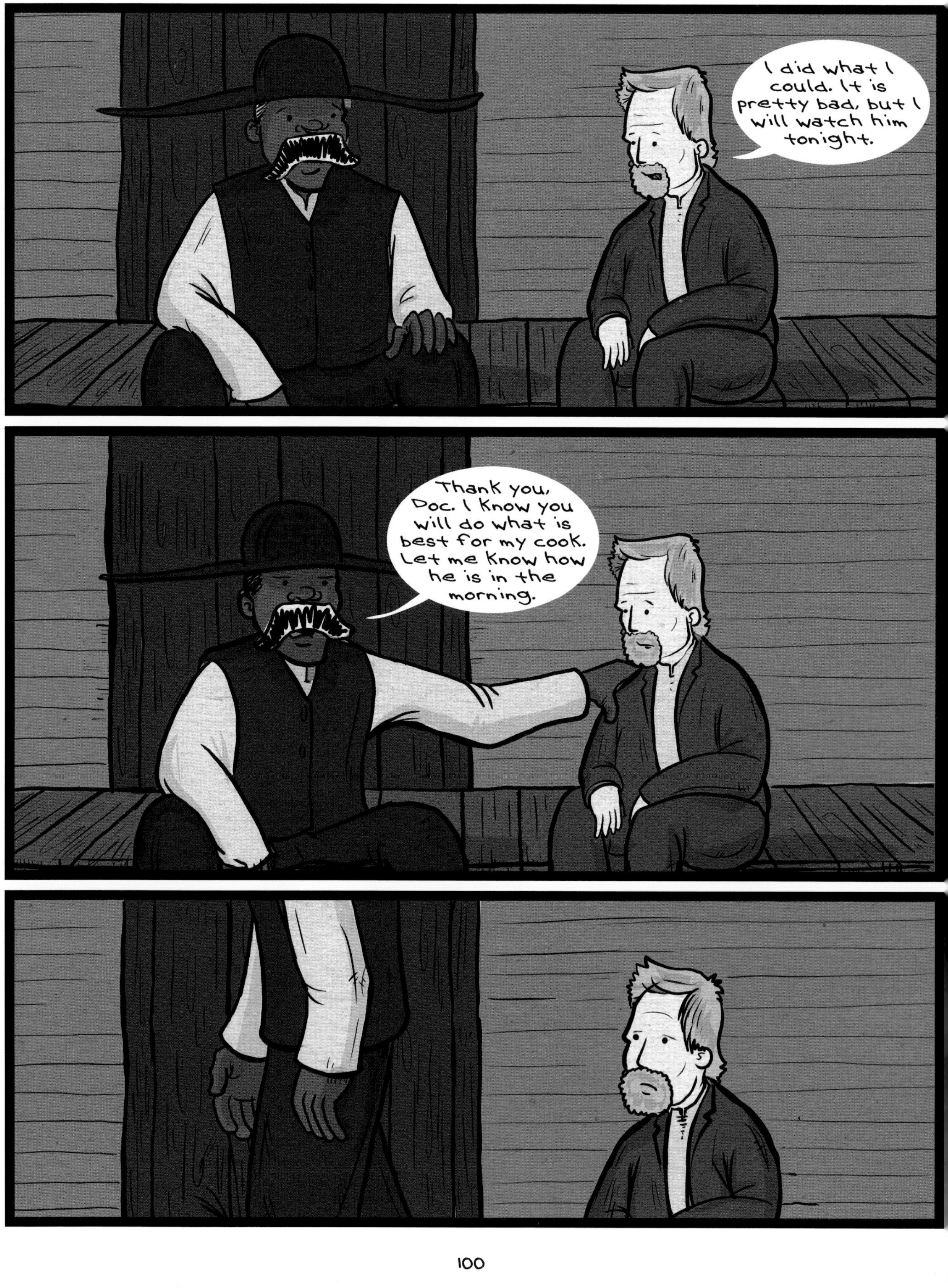
I did what I could. It is pretty bad, but I will watch him tonight.
Thank you, Doc. I know you will do what is best for my cook. Let me know how he is in the morning.

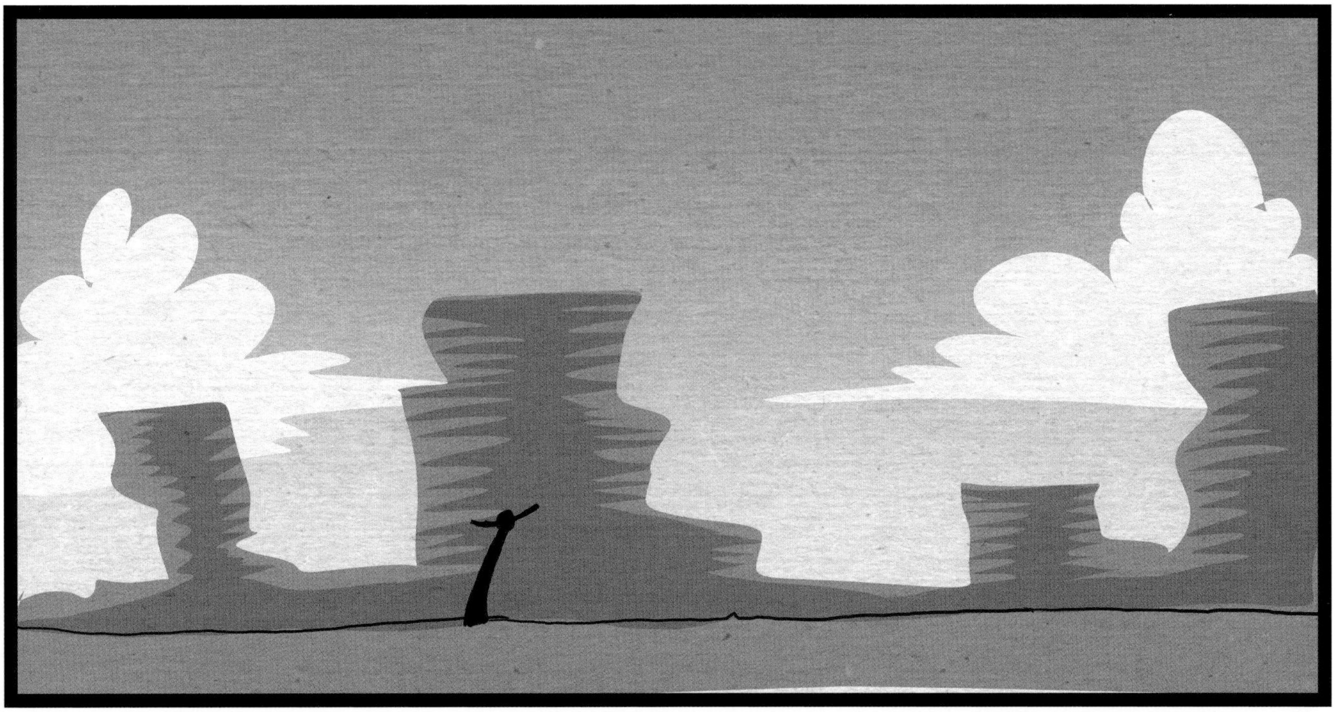

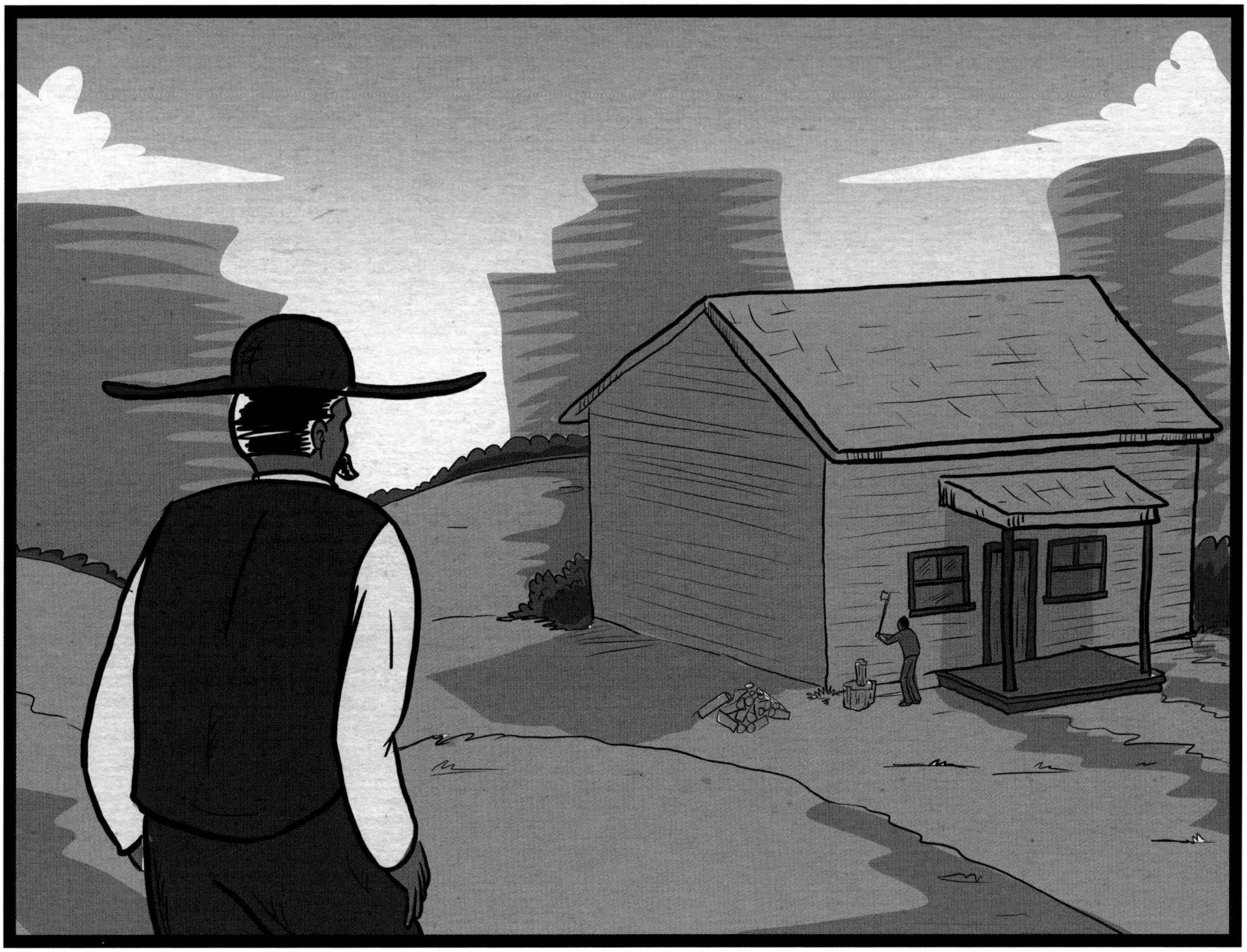

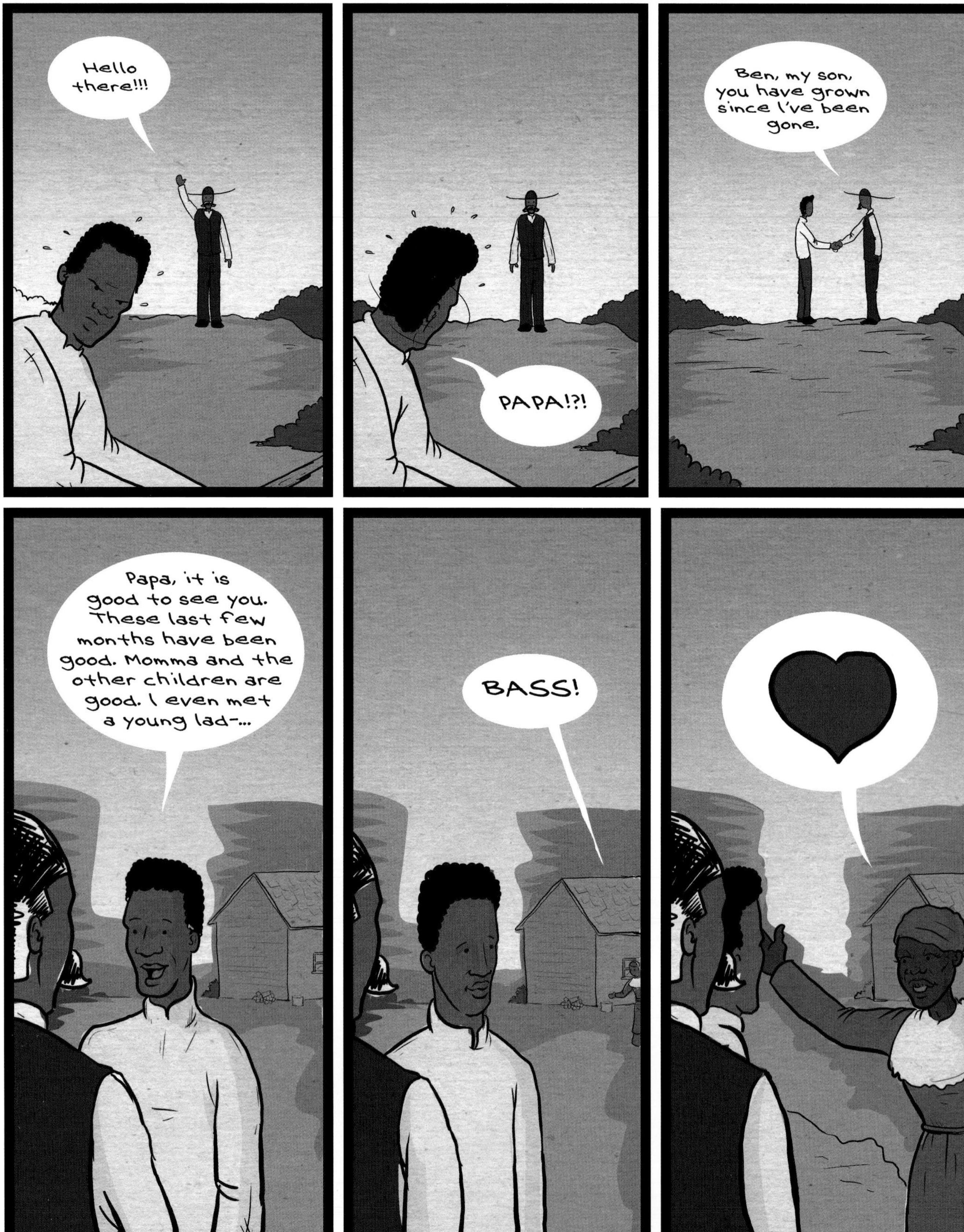
Hello there!!!
PAPA!?!
Ben, my son, you have grown since I've been gone.
Papa, it is good to see you. These last few months have been good. Momma and the other children are good. I even met a young lad-...
BASS!

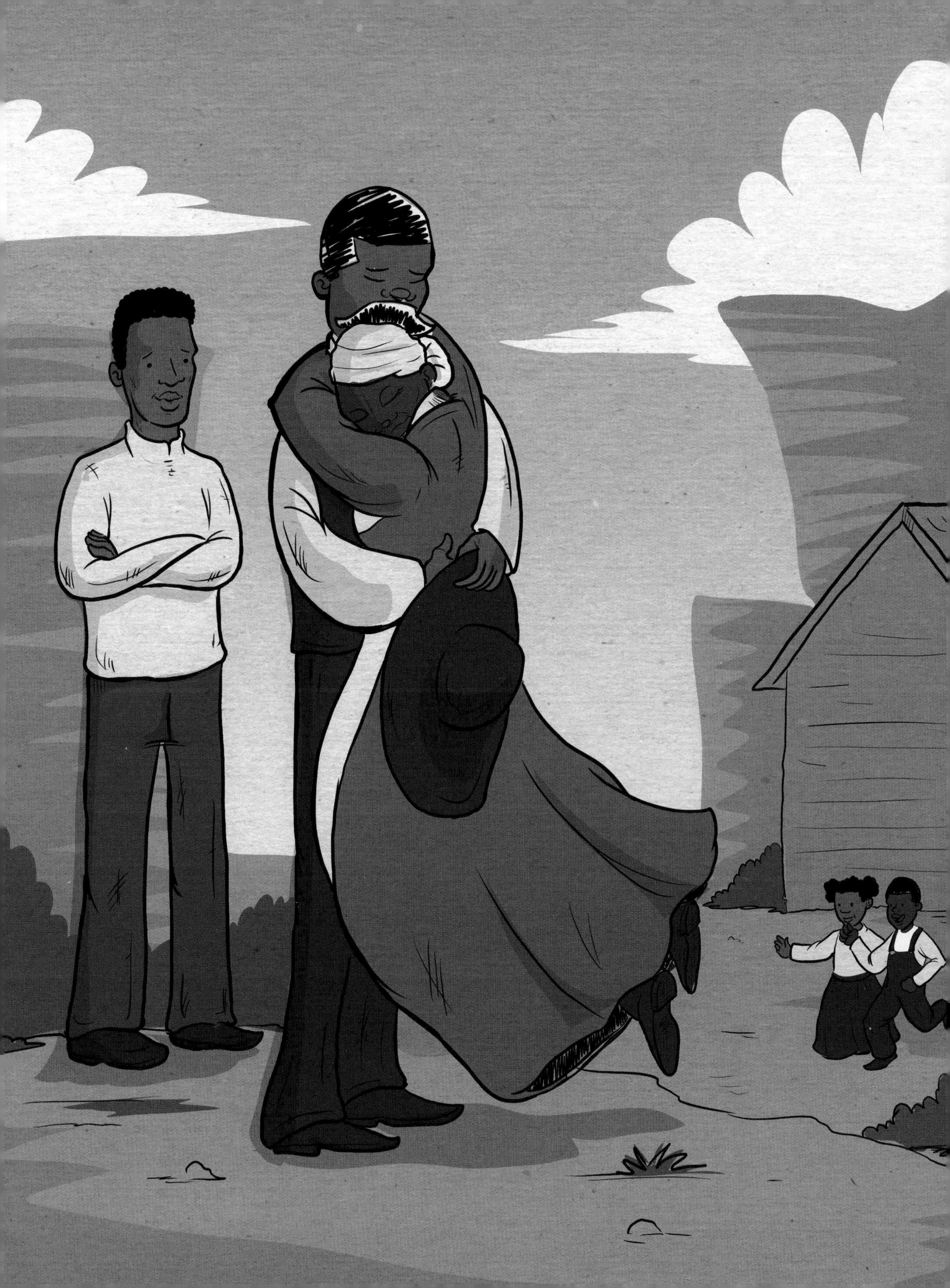

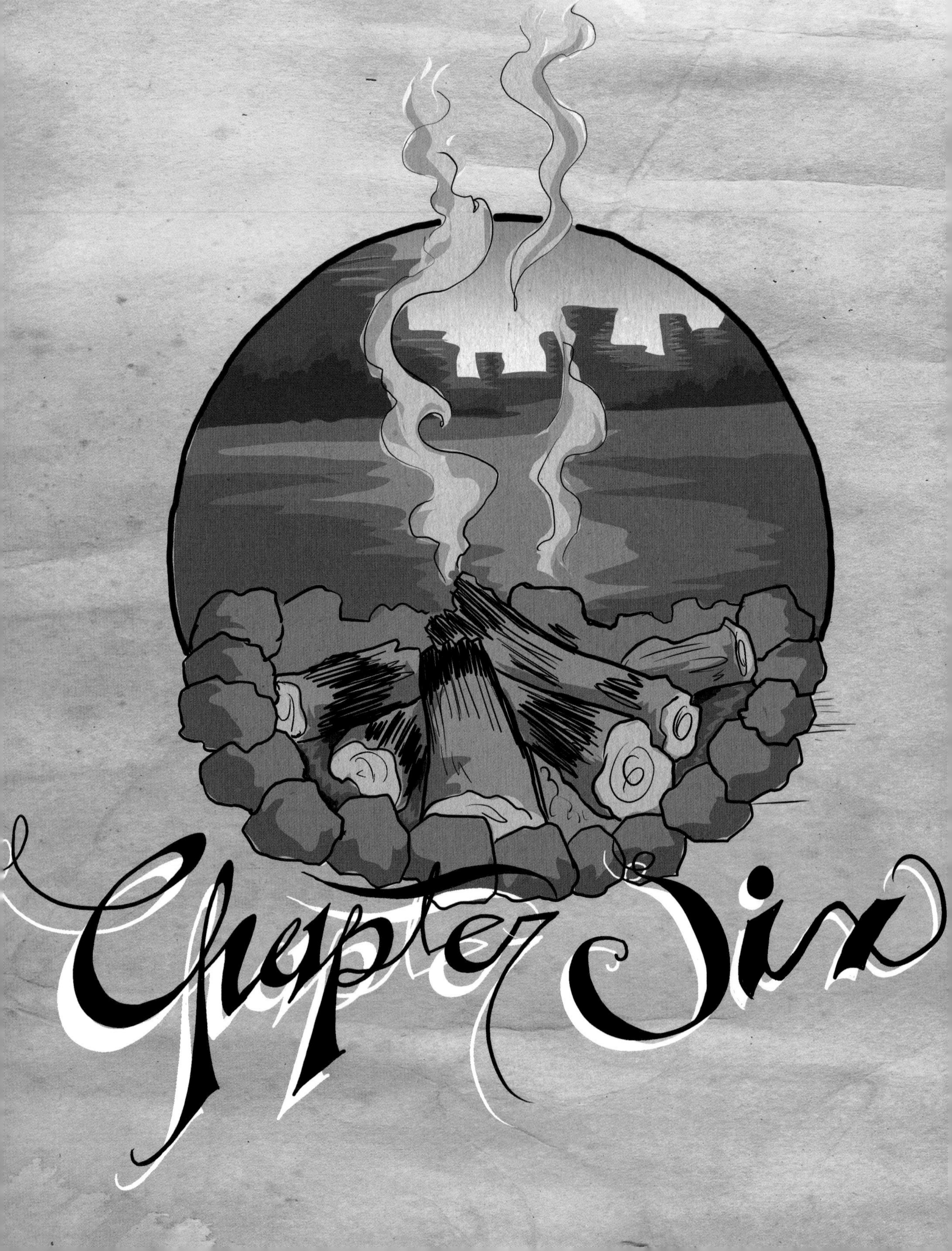

Chapter Six

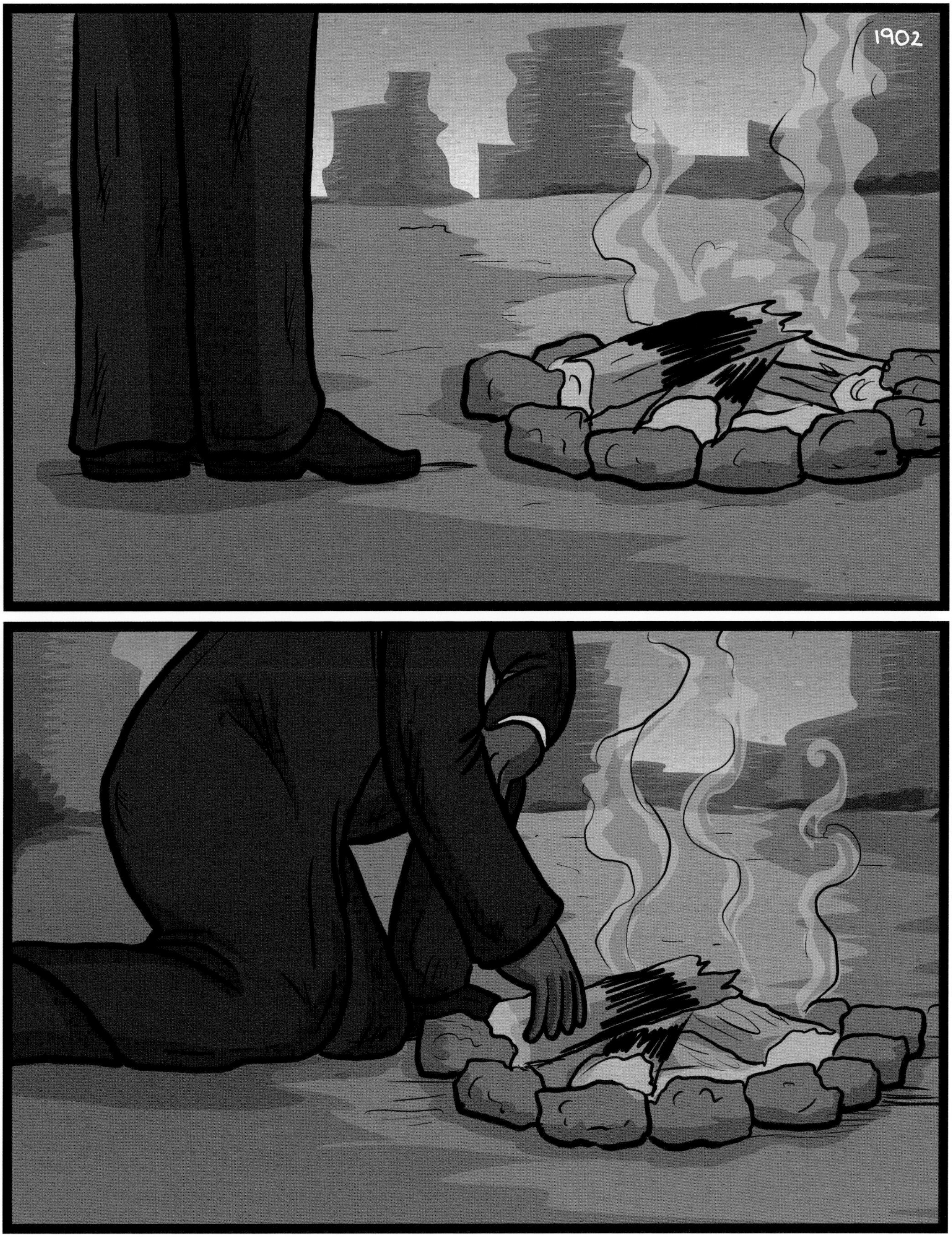
1902

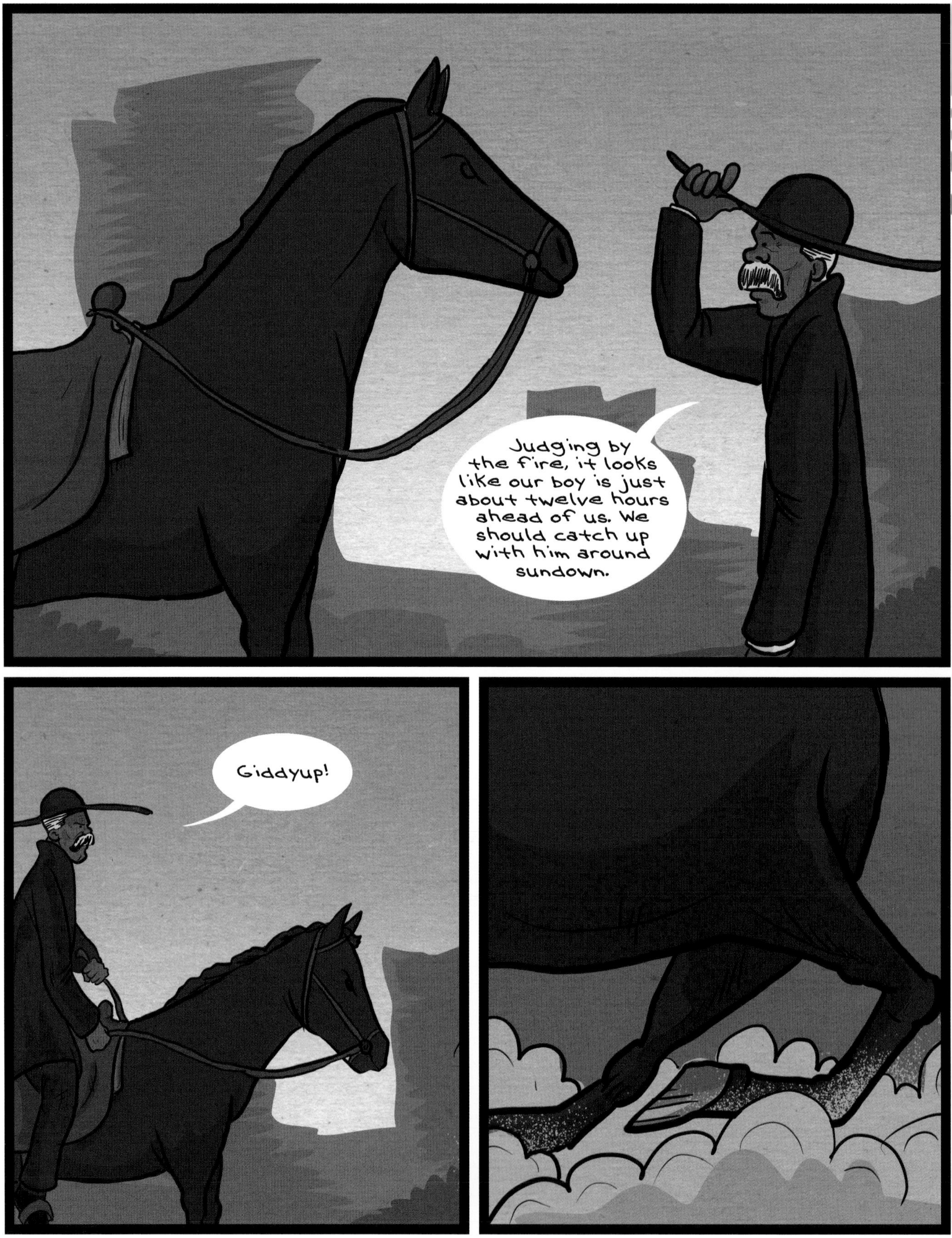
Judging by the fire, it looks like our boy is just about twelve hours ahead of us. We should catch up with him around sundown.
Giddyup!

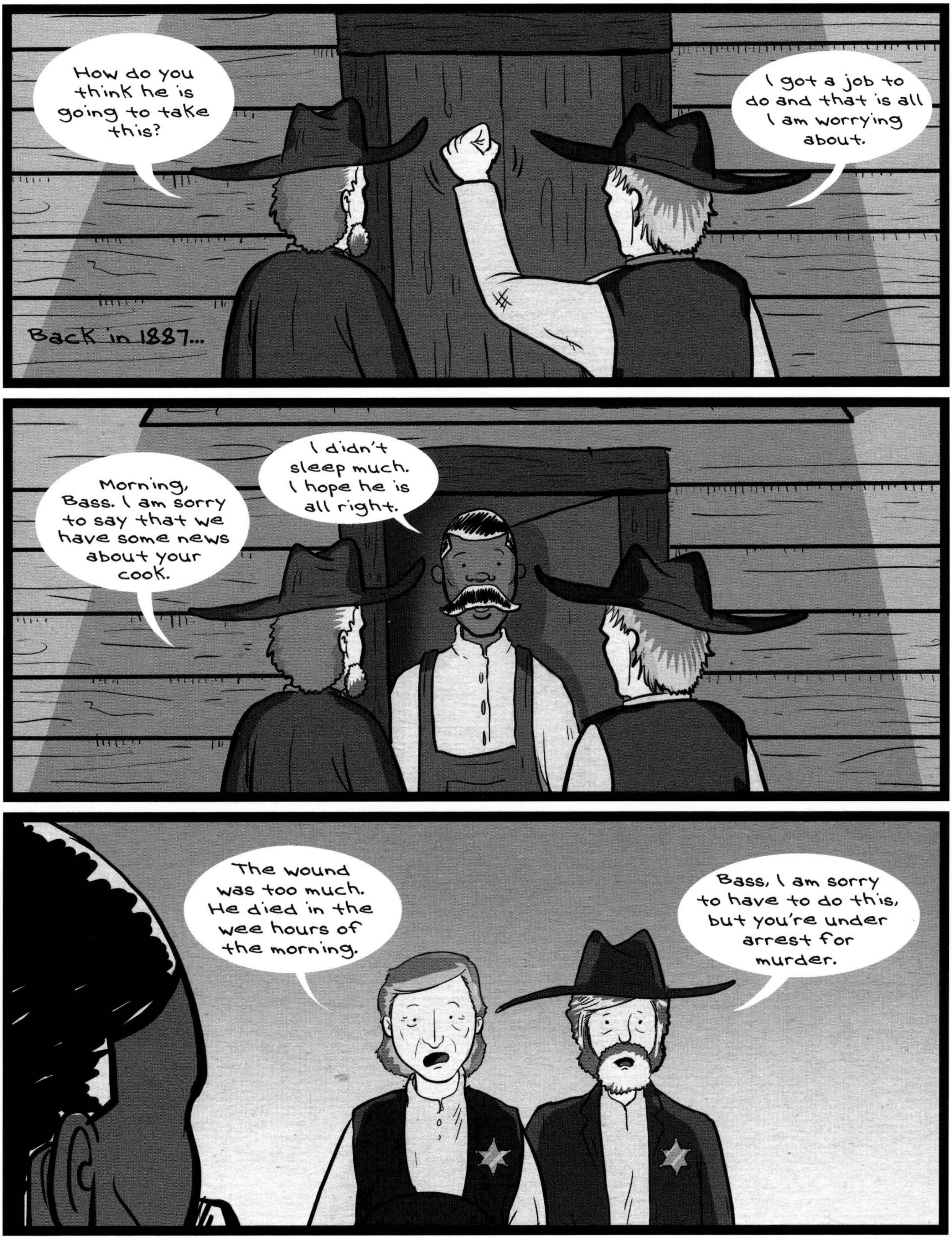
How do you think he is going to take this?
I got a job to do and that is all I am worrying about.
Back in 1887...
I didn't sleep much. I hope he is all right.
Morning, Bass. I am sorry to say that we have some news about your cook.
The wound was too much. He died in the wee hours of the morning.
Bass, I am sorry to have to do this, but you're under arrest for murder.

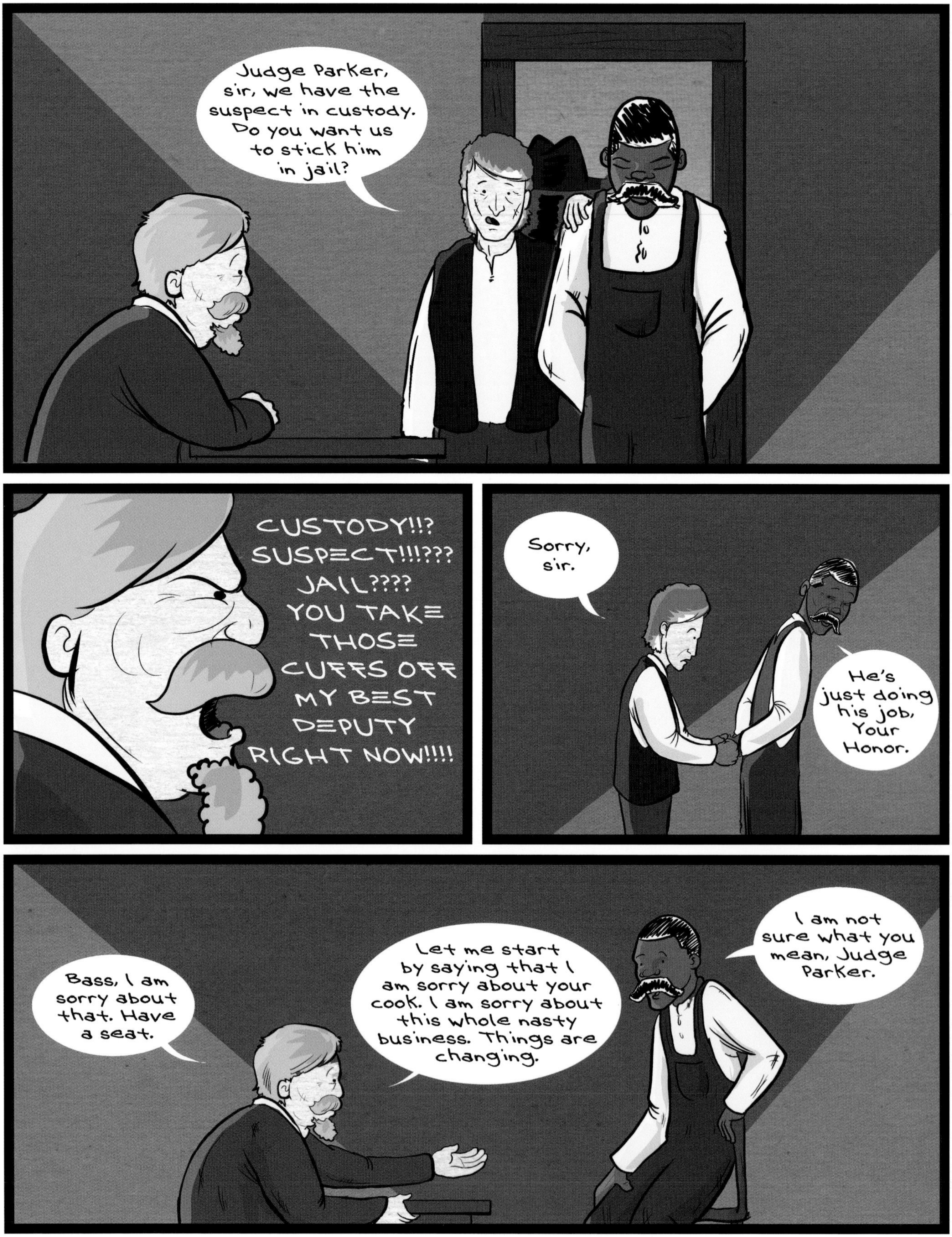
Judge Parker, sir, we have the suspect in custody. Do you want us to stick him in jail?
CUSTODY!!? SUSPECT!!!??? JAIL???? YOU TAKE THOSE CUFFS OFF MY BEST DEPUTY RIGHT NOW!!!!
Sorry, sir.
He's just doing his job, Your Honor.
Bass, I am sorry about that. Have a seat.
Let me start by saying that I am sorry about your cook. I am sorry about this whole nasty business. Things are changing.
I am not sure what you mean, Judge Parker.

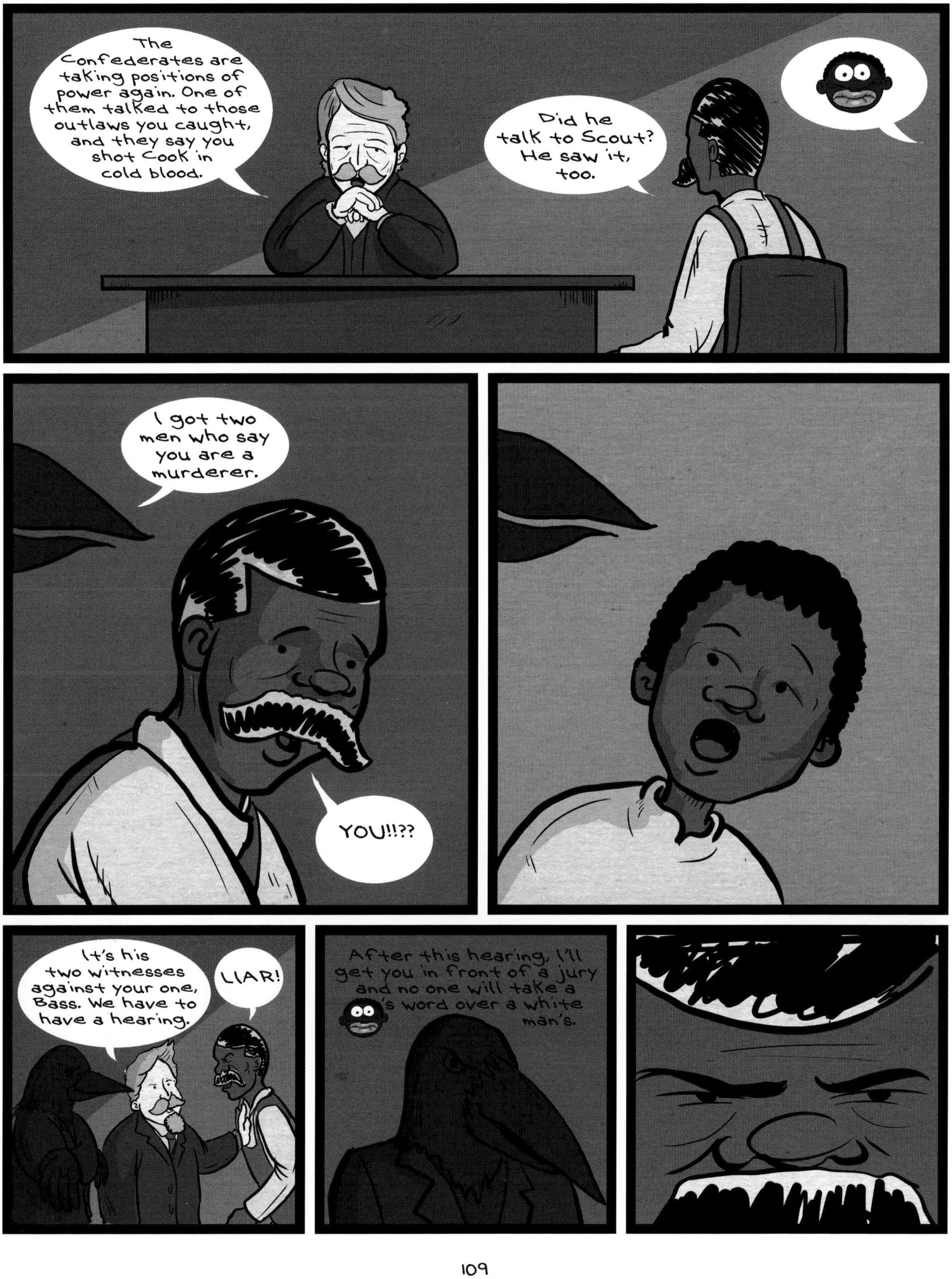
The Confederates are taking positions of power again. One of them talked to those outlaws you caught, and they say you shot Cook in cold blood.
Did he talk to Scout? He saw it, too.
I got two men who say you are a murderer.
YOU!!??
It's his two witnesses against your one, Bass. We have to have a hearing.
LIAR!
After this hearing, I'll get you in front of a jury and no one will take a
's word over a white man's.

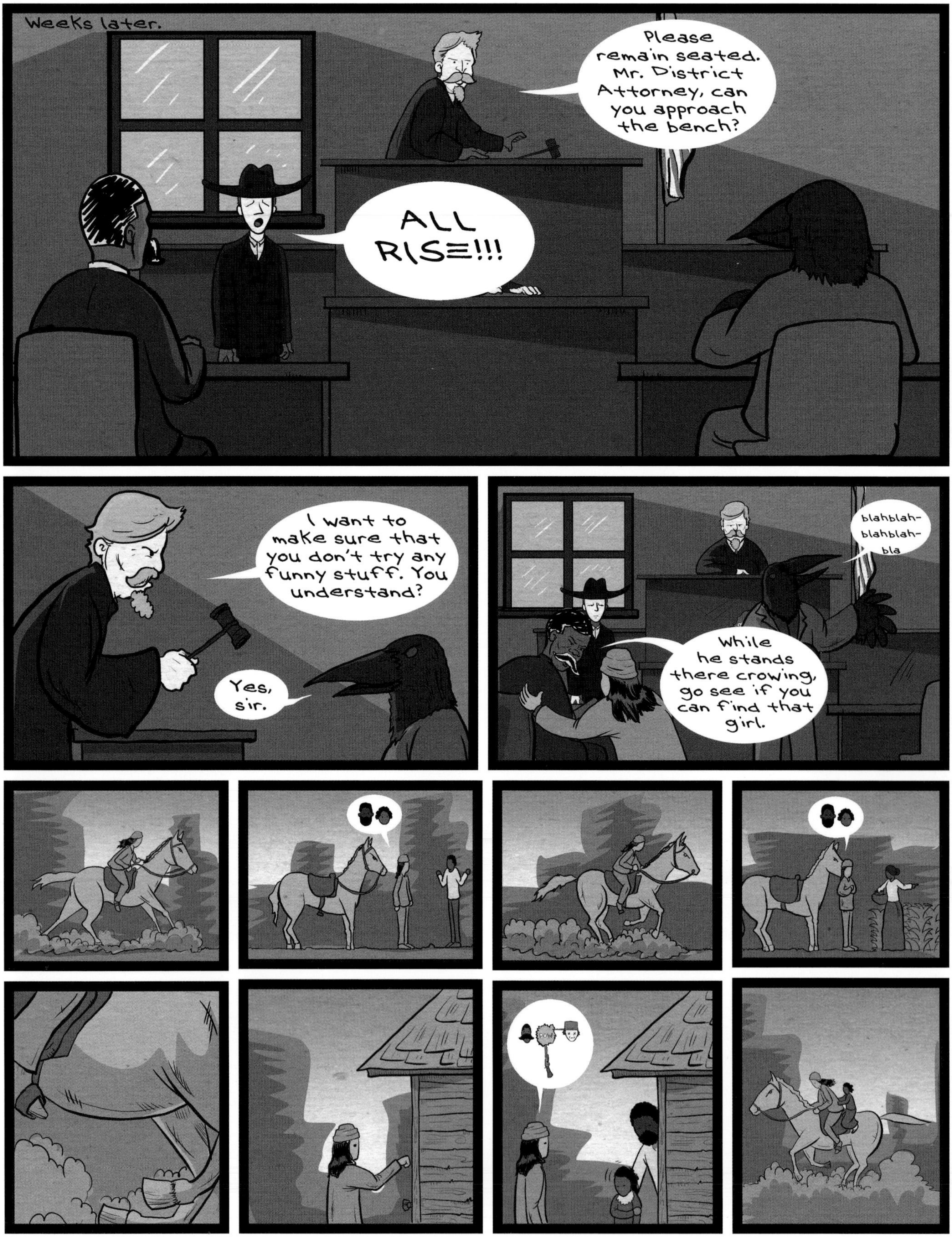
Weeks later.
ALL RISE!!!
Please remain seated. Mr. District Attorney, can you approach the bench?
I want to make sure that you don't try any funny stuff. You understand?
Yes, sir.
blahblah-blahblah-bla
While he stands there crowing, go see if you can find that girl.

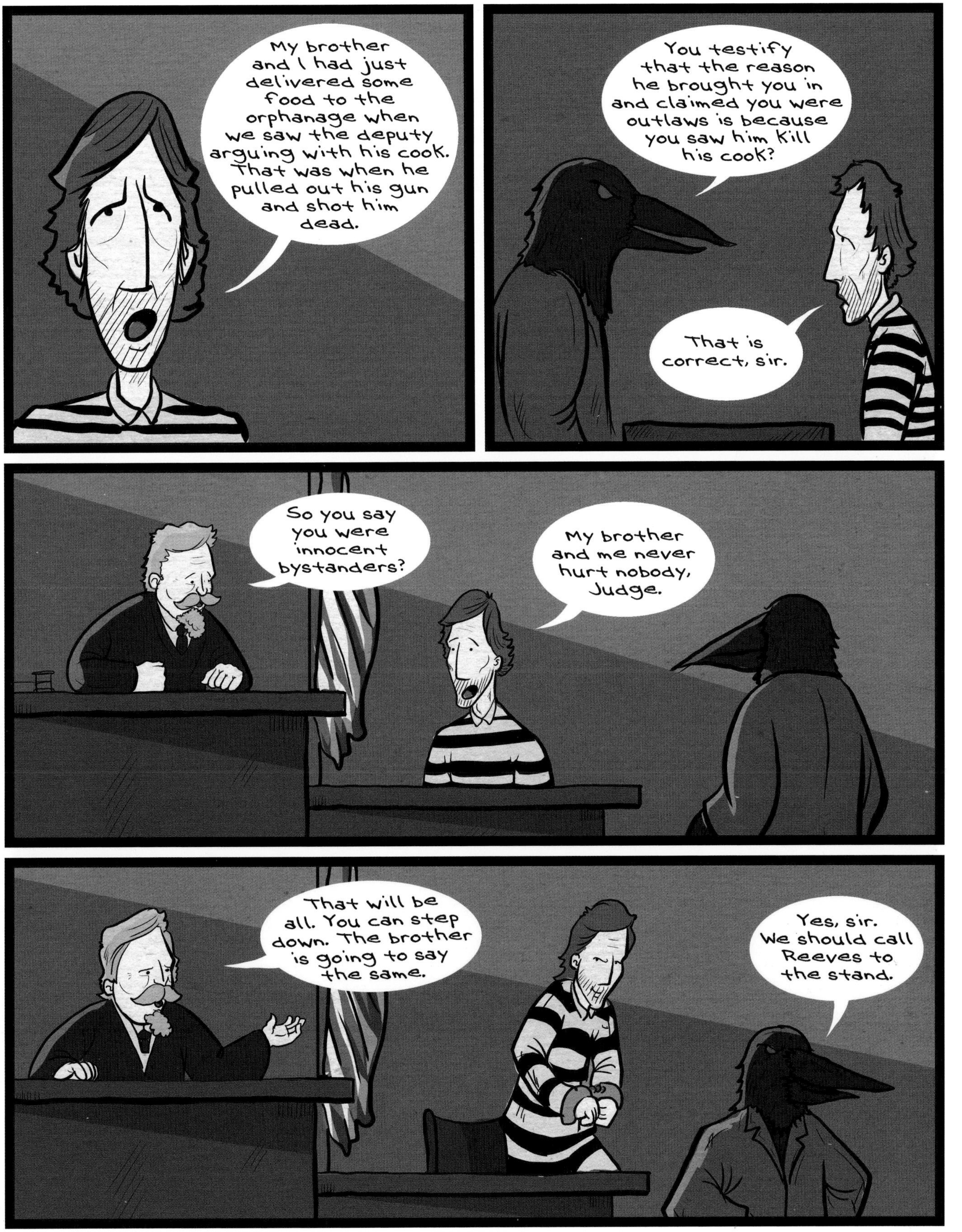
My brother and I had just delivered some food to the orphanage when we saw the deputy arguing with his cook. That was when he pulled out his gun and shot him dead.
You testify that the reason he brought you in and claimed you were outlaws is because you saw him kill his cook?
That is correct, sir.
So you say you were innocent bystanders?
My brother and me never hurt nobody, Judge.
That will be all. You can step down. The brother is going to say the same.
Yes, sir. We should call Reeves to the stand.

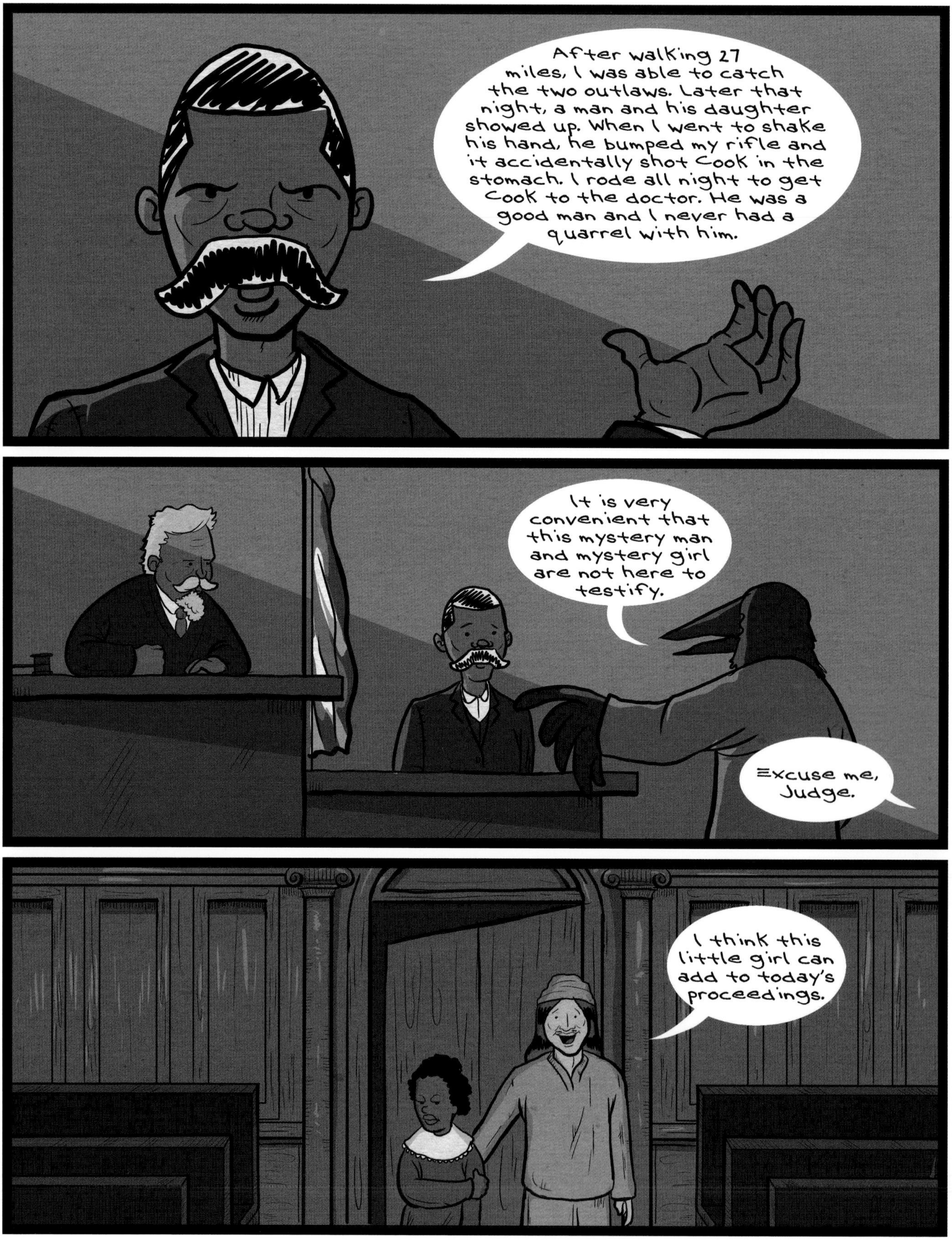
After walking 27 miles, I was able to catch the two outlaws. Later that night, a man and his daughter showed up. When I went to shake his hand, he bumped my rifle and it accidentally shot Cook in the stomach. I rode all night to get Cook to the doctor. He was a good man and I never had a quarrel with him.
It is very convenient that this mystery man and mystery girl are not here to testify.
Excuse me, Judge.
I think this little girl can add to today's proceedings.

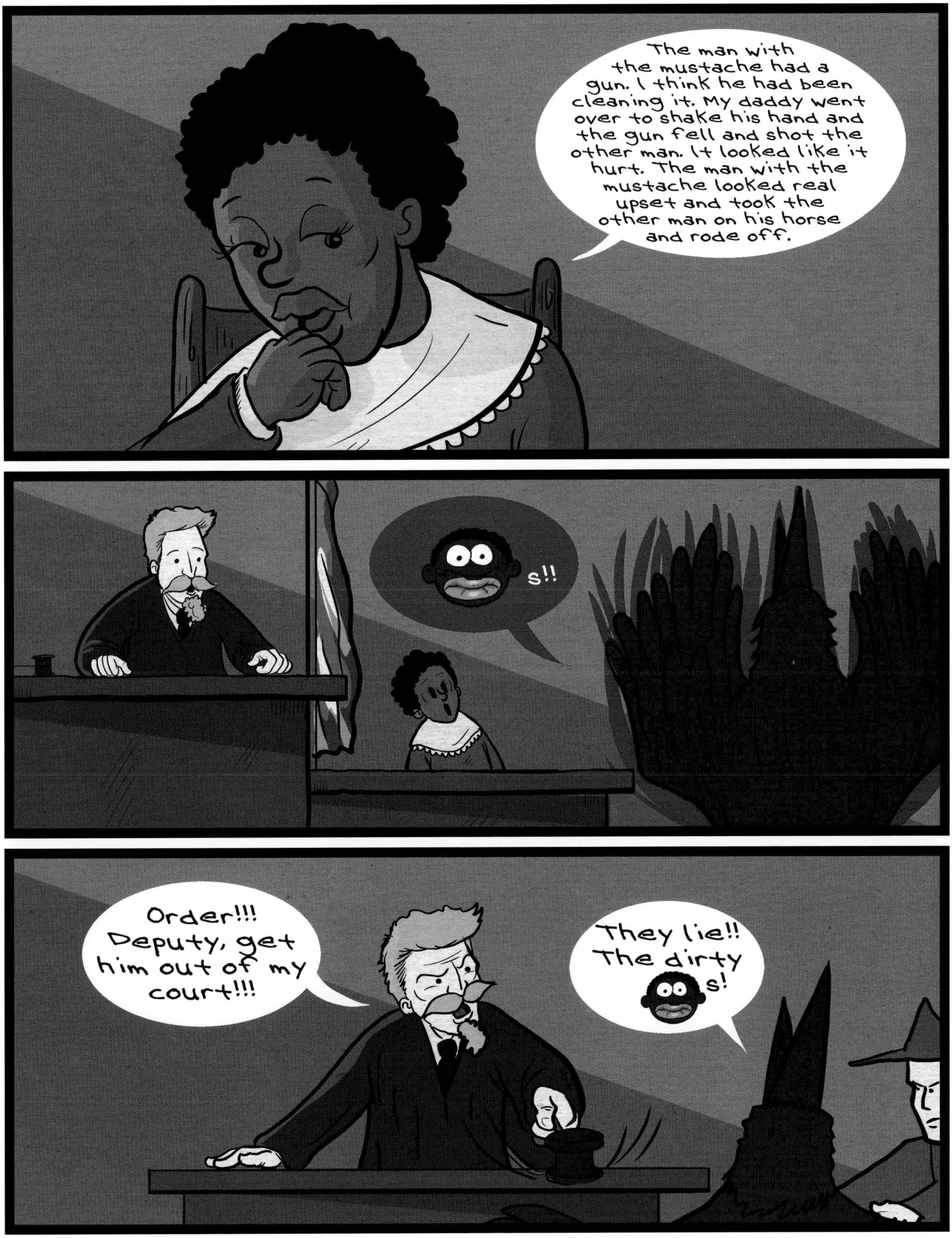
The man with the mustache had a gun. I think he had been cleaning it. My daddy went over to shake his hand and the gun fell and shot the other man. It looked like it hurt. The man with the mustache looked real upset and took the other man on his horse and rode off.
s!!
Order!!! Deputy, get him out of my court!!!
They lie!! The dirty s!

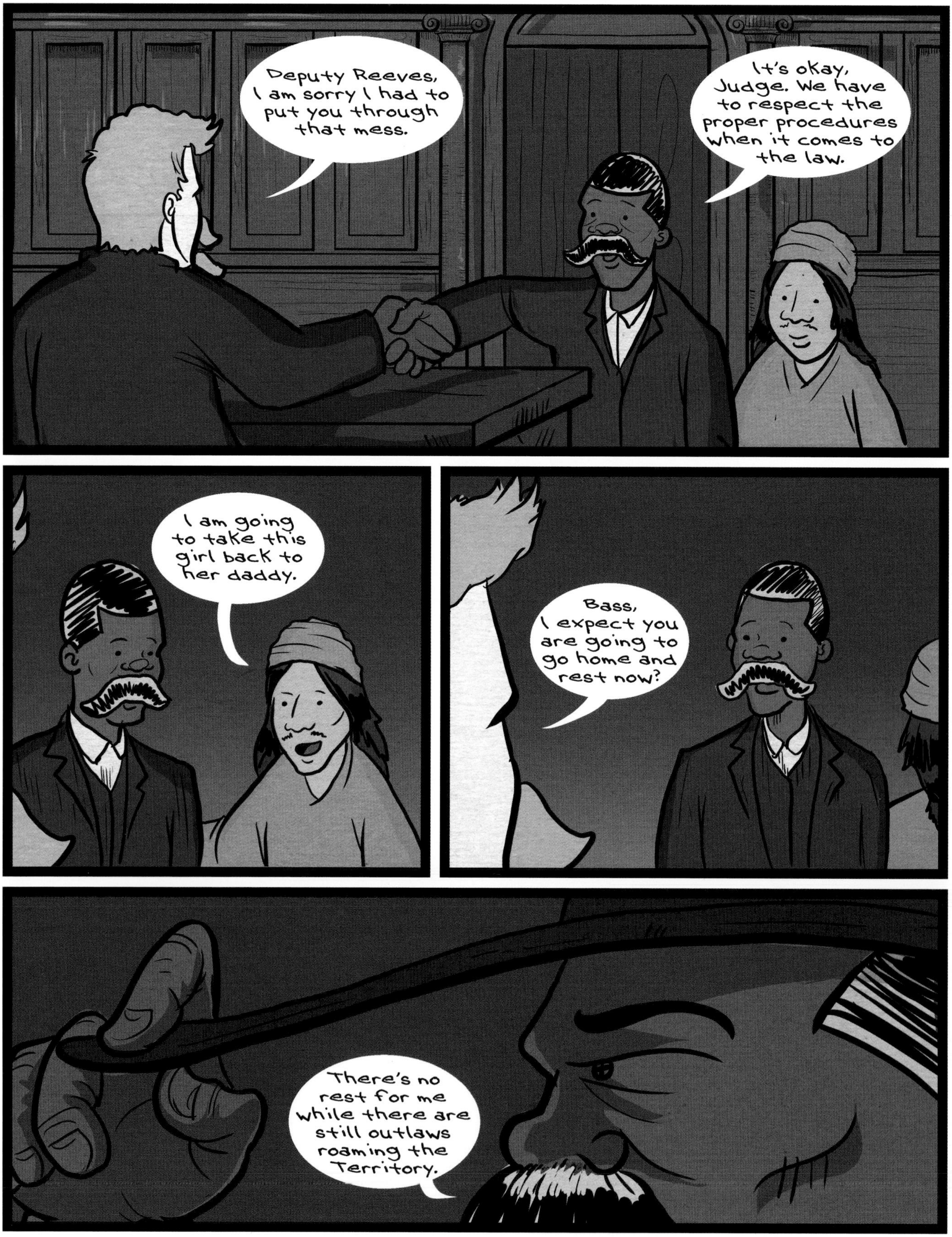
Deputy Reeves, I am sorry I had to put you through that mess.
It's okay, Judge. We have to respect the proper procedures when it comes to the law.
I am going to take this girl back to her daddy.
Bass, I expect you are going to go home and rest now?
There's no rest for me while there are still outlaws roaming the Territory.

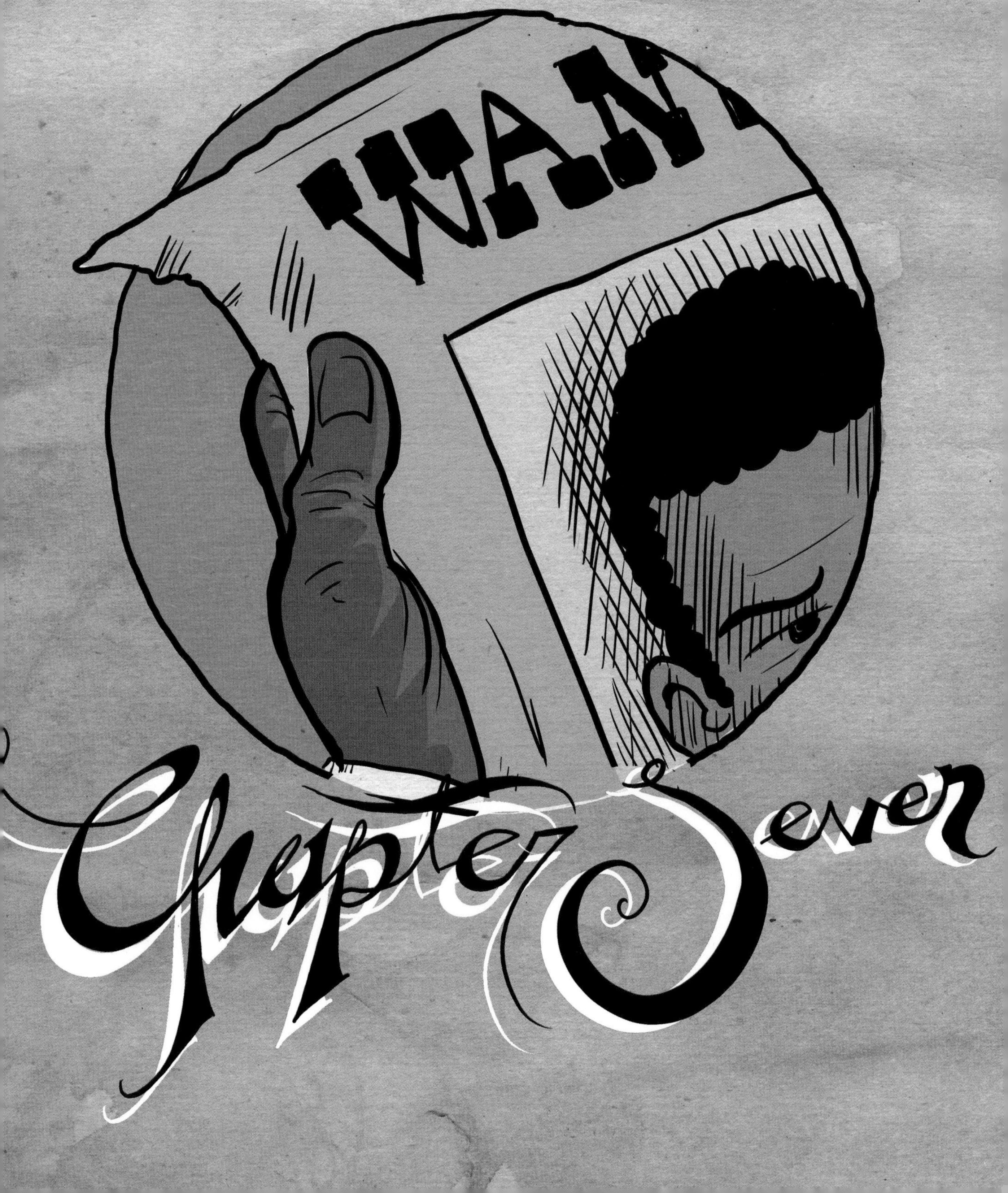
WAN

Chapter Seven

NO MAN'S LAND

Bass did not sleep. He spent the next decade and a half dressing in disguises, catching outlaws, and making the Territory safe for the people. He continued to complete acts of amazing law enforcement. He once brought in 21 outlaws at one time. He even helped to put down a race war in 1902. He was never shot—only shot at, and had to kill 14 outlaws over the course of his 32-year career. As progress brought the Old West into the 20th century, Bass worked as a police officer in Oklahoma, but not before he had to make his most difficult arrest...

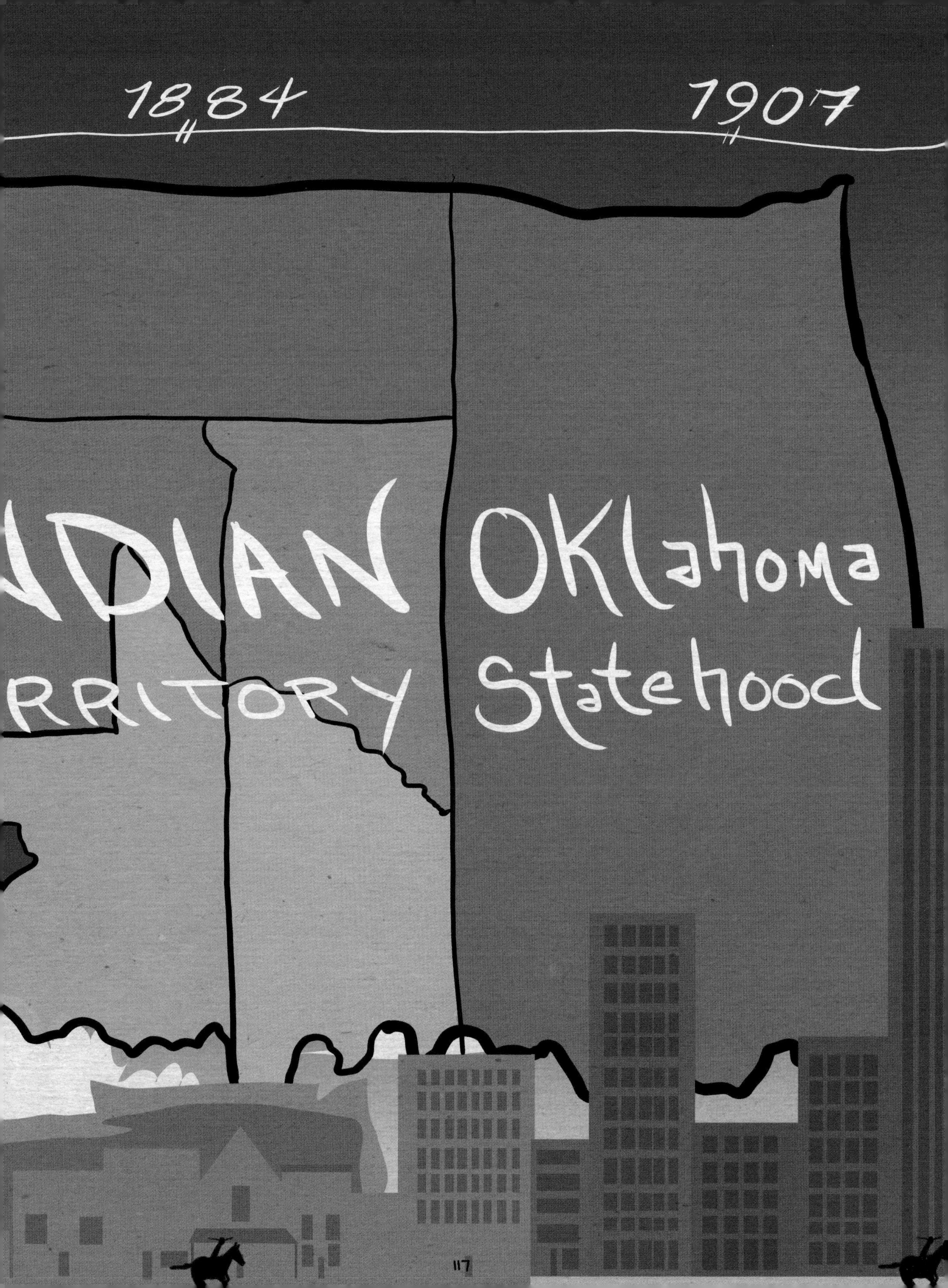
1884
1907
NDIAN
RRITORY
OKlahoma
Statehood

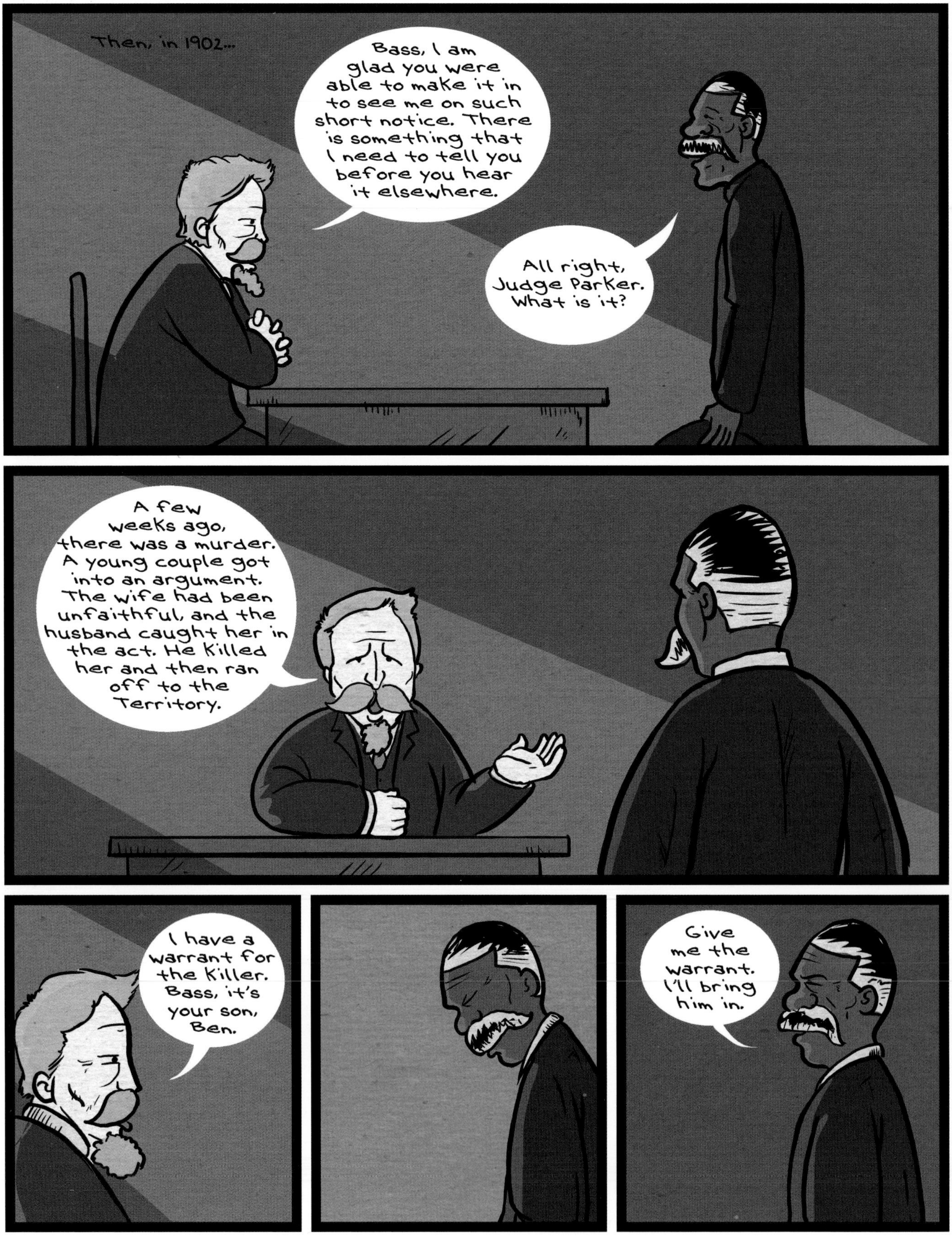
Then, in 1902...
Bass, I am glad you were able to make it in to see me on such short notice. There is something that I need to tell you before you hear it elsewhere.
All right, Judge Parker. What is it?
A few weeks ago, there was a murder. A young couple got into an argument. The wife had been unfaithful, and the husband caught her in the act. He killed her and then ran off to the Territory.
I have a warrant for the killer. Bass, it's your son, Ben.
Give me the warrant. I'll bring him in.

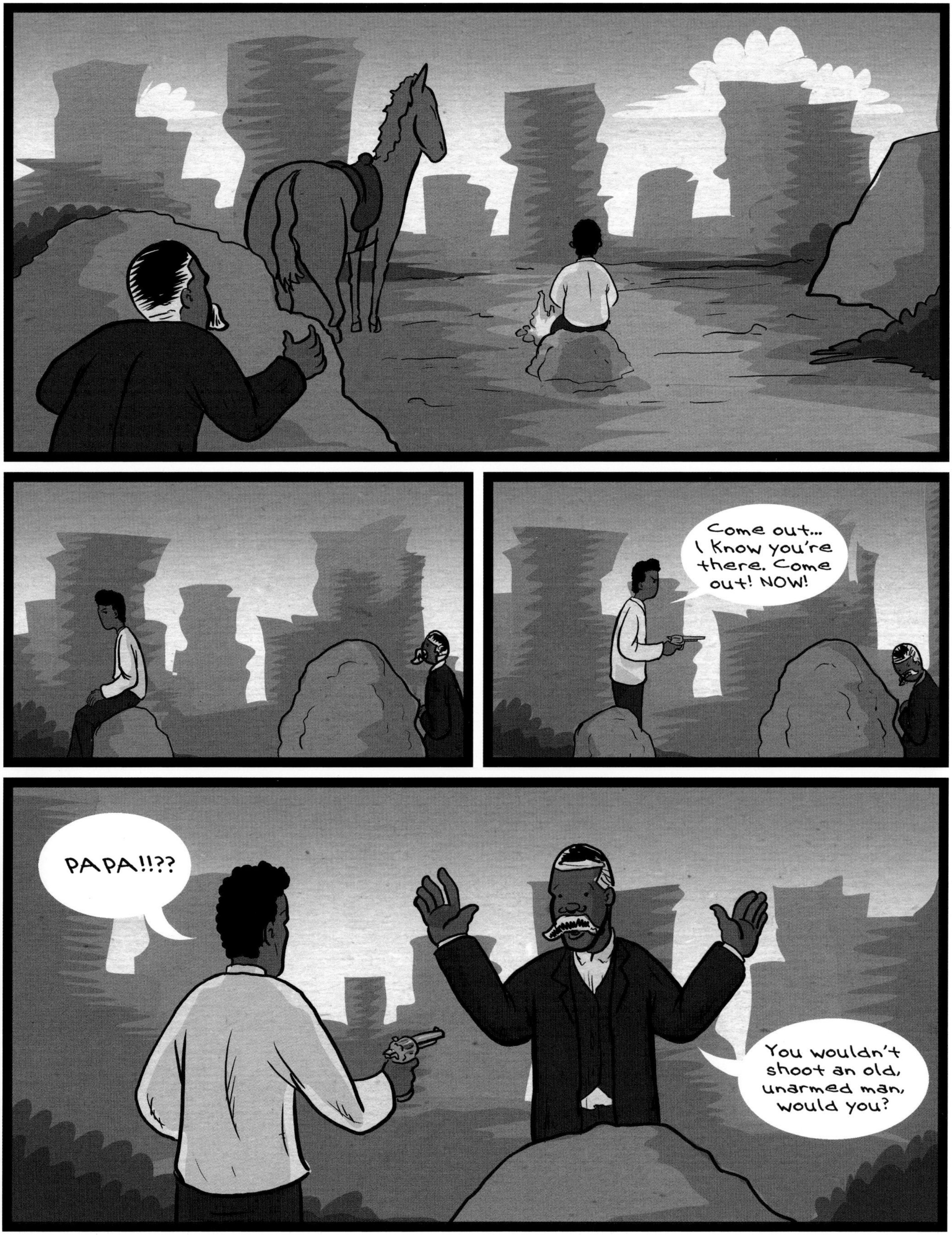
Come out... I Know you're there. Come out! NOW!
PAPA!!??
You wouldn't shoot an old, unarmed man, would you?

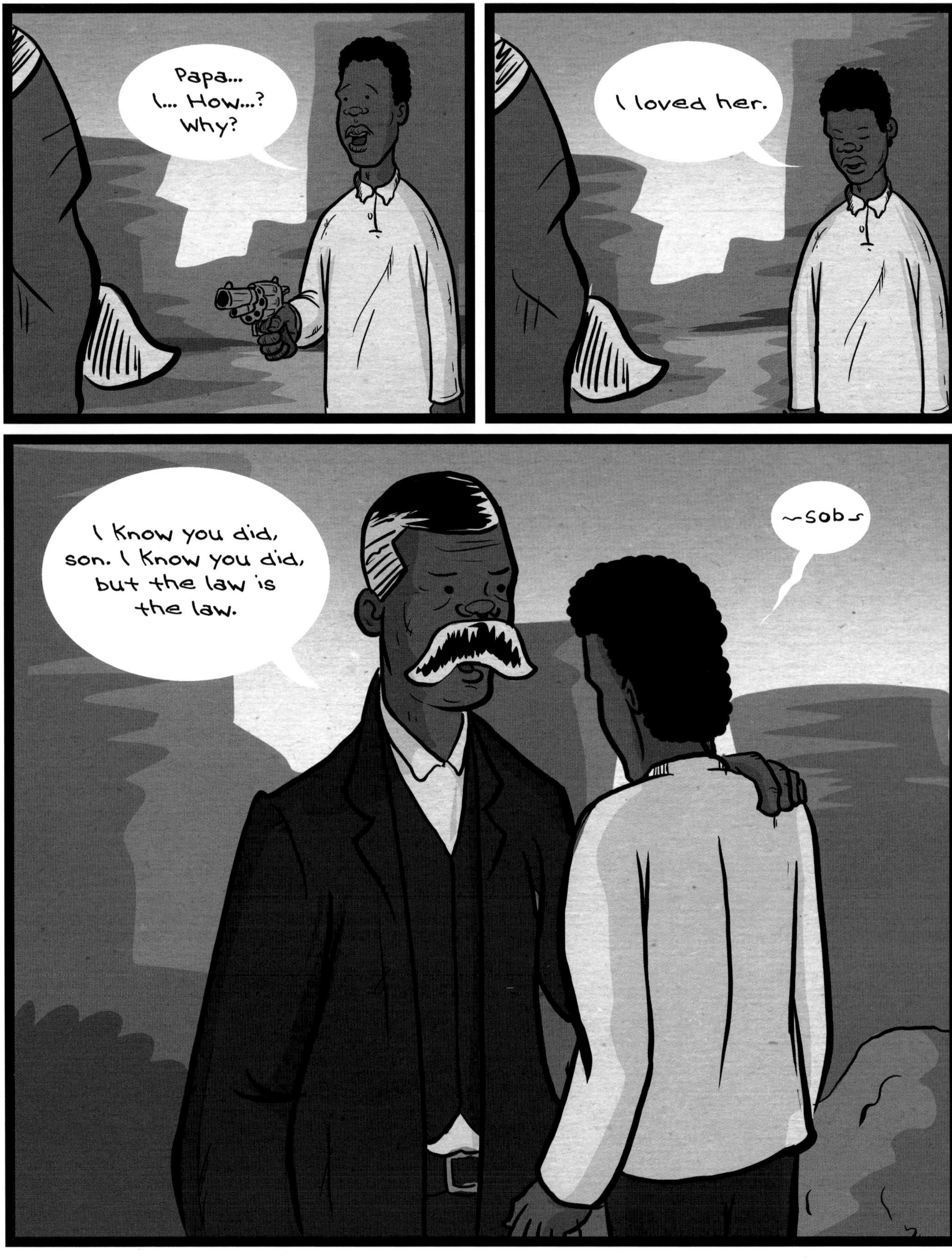
Papa... I... How...? Why?
I loved her.
I Know you did, son. I Know you did, but the law is the law.
~sob~

The apprehension of his own son added to the nearly 3,000 outlaws Bass caught over his 32-year career.

I am sorry about your son, Boss.

The law is there to keep people safe. We have to enforce it, no matter what.

His legendary sleuthing skills, incredible disguises, and...

Now let's get back to work.

...his habit of leaving behind a silver coin at the conclusion of his work...

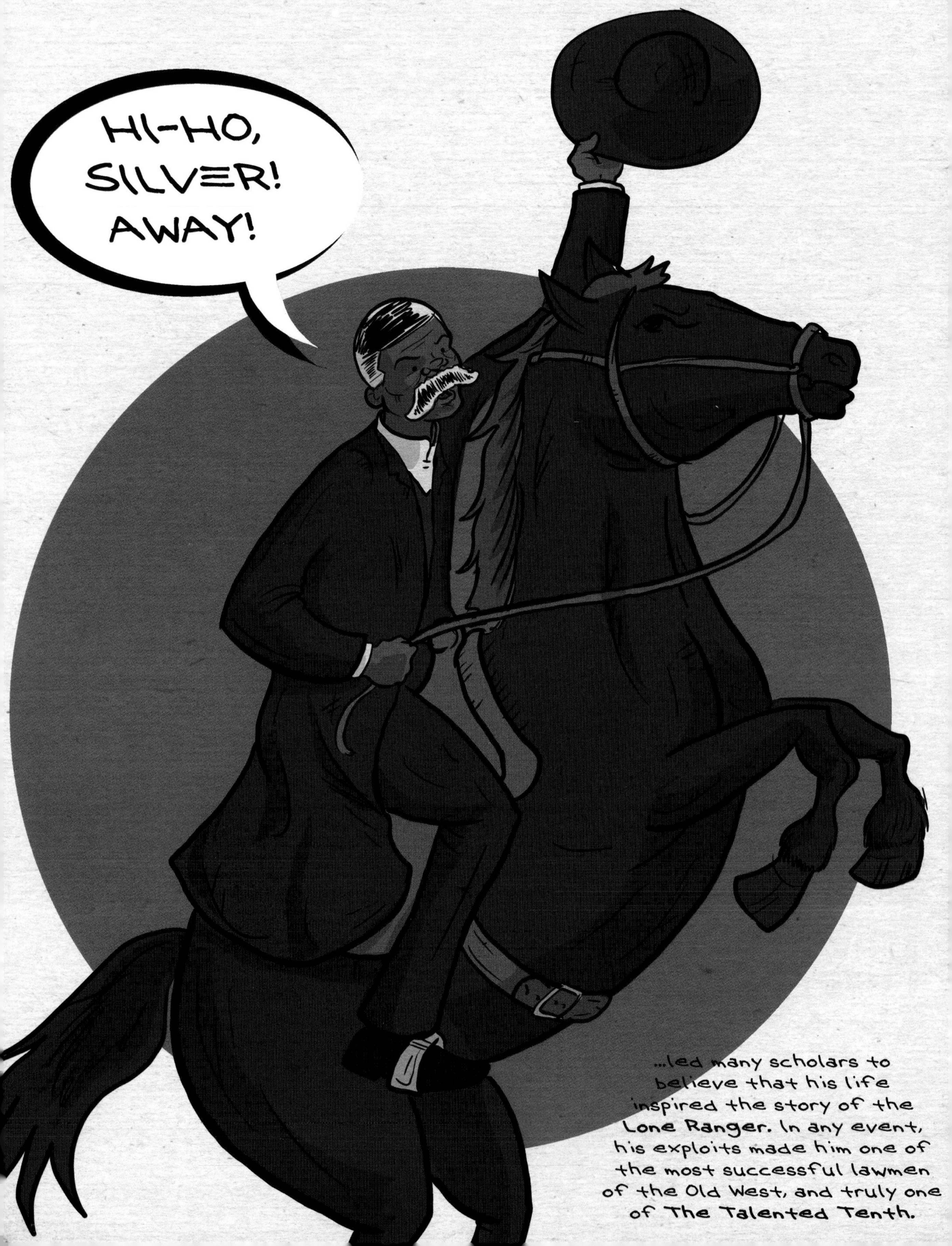
HI-HO, SILVER! AWAY!
...led many scholars to believe that his life inspired the story of the Lone Ranger. In any event, his exploits made him one of the most successful lawmen of the Old West, and truly one of The Talented Tenth.

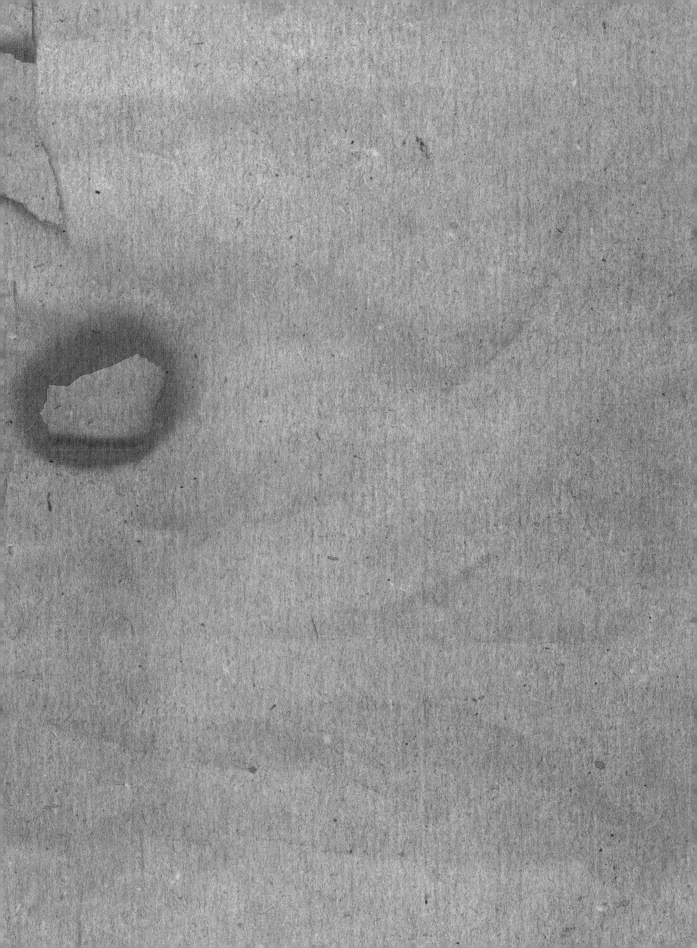

Bibliography

Burton, Art T. Black Gun, Silver Star: The Life and Legend of Frontier Marshal Bass Reeves. Lincoln: University of Nebraska Press, 2006.

Burton, Art T. "Lawman Legend Bass Reeves: The Invincible Man Hunter." Wild West 19.5 (2007): 50. MasterFILE Premier. Web. Retrieved June 12, 2013.

Soodalter, Ron. "Long Arm of the Father." Oklahoma Today 62.6 (2012): 38. MasterFILE Premier. Web. Retrieved June 12, 2013.

"Pictographs." Native Indian Tribes. Retrieved Nov. 26, 2013, http://www.warpaths2peacepipes.com/native-indian-art/pictographs.htm.

"Social Studies: Printables, Native American Picture Writing." Teacher Vision. Family Education Network. Oct. 1, 2013. Retrieved Nov. 24, 2013, https://www.teachervision.com/native-american-history/printable/7198.html?detoured=1.

Love the Fulcrum graphic novels?
Look for supplemental materials for
the classroom on our education website:

www.fulcrum-education.com

Bessie

Tales of the Talented Tenth

is a graphic novel series that focuses on the adventures of amazing African Americans in action. The subsequent volumes will tell the story of:

Bessie Stringfield, the motorcycle queen of Miami

Robert Smalls, an escaped slave-turned-politician

Mary Bowser, a freed slave who returned to the South as a Union spy during the Civil War

And more to come!

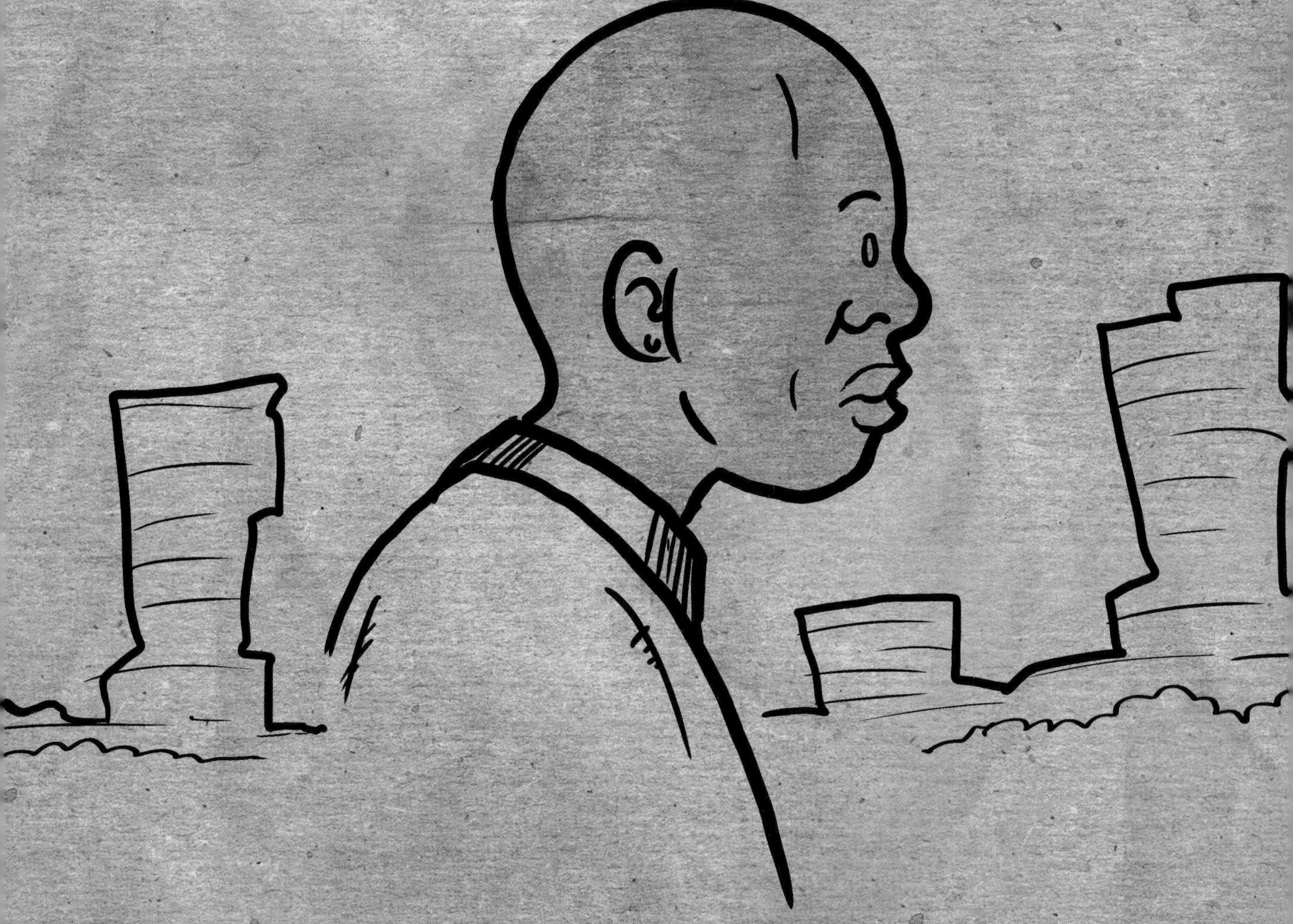

Joel Christian Gill is the Associate Dean of Student Affairs at the New Hampshire Institute of Art. He wrote the words and drew the pictures in Strange Fruit Volume 1: Uncelebrated Narratives from Black History and Bass Reeves: Tales of the Talented Tenth (the very book you are holding). The allegations that he ghost wrote Hamlet, The Voynich Manuscript, and started the Chicago Fire are completely unfounded. He also believes that #28daysarenotenough when it comes to black history. To learn more about Joel Christian Gill, see the beginning of this paragraph.